Architecture of
the 19th Century

Architecture of the 19th Century

Claude Mignot

evergreen

FORNT COVER:
Kew Gardens

BACK COVER:
Il Cisternone in Livorno (sketch by Pasquale Poccianti, 1827)

This book was printed on 100% chlorine free bleached
paper in accordance with the TCF-standard.

EVERGREEN is a lable of Benedikt Taschen Verlag GmbH

© 1983 Office du Livre, Fribourg
© for this edition 1994 Benedikt Taschen Verlag GmbH,
Hohenzollernring 53, D-50672 Köln
Printed by grafedit s.p.a., Azzano S. Paolo
Printed in Italy
ISBN 3-8228-9032-4

Table of Contents

Introduction

From the monuments that have become emblems of great cities (the Statue of Liberty in New York; Big Ben and Tower Bridge in London; the Arc de Triomphe, Sacré-Cœur and the Eiffel Tower in Paris) down to the church, school and town hall of the most humble village, the nineteenth century has left a profound impression on the architecture of our townscapes and country-sides. As architecture it is familiar enough but it disconcerts the eye by its abundance, its diversity and sometimes, it must be admitted, by its ugliness.

For a long time we have focused our attention solely on those elements of nineteenth-century architecture which foreshadowed the architecture of today. Instead of interpreting the century in its own terms, we have concentrated on iron-stanchioned warehouses, sparing a disdainful glance for the sumptuous houses of their owners; we were partial to the iron-and-steel halls of railway stations but smiled at their extravagant façades. We admired the architecture of the Crystal Palace and forgot that its simplicity was accepted by contemporaries only because there was nothing better to be had in the time available, and that it is modern only when seen in retrospect. We poked fun at the lavish façades of the Château de Ferrières, overlooking the fact that they were pleasing in the eyes of their owners. We followed with impatience the introduction of new materials and their frank statement in façades, forgetting that this was one of a number of aesthetic options which was *per se* neither more beautiful, nor more moral (or modern) than another. We admired the felicity with which Renaissance architects handled the forms of the antique world; but we made reservations when confronted by the similar way in which nineteenth-century architects handled medieval and Renaissance forms, felicitously or otherwise.

To understand nineteenth-century architecture we must rid our minds of deterministic conceptions of history and rationalistic conceptions of architecture, both of which are naïve. Iron-and-steel station halls are no more representative of the nineteenth century than their ornate façades are. Similarly, and contrary to what has often been written (paradoxically *since* the nineteenth century), it is no more absurd (and just as poetical) to place a triumphal arch in front of a station than it is to put the frontispiece of an antique temple in front of a Venetian country house, as Palladio did. Just as the industrial manufacture of textiles in sordid factories coexisted with the most elaborate feminine fashions, so the diversity of architectural styles must be examined against a background unconnected with the marketing of new materials.

To understand this architecture, we must rediscover the taste for quotation and evocation, for historical reminiscences and emotional associations which, to contemporaries, constituted its charm. We must interpret it, as we do that of earlier periods, as a free handling of forms and images, the final effect of which, being more than the sum of the out-of-place motifs used, may or may not be successful. Nineteenth-century buildings are so numerous and the formal experiments of such unequal quality that, seen as a whole, the impression is a little dull, if not ugly – just as nineteenth-century literature no doubt would be if it coexisted all together in our memory in the same way that the buildings constructed at that time coexist in our towns and villages.

Nineteenth-century architecture is first of all a simple matter of statistics. In 1800 Europe had a population of 187 millions, in 1850 266 millions, and in 1900 420 millions. These people who lived in an age of industrial revolution required hundreds of markets and stations, grammar schools and town halls, hos-

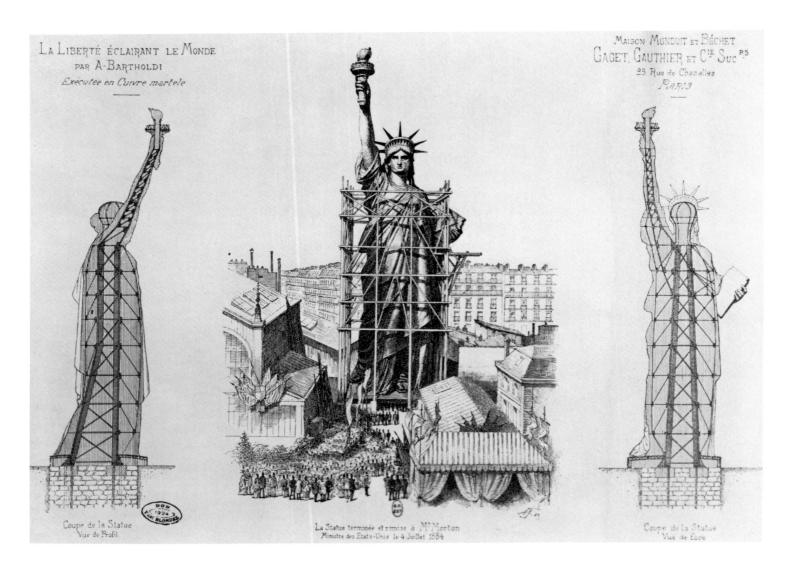

1   The Statue of Liberty, the new pharos of New York; stone base by Richard Morris Hunt; sculpture by Auguste Bartholdi; metal structure by Gustave Eiffel, 1884.

pitals and prisons, tens of thousands of schools and municipal buildings, and hundreds of thousands of houses and blocks of flats. In his collection of models for schools the French writer Léon de Vesly quotes the figure of 10,000 schools built between 1850 and 1868, but it is safe to estimate that some 40,000 schools were built in France up to the end of the century. Similar figures have been quoted for the United States. In Paris alone under Haussmann's administration 25,000 residential buildings were demolished and 70,000 new ones built.

This massive renewal of the stock of buildings affected every type of structure. In 1818 the British Parliament made funds available to help in the construction of churches, and between 1818 and 1856, 612 churches were built with subsidies from the Church Commissioners. A parliamentary report of 1876 stated that 1,727 churches and cathedrals had been newly built and 7,144 restored with public funds since 1840. In France the data are no less revealing. The figure of 200 Gothic churches under construction in 1852, quoted by Didron in his *Annales archéo-*

logiques, for a long time seemed to be an exaggeration, but the first statistical studies made in this field give reason to believe that it is probably accurate. In Brittany one third of the parishes of Finistère and of Morbihan and half those of Côtes-du-Nord and Ile-et-Vilaine rebuilt their churches during the nineteenth century.

This change in quantitative scale inevitably had an impact on the nature and quality of the architecture produced. In order to build quickly and on a large scale an attempt was made to perfect standard types which could serve as examples. The nineteenth century is the golden age of model collections of every kind, from the cottage to the city apartment block, from the church to the prison and mental hospital. The period can boast masterpieces comparable in distinction to the great works of the Renaissance (Charles Robert Cockerell's Ashmolean Museum,

2   Tower Bridge, London; J. W. Barry and H. Jones, 1886–94.

Karl Friedrich Schinkel's Academy of Architecture in Berlin, Henri Labrouste's Bibliothèque Sainte-Geneviève and Garnier's Opéra in Paris, Henry Hobson Richardson's Trinity Church in Boston); but the originality of this period doubtless lies as much in the mass of average works – little Victorian churches, Haussmann-style apartment blocks, American cottages – as in these few masterpieces. The individual building is less significant than the series to which it belongs.

Here we can see the effect of a major change in the system by which buildings are commissioned. It is not so much the conflict between architects and engineers, on which so much ink has been spilled, that explains the crisis in traditional plastic values as the development, side by side with traditional personal commissions, of more anonymous ones by official bodies and industrial concerns. 'Where can art be', asks Gabriel Davioud, 'when in a country the house is no longer the home of the father of a family, who built it to pass on to his children after seeing them born and grow up there, but a large civilian barracks where the layouts are as banal as the decoration, since both must be equally pleasing to the first potential tenant of a flat who comes along?'

It became the practice to make systematic comparisons between the costs of each design in terms of construction, layout and style: is iron more expensive than wood, neo-Gothic than neo-Romanesque? The private proprietor calculated the return on his investments; the civil servant the cost of each sick bed and each prison cell. Architecture became standardized, regulated and quantified. The modernity of the nineteenth century is due to the adoption of the typological approach just as much as to the use of new materials.

As early as the eighteenth century French architects saw the progress of their art in that of the art of layout. At that time all that was involved was the layout of town mansions and country houses. In the nineteenth century every type of building was affected – even the church marginally. The movement that began about 1770 was, as we shall see, significant in other respects: a new type of pavilion hospital was proposed, the specifications for a museum were pondered, the ideal of the panoptic prison defined. In the years 1820–30 another significant development took place: Leo von Klenze established a new model for an art museum, and John Haviland one for prisons; these were followed shortly afterwards by bazaars, winter gardens and the first railway stations, which were frequently modified until the end of the century. Yet to come were suburban villas, large hotels, department stores, swimming baths and so on.

Never had so much thought been given to the connection between the layout of spaces and people's mode of life, religious ritual, or patients' health. Never before had the architect been so dependent on the type of building he was engaged on, right down to details of design. The English neo-Gothic movement was partly due to a liturgical reform in the church; prison architecture was determined by the philosophy of penal reformers; and the complex layout of the Victorian country house reflected nineteenth-century social structure.

Thus questions of style were covertly relegated to a secondary status. Yet never before had they so perplexed architects. From 1820 onwards the desire to define the style of the nineteenth century was expressed with increasing insistence. No less insistent was the despair felt at the constant failure to do so. 'Each period has its own architectural style, why haven't we established our own?', wrote Karl Friedrich Schinkel in 1841. 'The great question is: are we to have an architecture of our period, a distinct, individual, palpable nineteenth-century style?', asked Thomas Leverton Donaldson, the first professor of architecture at University College, London, in 1847.

What had happened was that nineteenth-century architects had discovered the history of art and artistic liberty at the same time. Having found styles that were dominant in past centuries, they believed that an organic link existed between style and society; reasoning by analogy, they expected a style appropriate to the nineteenth century to emerge without realizing that the new conditions under which architecture was produced were destroying the mechanisms which, in past centuries, had ensured this arbitrary stylistic coherence. 'Once style imposed itself on the artists; today the artist must rediscover style,' Viollet-le-Duc noted with perspicacity.

Neo-classicism, Hellenism, Italianate classicism, neo-Gothic, neo-Romanesque, eclecticism, national-ism, free style, Art Nouveau – new experiences emerged throughout the century. These styles existed side by side instead of succeeding each other. Even eclecticism, which is sometimes claimed to be *the* style of the nineteenth century, is as diverse and controversial as liberalism in politics. A neo-classical Parliament building and a neo-Gothic town hall were built in the same city, Vienna. For the Valhalla near Regensburg von Klenze proposed two designs for one and the same project: a variation on the Parthenon and a neo-Gothic design. For the Glyptothek in Munich the same architect even suggested three designs, respectively in Greek, Roman and Italian style. Indeed, Sir George Gilbert Scott, in spite of his neo-Gothic convictions, had to adopt an Italian style in order to retain a commission. Never before had cultural, political, social, regional and national contrasts been stated in architecture as deliberately as they were in costume. Stations were divided into five categories, but they might be Moorish in Andalusia and Flemish in the north of Europe. Officials calculated the cost of a square metre of a university lecture-hall, but at Lille the arts faculty was in classical style and the school of Catholic theology in neo-Gothic. On the avenue Montaigne in Paris the medieval mansion of Prince Soltykoff stands next door to the Pompeian villa of Prince Napoléon.

Viollet-le-Duc claimed that structural design might constitute the universal principle of modern architecture. His mediocre creations demonstrate, as if in mockery, that this is not the case: one can be a theorist of genius and an admirable draughtsman yet a second-rate architect. Nor can the form really be determined by the specification: the architectural simplicity of nineteenth-century French hospitals was the result of the economic policy of the hospital administration (to build as inexpensively as possible) and of an aesthetic postulate, which might also be an alibi (utilitarian buildings must not be decorated). Under no circumstances was the style deduced logically from the specification, for English hospitals, which followed the same hygienic principles, were entirely different in their architecture.

Lastly some people believed that the new industrial civilization would give birth to new architectural forms. They had high hopes of the newly introduced materials – cast and wrought iron, glass and concrete – which, since they brought a visible break with past

3 Designs for a village school for 90 to 100 children; Ludwig Persius, 1845.

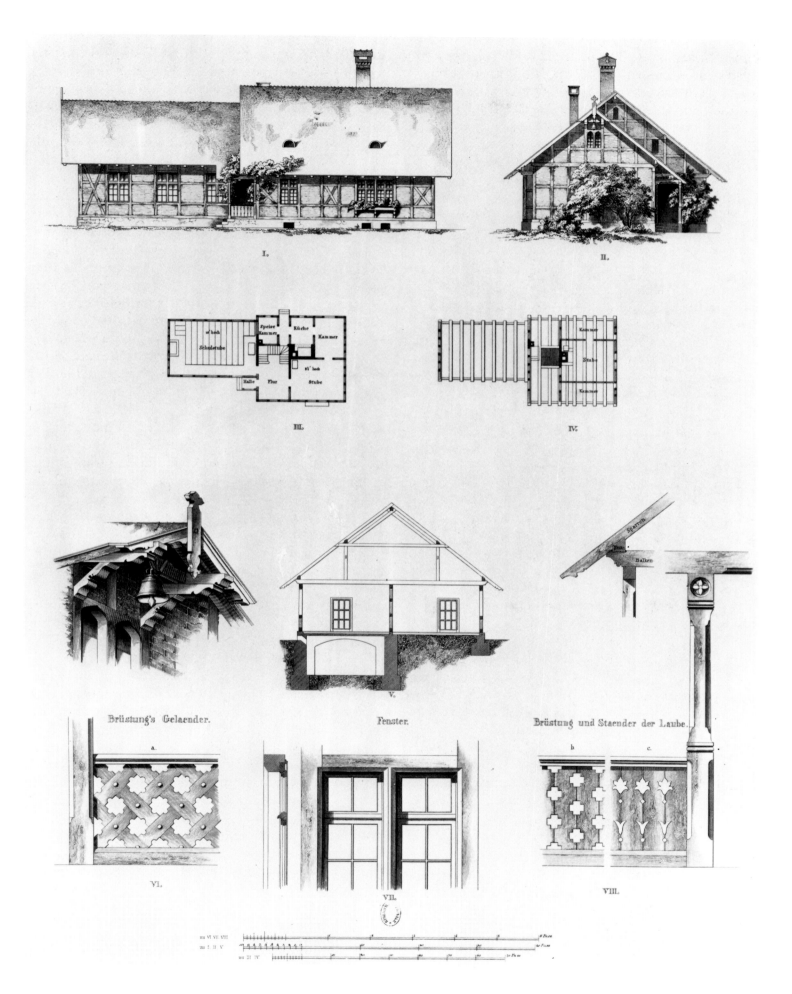

I.

II.

III.

IV.

Brüstung's Gelaender.

Fenster.

Brüstung und Staender der Laube.

V.

VI.

VII.

VIII.

I I

methods of building, might be a harbinger of a new architecture. But neither cast iron nor concrete can define a form, since they are capable of being fashioned into different shapes. As Charles Garnier remarked, it is no more natural to leave these materials exposed than it is to cover them up. Architectural 'writing', like literature, can maintain ambiguous and complex relationships with previous forms; like literature, too, it can escape the spirit that rules the age. This remains a slightly scandalous idea; but it alone explains the disconcerting variety of nineteenth-century architecture.

Today religious architecture is nothing more than an official formula made up of decorous reminiscences; royal and princely architecture died with the court and the high aristocracy; and the middle class, in spite of its admirable qualities, has long shown itself to be incapable of artistic creation in the architectural domain. However, we are witnessing the rebirth of an architecture which is private, stylish, comfortable and elegant; already we see rising a few great public buildings devoted to this new power (the crowd), town halls and theatres which are the palaces of our democracies; but if there is anywhere an original work which is truly new, for which the past provides no models, it is to be sought in our modern exhibition halls. These lines of Paul Planat, written in 1892, highlight the general characteristics of nineteenth-century architecture: the obvious and often unexpected inconsistency in the quality of churches; the emergence of a private middle-class architecture which combined elegance with amenity; the importance of public buildings which restored the architectural rhetoric of royal and princely palaces; and original new types of buildings suited to an industrial era in which architects went in deliberate quest of innovation.

The originality of architectural culture lies in these contradictions and experiments. Never before had the variety of styles been so great or the effort at standardization so persistent. Never had the quest for novelty been so deliberate or imitation so common. International exchanges were so frequent that to talk of 'free-trade taste' was natural, but everywhere it was above all a national architecture that was sought. Never before had there been so much reflection and writing about architecture, but between the nostalgic return to the past and the confidence in progress a certain pessimism often slipped in as regards the quality of contemporary work. Antique polychromy and iron-and-steel futurism, the taste for the picturesque and the quest for modern amenities – these were various facets of the same naïve hope of producing what Viollet-le-Duc called 'a form of art appropriate to our time'. Nevertheless the originality of the nineteenth century was reflected in systematic thought on building types and specifications and in the strained relationship with the whole tradition of architecture.

Classicism and Questions of Style

'Architecture and the entire Academy are nowadays in danger of becoming pioneers.' (Quatremère de Quincy, 1829)

The Legacy of the Enlightenment and Classical Ideal

The pattern of history rarely coincides with the artificial divisions of the past into centuries. In many respects innovations and discontinuities are more frequent during the years 1765–70, 1835–40 and 1915–20 than around 1800 or 1900. The nineteenth century inherited a style, or rather an architectural ideal, which by common consent is still called 'neo-classicism' or 'Romantic classicism', although we are now more aware of the heterogeneity of its constituent parts. In Europe and America it was dominant until about 1835–40. Its internal contradictions, the progress achieved in national archeologies, the Gothic Revival quarrel, and the development of new technologies shattered its certainties and gave rise to a dual aesthetic of eclecticism and rationalism. The antagonism between these aesthetic principles was scarcely resolved by the end of the century. It became identified with the nineteenth century in the public mind about 1850, which is precisely the moment when the last links with the Age of Enlightenment were severed.

About 1770 the shifts within the Renaissance tradition (neo-Palladianism, neo-Mannerism), the archeological revival (discovery of ancient Greek art and a new feeling for the architecture of Imperial Rome), and the return to nature, reason and sensibility had fostered the emergence (through mechanisms which are still largely obscure) of a new architectural idiom in which certain features constantly recur: clear-cut lines which eschew the easy charm of cornice mouldings; monochrome surfaces which are either smooth or harshly scored with the grooves of joints; simple masses which with the aid of certain antique archetypes (tholos, temple, peripteros, pantheon) allude ever more explicitly to elementary geometrical forms (cube, sphere, pyramid, cylinder); contrasts emphasized by light and shade; regular colonnades and porticos contrasting boldly with great bare walls of sublime simplicity; and finally cupolas and barrel-vaults with austere coffering in a chiaroscuro cast by toplighting.

At the same time a new type of garden where dells, groves, sheets of water, winding avenues and pavilions were laid out with pleasing irregularity had appeared in England and soon replaced the terraced garden with regular flower beds of the Italian and French tradition throughout Europe. These gardens were composed in the manner of paintings and enlivened by ancient ruins and Italian summerhouses, the roots of which are to be found in the bucolic landscapes of Poussin and Dughet, by peasant cottages and mills, which recall the works of Ruysdael or Salvator Rosa, or by Chinese pagodas and Indian pavilions, which flattered the cosmopolitan aristocracy's taste for the exotic.

To provide a vocabulary for these reorientations, the traditional notion of the 'beautiful' under the arbitrament of good taste was supplemented by notions of the 'sublime' and the 'picturesque' which, without conflicting, made up a dual aesthetic. Unity was achieved through the identification supposed to exist between nature, antiquity and reason and through a refocusing of the architectural effect on the subjective feelings of the spectator. By means of an ordered interplay of visual and symbolic associations architecture was to speak to the spirit and move the soul.

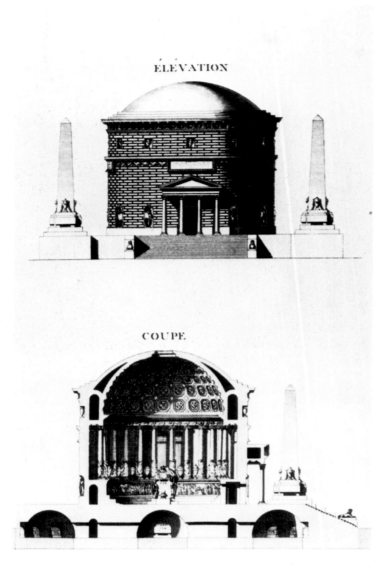

COUPE

4 Elevation and section of a mausoleum. After Joseph Peyre, 1795, Pl. 6. The paradigm of the Pantheon.

Whether due to a pause after the turbulence of the French revolution or to pure chance (the slow and oblique progress of history never fails to afford historians an opportunity to exercise their ingenuity by picking out significant events from the wide array available), there appeared round 1800 several books which seemed both to sum up the experience derived from the past and to embody the problems of the new century.

In 1765 the *Œuvres d'architecture* by Joseph Peyre (1730–85) had given dramatic expression to a new sensitivity, born in Rome in the international circle of the Piranesians, to the grandeur of the architecture of Imperial Rome. The work's republication in 1795 reaffirmed this taste for these somewhat megalomaniac designs, with their predilection for colonnades endlessly multiplied, imposing domes and huge ther-

mal baths. It was an essential element in the architecture of the French and Russian empires, and also of certain small autocracies, and foreshadowed the megalomania of the grand style of the École des Beaux-Arts. Étienne-Louis Boullée (1728–99) passed away before he could publish his *Essai sur l'art*, in which he presented the new ideal of the 'sublime' which he had formulated. However, he passed it on to numerous pupils, among them Claude Nicolas Ledoux (1736–1806), who in 1804 published *De l'architecture considérée sous le rapport de l'art des mœurs et de la législation*. He accompanied this anthology of his work with a rationalist discourse that had a visionary and clandestine masonic element. The new models of private mansions, churches – Saint-Philippe-du-Roule, 1772–84, by Jean-François Chalgrin (1739–1811) – and public buildings – the École de Chirurgie, later the École de Médecine, 1769–75, by Jacques Gondouin (1737–1818) – would remain essential landmarks for three decades; their plans were published by Jean Charles Krafft and Nicolas Ransonnette (*Plans, coupes et élévations des plus belles maisons et hôtels construits à Paris*, 1802). It was in England, however, that William Gilpin (*Three Essays on Picturesque Beauty*, 1794), Uvedale Price (*Architecture and Buildings connected with Scenery*, 1794–8 and *Essays on the Picturesque*, 1810) and Richard Knight (*An Analytical Inquiry into Principles of Taste*, 1805) gave the aesthetic of the picturesque its most potent expression.

In 1802 Jean-Baptiste Rondelet (1743–1829), who in 1799 became professor of building at the reorganized École des Beaux-Arts, published the first volume of his *Traité théorique et pratique de l'art de bâtir*. This embodied the fruit of the experience he had acquired with Jacques-Germain Soufflot (1713–80) in building Sainte-Geneviève, which, polemics aside, remained a work of reference for the whole nineteenth century – from the cathedral at Helsinki to the Palais de Justice in Brussels. It comments on Vitruvius, synthesizes the progress made in the art of stereotomy by Jean Rodolphe Perronet (1708–94), whose bridges remained models for the following generations, and gives an account of the first experiments in the structural use of cast and wrought iron. The fact that it was republished in 1847 with a *Supplement* by G. Blouet (1795–1853) highlights the continuity between the eighteenth and nineteenth centuries. The later period inherited that universal curiosity characteristic of the Age of Enlightenment: an interest in technological innovation, a spirit of inquiry into the world in all its diversity, and a return to the antique past.

5   Admiralty, St Petersburg (Leningrad); Adrian Zakharov, 1806–23.

6   Marktplatz, Karlsruhe, W. Germany; Friedrich Weinbrenner, 1804–24. Left, the church (1807–16); right, the town hall (1821–5); the pyramidal monument was erected in 1823.

In the mid-eighteenth century there had been a remarkable upsurge of interest in archeology. This discipline emerged from the narrow confines of scholarship and acquired a more worldly tone – evident in works ranging from *Pausanias ou voyage historique de la Grèce*, published in Paris in 1731 and translated into every language by the end of the century, to *Voyage pittoresque de la Grèce* by the Comte Choiseul-Gouffier in 1782, reissued in 1809. At the same time archeologists adopted a more scientific approach. In 1732 excavations began at Herculaneum under the auspices of the king of Naples, and in the same year London witnessed the establishment of the aristocratic 'Society of Dilettanti', whose touristic hedonism set the tone for dozens of archeological expeditions for more than a century. Curiosity expanded to embrace the whole of the ancient Mediterranean world, from the Orient (Robert Wood and James Dawkins, *The Ruins of Palmira in the Desert*, 1753, and *The Ruins of Balbek . . .*, London, 1757) to Greece (Julien-David Leroy, *Les Ruines des plus beaux monuments de la Grèce*, Paris, 1758, translated into English in 1759 and into German in 1769).

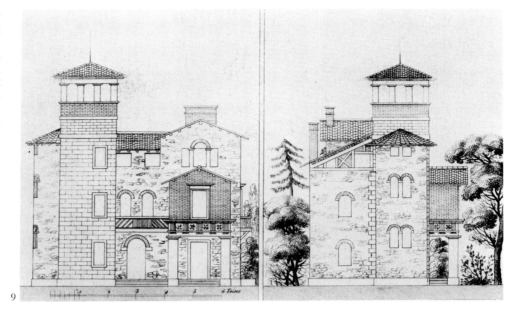

These efforts continued unabated. The first volume of *The Antiquities of Athens*, which became the bible of Hellenizing classicism, was published by James Stuart and Nicholas Revett in 1762, the second in 1787, the third in 1795, and the fourth in 1816. Studies of the ruins of Paestum were published in Paris by Dumont and Soufflot in 1764, in London by Mayor in 1768, in Rome by Piranesi in 1784, and again in Paris by Delagardette in 1799.

A similar interest was aroused by civilizations outside Europe. The taste for chinoiserie took a more architectural turn when, on his return from a journey to Canton, Sir William Chambers (1723–96) published his *Designs of Chinese Buildings, Furniture . . . Gardens . . .* (London, 1757), in which he recognized the unity of Chinese culture, which was both different and complete in itself.

Changes that occurred on the political scene led to certain shifts of direction. The maritime supremacy of Britain and the Napoleonic blockade were no doubt the reason why the itinerary of English architects was transferred from Italy to Greece early in the century, and the establishment of the Académie de France in the Villa Medici at Rome under the Empire provided a permanent setting for the institutional trend of French archeological research into Roman antiquity. Bonaparte's expedition to Egypt in 1798 was instrumental in turning a decorative and picturesque Egyptomania of a Piranesian character into Egyptology. In England the activities of the East India Company fostered neo-Indian taste (Richard Gough, *A Comparative View of the Ancient Monuments of India*, 1786; William Hodge, *Select Views of India*, 1786; Thomas Daniell, *A Picturesque Voyage to India*, 1810) which had no counterpart on the Continent.

But exchanges were too international in character for these trends to be exclusive: in 1808 Legrand produced a French edition of Stuart and Revett's *Antiquities of Athens*, and the *Voyage dans la Basse et Haute Egypte* by Vivant Denon (Paris, 1802) was published in London in 1803, and in New York in 1807.

Just as the neo-classical style reawakened an interest – palpable in Ledoux, George Dance (1741–1825) and Hans-Christian Hansen (1803–83) – in Giulio Romano's (1499–1546) stark Mannerist architecture, it also fostered a new appreciation of the effects produced by the cubic mass and the solid surfaces of the *palazzo* of the Italian Renaissance. Between the pretty-prettiness of Rococo and the severity of the Greek style, the firm and elegant lines of these palaces pointed to a middle way which Charles Percier (1764–1838) and Pierre François Léonard Fontaine (1762–1853) were the first to explore: 'One must remember,' wrote the latter, 'that the beauties and perfections of fifteenth-century works are more applicable to our purposes than those of Greek and Roman buildings.' With their variety of expression, ranging from the rather rough severity of the Florentine palaces of the Quattrocento to the smiling graciousness of the Venetian palaces of Jacopo Sansovino (1486–1570), these models were perfectly fitted to the specifications for certain public buildings (libraries, archives, seminaries, universities) as well as for residential blocks and private houses in towns. To put them into effect architects very soon had in their hands the records made by Percier and Fontaine, *Palais, maisons et autres édifices modernes dessinés à Rome* (1798) and *Choix des plus célèbres maisons de plaisance de Rome et des environs* (1806), which became reference works for Europe throughout the century; Auguste

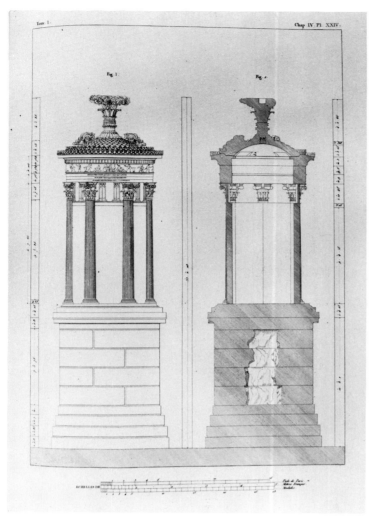

10   Monument of Lysicrates, Athens. After James Stuart and Nicholas Revett, *Les Antiquités d'Athènes*, vol. I, chap. IV, Pl. 24.

11   Ionic temple on Illissos. After James Stuart and Nicholas Revett, 1808, vol. I, chap. II, Pl. 8.

Henri Victor Grandjean de Montigny's (1776–1850) *Architecture toscane* (1806–19) was done explicitly in imitation of them. This return to the Italian architecture of the High Renaissance beyond the seventeenth century grand style has a picturesque companion piece. The rural architecture of the Roman landscape, with its asymmetrical belvederes and simple lime-washed walls, naturally caught people's attention in a general climate of pastoralism and Italophile attitudes. Significantly enough, Pierre Clochar mingled academic and vernacular architecture in his *Palais, maisons et vues d'Italie*, published in 1809.

All these publications were the first manifestations of an international 'bibliographic revolution' which, between 1750 and 1850, drastically changed the 'museum of the mind' (Malraux) of architects, their employers and clients. The *Recueil et parallèle des édifices de tous genres anciens et modernes*, published in the very year 1800 by Jean Nicolas Louis Durand (1760–1834), which shows side by side and on the same scale the buildings of every age and country, bears striking testimony to the broadening of cultural horizons that took place in the second half of the eighteenth century. At one and the same time architects became aware of the historical distance separating modern architecture from that of the Renaissance and the ancient world and also of the latter's varied character. Precisely at the beginning of the century there took shape three architectural responses to the European crisis of conscience – eclecticism, rationalism and archeological imitation – between which the nineteenth century could never make up its mind.

Although rejected in the name of good taste by Pierre Patte (1723–1814) and by Sir William Chambers, the new architectural images were for the most part well assimilated by an eclectic classical culture long before the term eclecticism was coined. It was not simply that the aesthetic of the picturesque sanctioned the multiplication of Egyptian, Greek, Chinese and Indian motifs in garden pavilions; like the rustic order of Giulio Romano in the sixteenth century, the archaic Doric of Paestum, burly and without base, and the Corinthian splendours of Baalbek also added their adornments to the classical range. In 1786 Matthieu Delagardette (1762–1805) had no compunction about adding to his *Règle des cinq ordres de Vignole* the Doric order of Paestum. Pyramids and Egyptian obelisks, grandiose Sicilian temples, propylaea, and Athenian temples of the winds were added to the repertoire of antique archetypes upon which the architectural imagination had worked since the Renaissance. But the historical variety of these forms exploded the basic myth of classicism. Thus

Klenze (1784–1864) proposed for the Munich Glyptothek three designs in Greek, Roman and Italian style respectively, accentuating in this way the conventional and cultural character of the architectural idiom and marking for the first time the distinction between *style* and *styles* which is basic to an understanding of nineteenth-century architecture. With aesthetics once more focused on architectural effect, a subjective associative symbolism insinuated itself in place of the ideal identification of nature with antiquity. The way was thus opened for the assignment of styles according to the type of building, a characteristic feature of mid-century eclecticism: severe archaic Doric would be thought suitable for prisons and law courts, Egyptian style for cemeteries, and late Corinthian for imperial palaces.

Setting their minds against this stealthy eclecticism, a group of English amateurs and architects suggested replacing Roman orders by the purer range of Greek ones. The start of this Greek revival or Hellenizing classicism was marked by the foundation in London in 1803 of the 'Athenian Society for the Study of the Most Perfect Art' and the pamphlet issued in 1804 by Thomas Hope (1769–1831), one of these philhellenic dilettantes, against the Roman design proposed by James Wyatt (1746–1813) for Downing College, Cambridge. The Greek Doric column, which Chambers judged to be ugly because of its bad proportions, or had been used by Ledoux or Friedrich Gilly (1772–1800) because of its bulk, now appeared to be beautiful because it was Greek.

As in fifteenth-century Italy, archeological studies led to the deliberate revival of an architectural system at odds with preceding tradition. Just as the 'beautiful antique style' of Filippo Brunelleschi (1377–1446) and Leone Battista Alberti (1404–72) sprang from a new awareness of a *medium aevum*, this Greek Renaissance was made possible by the discernment of essential differences between the principles of Greek and Roman architecture.

For its advocates it was not a question of subjective choice but rather of a return to the purity of the primi-

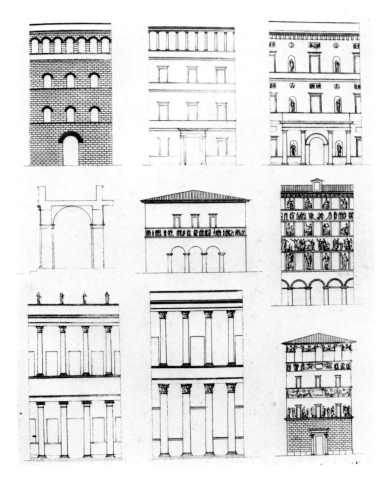

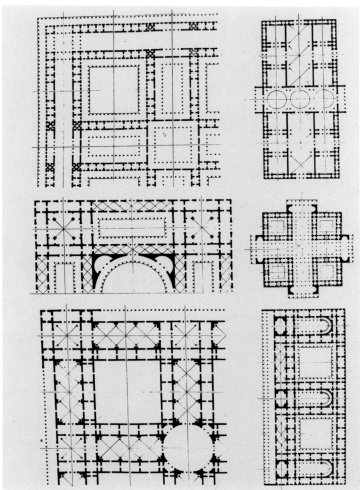

12   Vertical combinations of columns and arches. After Jean Nicolas Louis Durand, 1802–9, vol. I, 2, Pl. 3.

13   Ground plans of buildings. After Jean Nicolas Louis Durand, 1802–9, vol. I, 2, Pl. 22.

14, 15　Two designs for the Glyptothek of Munich, Leo von Klenze, 1815: above, in Roman style; below, in Renaissance style. Klenze put forward three variants.

tive forms that had existed prior to the distortions that had allegedly been perpetrated, not by the Middle Ages as was thought in the fifteenth century, but by the Romans. However, the Greek style could become the true criterion of architectural distinction only in a general climate of philhellenism. Literary evocations, subjective associations, fashion and archeology conspired together in a manner foreshadowing all subsequent 'renaissances'. Viewed in retrospect, this Hellenizing classicism may be seen as the first of the revivals characteristic of the nineteenth century.

An entirely different avenue of investigation was chosen by Jean Nicolas Louis Durand, a pupil of Boullée, in the architectural courses which he gave at the École Polytechnique from the time of its foundation. The first *Précis* of these lectures was published in 1802. Republished in 1817–18 with an illustrated supplement, this became a reference work throughout Europe for half a century. As if reacting in opposition to the general spread of eclecticism and the increasing number of parallel revivals, Durand proposed that

architecture should be based on an ageless rational principle: economy of geometry and layout.

As far back as 1753 Abbé Marc-Antoine Laugier (1713–69) had attempted, in his *Essai sur l'architecture*, to place architectural theory on a more solid basis than antique tradition or modern taste when he reflected on the natural model of the primitive hut. Between this first attempt at rational analysis, quite touching in its naïveté, and Durand's rationalism there is the same distance as between Soufflot's architecture and that of Boullée. Durand backs up his analysis by a critical appraisal of Sainte-Geneviève (Panthéon): 'It is arrangement alone which should concern the architect, even if he sets store only by architectural decoration and seeks only to please, since this decoration can be called beautiful, can yield true pleasure, only if it is the result of the most suitable and the most economical arrangement' (*Précis*, p. 21). It must be remembered that the desire to persuade and please a difficult public of young scientists may have fostered the crystallization of these ideas, but Durand, by making rational fulfilment of the specification the guiding principle of architecture, defined the common ground for all those who, through-

16 Glyptothek of Munich, Leo von Klenze, designed 1815, executed 1816–30. Ludwig I of Bavaria, who had acquired the Aegina sculptures in 1812, chose for the new museum of sculpture he had resolved to build the third variant, in Greek style, which Klenze had put forward.

17 Glyptothek of Munich, interior view. In his design for the interior, Klenze was inspired by a model published by Jean Nicolas Louis Durand, vol. I, 2, Pl. 12, Fig. 15.

out the century, were offended by the multiplicity of styles.

After stating these principles, Durand went on to develop a progressive system of teaching: starting with the study of the elements of architecture, 'which are to architecture what words are to speech and notes to music', he proceeded to their vertical and horizontal combinations and the design of parts of buildings, and then showed 'how they should be combined in their turn in the overall composition of structures' (*Précis*, p. 29). The graphic section accompanying his course was illustrated by admirably lucid drawings. So successful was he in abstracting the essentials in his graphic work that these diagrams attained the desired universal value. As well as a distillation of the new neo-classical language into terms suitable for teaching, they paved the way for a separation of architectural syntax and vocabulary which, by transcending the variety of motifs, ensured the unity of eclecticism.

Thus those major themes of the nineteenth century – desire for Roman grandeur and picturesque asymmetry, rationalism of structure and layout, subjective historical symbolism, eclectic classicism and archeological dogmatism – are already present in embryo on its threshold.

18   The Madeleine in Paris: façade; Pierre Vignon, 1807–45. In accordance with the wishes of Napoleon I, the building was designed to be a temple of glory dedicated to the heroes of the Grande Armée: when it was decided at the Restoration by royal decree (1816) to make it into a parish church, the interior was altered.

Neo-Classical Poetics: Rome, Greece and Italy

Neo-classical poetics is characterized by its return, over and beyond the syncretic types of the Renaissance, to antique archetypes (pyramids and obelisks, temples and tholoi, triumphal arches and thermal baths). Its strength and charm derive from the tension sustained between the almost transparent references to elementary geometrical forms (cube, sphere, pyramid) and the almost literal imitation of exemplary monuments (Choragic Monument of Lysicrates in Athens, tomb of Cecilia Metella in Rome). The allusions are no longer to the portals of Giacomo da Vignola or the Italian-style salon, St Peter's in Rome or the Gesù, but rather to the Propylaea of Athens (project for Downing College, 1806, by W. Wilkins) and the atrium of Pompeian houses (Belsay Hall,

1806–17, by John Dobson), the Parthenon (Valhalla near Regensburg, 1830–42, by Leo von Klenze) or the Pantheon (University of Virginia, 1804–17, by Thomas Jefferson).

The commemorative columns which appeared in growing numbers all over the world throughout the century were derived from prototypes such as the Vendôme column raised in Paris by Jacques Gondouin and Jean-Baptiste Lepère (1761–1844) – a Napoleonic version of the Trajan column (1806–10) – the Nelson pillar (1808–9, destroyed in 1966), set up in Dublin by William Wilkins, the Washington column by Robert Mills at Baltimore (1815–29), and the Alexander column by Auguste Ricard, alias de Montferrand (1786–1858) in St Petersburg (1829).

Reflections of the Propylaea of Athens engraved by Leroy, which served as a frontispiece to Durand's *Précis*, were to be seen everywhere: entrances to towns, castles, gardens or cemeteries. So too was the related motif of the Roman triumphal arch, which imperial rhetoric seized upon without being its exclusive exponent. In their Arc du Carrousel (1806–8), the monumental entrance to the Tuileries and the memorial to Austerlitz, Percier and Fontaine recalled

19 Valhalla, near Regensburg; Leo von Klenze, 1830–42. After the defeat of Napoleon at Leipzig in 1813 Ludwig I of Bavaria decided to build a 'hall of fame of famous Germans'. The first competition was held in 1814-15; the second, in 1829, was won by Klenze.

20 Monopteral temple in the English Garden, Munich; Leo von Klenze, 1827. One of Klenze's drawings, preserved at the R.I.B.A. in London, shows the colour lithograph intended for this pavilion, which is typical of a Hellenized picturesque style.

21 Valhalla, near Regensburg: interior; Leo von Klenze, 1830–42.

22 Altes Museum, Berlin: the rotunda; Karl Friedrich Schinkel, designed 1823, executed 1824–8. Jean Nicolas Louis Durand published in his work a design for a museum round a circular hall with a dome.

23 Altes Museum, Berlin; Karl Friedrich Schinkel, designed 1823, executed 1824–8. Through the slenderness of its proportions the Greek Ionic order mitigates the majesty severity of the colossal portico crowned by a small attic which screens the central rotunda.

the Arch of Septimus Severus, which they had examined in Rome. In Marseilles, on the other hand, Michel Robert Penchaud (1772–1832) was inspired rather by the Arch of Titus (1823–32). In Milan the programme of monumental gates started by the French was continued by the Austrians: from the Porta Ticinese (1801–13) by Luigi Cagnola (1762–1833) to the Porta Venezia (1827–33) by R. Vantini (1791–1856). In Paris the Arc de Triomphe de l'Étoile, designed by Jean-François-Thérèse Chalgrin in 1806, was completed under the July monarchy by Abel Blouet (1795–1853); and in Germany the Brandenburg Gate in Berlin, constructed in 1789–93 by Carl Gotthard Langhans (1732–1808), has its counterpart in the Propylaea of Munich (1846–53) by Leo von Klenze. In 1837 Philip Hardwick (1792–1870) had the Propylaea of Athens in mind for his treatment of the entrance to Euston station.

The model of a temple standing alone on a high podium arouses no less interest. It is echoed in examples ranging from the 'Temple de la gloire' drawn in 1806 by Pierre Vignon (1762–1828), which became the church of the Madeleine (1807–45), to the National Monument in Edinburgh (1822–5) by Charles Robert Cockerell (1788–1863) and William Henry Playfair (1789–1857), which was not completed, and von Klenze's Valhalla.

It is significant that when it was desired to add a monumental façade to the National Assembly in Paris, installed for better or worse in the Palais Bourbon, Bernard Poyet's (1742–1824) mind naturally turned to a peristyle (1806). In France this motif is to be found in ten or more law courts, from the severe Doric of Rheims (1841–5) by Augustin Nicolas Caristie (1783–1862) to the elegant Ionic of Périgueux by Jean-Baptiste-Louis Catoire (1806–50). It recurs in the majority of American capitols: from the Virginia state capitol at Richmond (1785–8) by Thomas Jefferson to Vermont state house by Ammi B. Young with its cupola (1832) and the Tennessee state capitol at Nashville (1845–59) by William Strickland (1788–1854) with its pinnacle, copied from the Choragic Monument of Lysicrates. More generally, a temple frontispiece was chosen for the façades of temples of the law (law courts, legislative assemblies, capitols) and of art (museums and galleries) since to the Enlightenment mind these buildings symbolized the progress of civilization. Examples include the Glyptothek in Munich (1816) by Klenze, the Altes Museum in Berlin (1824–8) by Schinkel, the British Museum in London (1847) by Sir Robert Smirke (1780–1867), the National Gallery of Scotland (1850–4) by Playfair.

24 Siegestor, Munich; Friedrich von Gärtner, begun 1844. The arch, modelled on the Arch of Constantine in Rome, was built to commemorate the Bavarian troops who fought in the Wars of Liberation in 1813–15. It stands at the northern end of the Ludwigstrasse.

If the frontispiece has clearly become a feature to be expected for the façades of churches, starting with the prototype of Saint-Philippe-du-Roule by Chalgrin, it also provides a face for banks (Second Bank of the United States, Philadelphia, 1818–24; Old Savings Bank, Cork, Ireland, 1824), stock exchanges and even private houses. The combination of a peristyle and two simple volumes, a cylindrical drum and a hemispherical dome with austere coffering, explains the predilection for the theme of the Pantheon. An archaic flavour was often lent by the substitution of a Greek Doric portico, as in the Tempio of Antonio Canova (1757–1822) at Possagno (1819–22).

There were nevertheless marked differences in the cultural climate from one country to another; witness the contrast between the Continent, where the aesthetic of the sublime was more vigorously asserted, and England, where the picturesque found earlier and more ambitious expression; between the Roman rhetoric of the French and Russian empires and the Greek style of the young American democracy; between French Raphaelism and English Philhellenism; between the narrow-horizoned culture of the smaller Scandinavian and Italian states and the capacity for assimilation shown by certain German architects such as Schinkel or Klenze.

25 Propylaea in Munich; Leo von Klenze, 1846–53.

26 Ruhmeshalle, Munich; Leo von Klenze, 1843–50. The site, high above the Theresienwiese, was chosen by Klenze at the behest of King Ludwig I, but while work on the statue was in progress it was decided that it should be in 'Old Germanic' style; it was cast in iron by Ferdinand Miller in 1844–50 after a design by Ludwig Schwanthaler.

The faster pace at which political and military history moved and the necessity of digesting the vast heritage of buildings nationalized by the Revolution no doubt explain why the most vigorous expressions of 'sublime' neo-classicism were built not in France but in the autocratic countries of northern Europe, where the ideal of the enlightened prince still survived, and in the small princedoms of Italy.

In Russia, from the reign of Catherine II (1762–96) onwards, there had been a close association between enlightened absolutism and neo-classicism. Under Alexander I (1801–25), to whom Ledoux dedicated *De l'Architecture. . .* in 1804, the planning on a monumental scale of St Petersburg, founded in 1703, continued without interruption. The most remarkable of these edifices, in which the new ideal of Boullée and Ledoux was embodied, are the Stock Exchange, built in 1804–16 by the Frenchman Thomas de Thomon (1754–1813), with the sturdy simplicity of its archaic Doric order, the Admiralty, built in 1806–15 by Adrian Zakharov (1761–1811), a pupil of Chalgrin, with its square colonnade crowning a massive cube, and the Academy of Mines in 1806–11 by Andrei Voronikhin (1759–1814), who was a pupil of Charles de Wailly (1730–98) in Paris. After 1816 a younger generation abandoned this sublime neo-classicism for a more tempered version. In the General Staff Headquarters in 1819–29 and the Senate in 1829–34, built by Karl Ivanovich Rossi (1775–1849), who received his training in Russia, the effect is due only to the colossal scale of regular colonnades on a massive base. In St Isaac's cathedral of 1817–57, a variation on the

27 Senate Square, Helsinki; Johann Carl Ludwig Engel, designed 1818. The square is framed by the Senate Building (1818–22) and the University (1828–32), and dominated by the Lutheran Cathedral, designed in 1818 and built between 1830 and 1852.

theme of Soufflot's Sainte-Geneviève (Panthéon), the Frenchman Auguste Ricard, called de Montferrand, lavished materials with a sumptuousness that rivalled the architecture of Imperial Rome. In this respect he emulated his master Percier.

An architecture of somewhat less impressive dimensions and more austere appearance prevailed in the Scandinavian kingdoms. Christian Frederik Hansen (1756–1845) utilized for Copenhagen's prison and the law courts (1803–16) a sturdy rustic style which recalls Ledoux. For the cathedral, Vor Frue Kirke (1811–29), he took the basilical design of the royal chapel at Versailles and reinterpreted it in terms of archaic sublimity. An archaic Doric colonnade, dominated by a large coffered vault, was superimposed upon vast bare arcades.

28 University of Helsinki: atrium; Johann Carl Ludwig Engel, 1828–32.

29 Former Senate House, Helsinki: the great staircase; Johann Carl Ludwig Engel, 1818–22.

30 Piazza del Plebiscito, Naples; Leopoldo Laperuta, 1809. With its fine colonnades in the Doric order, inspired by Murat, the piazza – formerly the Forum Murat, then the Forum Fernandino – lies between the south-western façade of the Palazzo Reale and the church of San Francesco di Paolo, by Pietro Bianchi, 1817–31; on either side stand the Palazzo Salerno (eighteenth century) and government buildings (1815).

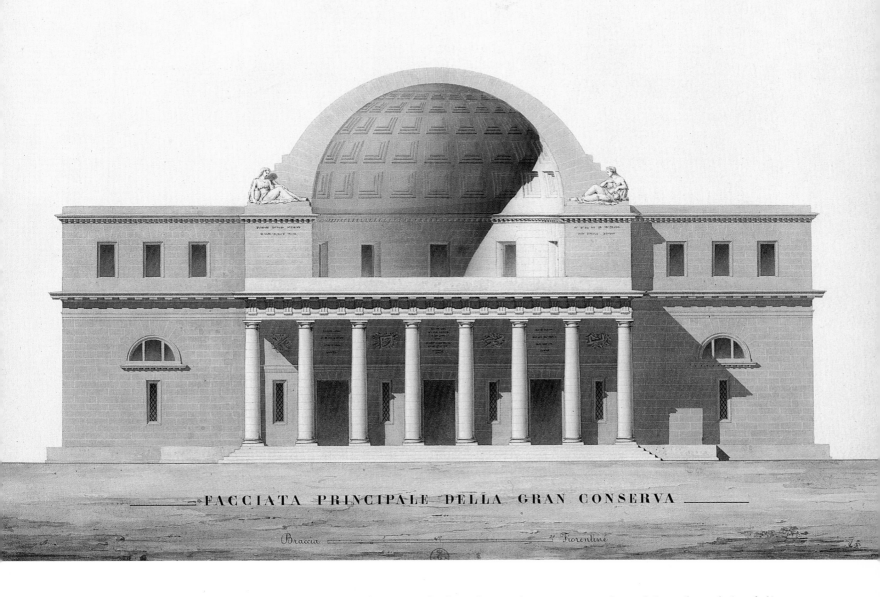

FACCIATA PRINCIPALE DELLA GRAN CONSERVA

Braccia *Fiorentine*

31 Il Cisternone, Leghorn; Pasquale Poccianti, designed 1827. The monumental cistern was executed between 1837 and 1848.

The creation of the Grand Duchy of Finland in 1809 gave Carl Ludwig Engel (1778–1840) an opportunity to create what is beyond doubt one of the finest neo-classical urban layouts, the great Senate Square of Helsinki. This is flanked by the Senate (1818–22) and the University (1818–32) and dominated by the steps which lead up spectacularly to the Lutheran cathedral (1830–52), a rather successful variation on Soufflot's Sainte-Geneviève (Panthéon). In the neo-Greek atrium of the university library, which has a fine adjoining staircase (1836–44), Engel played skilfully on the contrast between the squat and archaic profile of the baseless columns, smooth and fluted, and the delicacy of the sculptured friezes.

The separation of Norway from Denmark in 1814 afforded Christian Henrik Grosch (1801–74), a pupil of Hansen, similar opportunities in Oslo. At Gdańsk (Danzig), then under Prussian rule, in the municipal theatre, Held almost attains the poetry of Ledoux. In the various Italian states, certain constructions (San Francesco di Paola in Naples, 1816–24; the Cisternone at Leghorn, 1837–48) and countless projects bear witness to the same aspirations.

The adoption of new rules of hygiene together with the progress achieved by the Enlightenment, whose luminaries banished cemeteries to the outskirts of towns, the new cult of great men and the traditional importance of the funeral liturgy – all these en-

29

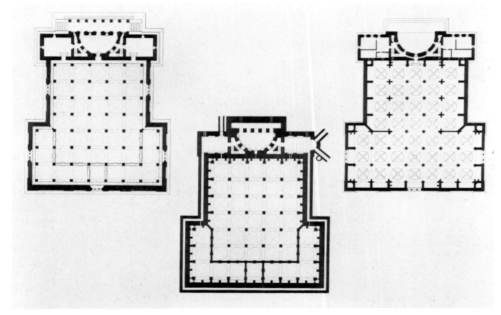

couraged here, as on a smaller scale in Spain, the creation of vast cemeteries of monumental architecture which are among the finest and least known manifestations of the aesthetics of the sublime. Neo-classical megalomania found fitting scope in these vast courtyards lined with porticos and centred on one or more 'little pantheons', consecrated to the cult of the great men of the city: the cemeteries of Campo Santo, above Genoa, designed in 1825 by Carlo Barabino (1768–1835), of Verona by Giuseppe Barbieri (1828), of Brescia by Rodolfo Vantini. In Spain, we find similar cemeteries at San Isidoro in Madrid by J. Aléjandro y Alvarez (1842).

In France the examples are on a more modest scale: the expiatory chapel in Paris (1816–24) by Fontaine,

monuments to the dead Royalists of Quiberon (1825) by Caristie, whereas in England and the United States picturesque designs were created for small parish cemeteries, and also the large landscape cemetery of the kind proposed by Alexandre-Théodore Brongniart for le Père-Lachaise (1804).

In England the complete decentralization of centres of decision, the absence of an Academy as the arbiter of good taste, and the importance of an aristocracy whose culture was cosmopolitan were conducive to great variety. Sir John Soane (1753–1837) pursued his own solitary graphic meditations aloof from all the conventional forms of classicism, producing smooth and gentle surfaces of a linear pattern which capture shadows with great deli-

34 Cemetery of Staglieno, Genoa; Carlo Barabino, designed 1825, executed 1844–51. The archetype of the Pantheon has been Hellenized by the use of a 'Greek' Doric order: also to be noted is the use of the slope and the interplay of the flight of steps and the vegetation.

35 Cumberland Terrace, Regent's Park, London, 1826–7; John Nash and James Thomson. This 'terrace', the most spectacular of those surrounding Regent's Park, is to be compared to the rue de Rivoli by Charles Percier in Paris. Like Blaise Hamlet (1811, John Nash) it recalls the ideal of a composed architectural landscape made up of pictures.

cacy; Thomas Harrison (1744–1829) at Chester Castle (1793–1820) and George Dance junior (1741–1825) at Stratton Park, Hants (1801–3) fell little short of the sublime neo-classicism of the Continent.

However, from the first decade of the nineteenth century onwards, two phenomena – the widening scope of the picturesque aesthetic and the growth of an uncompromising Hellenic classicism – bestowed on English architectural culture a specific character that lasted a long time. John Nash (1752–1835) extended the principles of picture composition to whole villages (1811, Blaise Hamlet), to country houses (about 1802, Cronkhill) and the urban landscape. Regent Street (from 1811 onwards) and the terraces surrounding Regent's Park are composed with a

sense of pictorial contrast and surprise as a park. Cronkhill is organized asymmetrically round a circular tower reminiscent of the Italian buildings decorating the landscapes of Claude Gellée. The contrast between the plans and elevations with their continental right-angled symmetry and the asymmetrical British overall design was to remain noticeable until the end of the century.

The most striking feature of these first decades was the success of 'Hellenic classicism'. This was given impetus by a new generation of architects who had travelled in Greece. Sir Robert Smirke and William Wilkins were associated with Lord Elgin's team in Athens around 1800. In the following decade Cockerell, John Foster (1787–1846) and Henry William

36   All Souls Church, Langham Place, London; John Nash, 1822–4. The church serves as a pivotal point for the whole of Regent Street as laid out by J. Nash; it is a variation on the classical motif of the tempietto and topped by a spire, an interesting translation of a Gothic feature into neo-classical language. Here the orders are in the Roman, not Greek, idiom.

37   St Pancras Church, Euston Road, London; William and Henry William Inwood, 1819–22. A Hellenized version of a type of church fixed by James Gibbs early in the eighteenth century. The portico has the proportions of the Greek and not the Roman Ionic order; the octagonal steeple is a variation on the Tower of the Winds in Athens with a top borrowed from the Monument of Lysicrates; and the side portico is a pastiche on that of the caryatids of the Erechtheum.

Inwood (1794–1843) found Lord Byron there along with thousands of moneyed tourists. (In 1826 a traveller commented with disgust on the thousands of names cut in the columns of Sunium.) On their return these architects published learned reports and substituted Greek Doric and Ionic profiles for the Roman orders. The success of William Wilkins's neo-Greek designs for Downing College in 1804 and for the East India College at Haileybury in 1805 marked the beginning of this movement, which soon spread all over England – to Plymouth with John Foulston (1772–1842), to Manchester with Francis Goodwin (1784–1835) and to Liverpool, where John Foster took up his abode. Scotland was also affected: Aberdeen, Glasgow and particularly Edinburgh, which became the 'Athens of the North' with contributions by William Henry Playfair and Thomas Hamilton (1784–1858), whose knowledge of Greece, however, was second-hand. Their works acquire their vigour

from the scenographic dispositions of masses on a 'sublime' site, for the elegance and precision of this archeological Hellenism, which has a charming effect in a small church (St Pancras by Inwood), did not suffice to give character to a monumental composition (British Museum, by Smirke). Consequently, after 1840 everywhere except Scotland this style fell into a disfavour just as violent as the initial infatuation had been.

In America Thomas Jefferson pursued his meditation on classic, Roman and Palladian themes with great distinction. Benjamin Henry Latrobe (1764–1820), who arrived there in 1796, introduced the ideal of the neo-classical sublime into the cathedral at Baltimore (1805–18) along with the first echoes of British Hellenism (Bank of Pennsylvania, 1798–1800). Trained in his studio, Robert Mills remained more faithful to the idea of the sublime, whereas William Strickland did not hesitate to adopt

38 Royal High School, Edinburgh; Thomas Hamilton, 1825-9. The picturesque way the masses and colonnades are handled owes a great deal to the Acropolis in Athens, known directly or, in this case, indirectly, and was to remain one of the essential dimensions of the Greek Revival in Scotland.

39 Royal High School, Edinburgh: the hall. Note the cast-iron columns supporting the gallery.

40 Royal College of Physicians, Queen Street, Edinburgh; Thomas Hamilton, 1844.

41 Second Bank of the United States, Philadelphia, Pa.: south portico; William Strickland, 1818–24. Strickland's design was modelled on the Parthenon, reduced by three fifths.

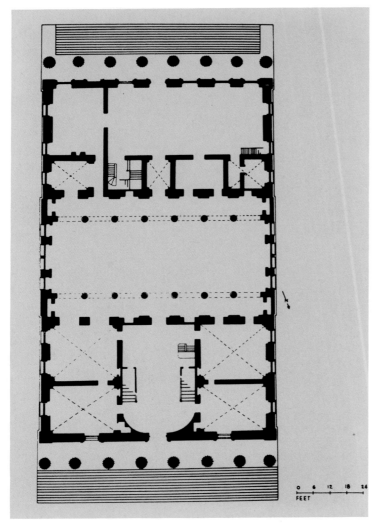

Hellenic elegance. In the 1820s the 'Greek Revival' was triumphant in public buildings, as well as in simple houses built of wood in the vernacular style; here books of models popularizing the Greek orders produced what might be called 'carpenter's Hellenism'.

The nationalization of the assets of the clergy and emigrants in France, and then throughout revolutionary Europe, suddenly placed in the hands of the state an immense heritage of property (convents and churches, abbatial palaces and aristocratic mansions) in which were installed the public departments, prefectures, law courts, prisons, hospitals that the new administration set up. There was no lack of ambitious projects (project for enlarging Versailles by Antoine François Peyre, junior, the Palace of the King of Rome at Chaillot by Percier and Fontaine, 1811, etc.). Chalgrin turned the Palais de Luxembourg into the Senate; Antoine Vaudoyer (1756–1846) installed the Institut in the Collège des Quatre-Nations. Charles Percier (1764–1838) and Pierre François Léonard Fontaine, the architects of the Emperor Napoleon, were engaged in multifarious conversions at Malmaison, the Tuileries and Fontainebleau.

The influence of Percier, who trained several generations of architects, seems to have been a determining factor in the success of this mode. Designed in 1810, the Ministère des Relations Extérieures (later Cour des Comptes, burned down in 1871) by Jacques-Charles Bonnard (1765–1818) was the first building in Paris 'to recall the character of the sumptuous palaces of modern Rome, both in the development of the plan and in the decoration of external and internal elevations. Its façades will be decorated with two orders of architecture like the first two floors of the Farnesi palace in Rome.' Following Percier, French architects were partial to the somewhat cool mouldings of the Chancellery Palace or the linear rustic work of the Lancellotti Palace rather than to Florentine vigour. This linear style, which goes perfectly with that of the line drawing then in fashion and with the chilly elegance of the Restoration, culminates in the seminary of Saint-Sulpice in Paris (1820–38) by Étienne Hippolyte Godde (1781–1869) and in the town library of Moulins (1821–9) by François Agnety. It almost tended to become the official style of the Conseil des Bâti-

42 Second Bank of the United States, Philadelphia, Pa.: plan; William Strickland, 1818–24.

43 University of Virginia, Charlottesville: view looking towards the library; Thomas Jefferson, 1817–26.

44 University of Virginia, Charlottesville; Thomas Jefferson, 1817–26. After a lithograph by Bohn, 1856. The idea of a university as an academic village had been conceived by Jefferson as early as 1804.

45 University of Virginia, Charlottesville: one of the ten pavilions; Thomas Jefferson. Jefferson wanted each pavilion to be different so that 'the buildings could serve as a model for professors of architecture'.

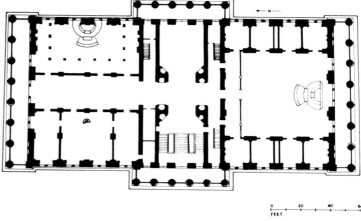

46 Tennessee State Capitol, Nashville: south façade; William Strickland, 1845–59. With its Ionic colonnades modelled on those of the Erechtheum and its turret, which is a variation on the Monument of Lysicrates, it is one of the last monumental expressions of the Greek Revival in America.

47 Tennessee State Capitol: plan; William Strickland, 1845–59.

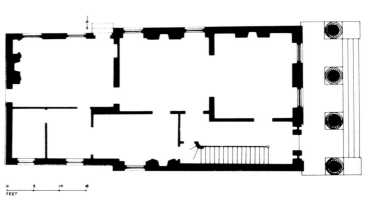

48 The house of Judge Wilson, Ann Arbor, Michigan, 1843. Built at a time when the first Italianate houses were appearing in the United States, it is a fine example of the house-temple, the prototype of which is the Samuel Russell House at Middletown, Connecticut; Ithiel Town and Alexander Jackson Davis, 1828–30.

49 Wilson House, Ann Arbor, Michigan: plan; 1843.

50 Rue de Rivoli, Paris; Charles Percier and Pierre François Léonard Fontaine, 1802–55. A type of apartment block developed in Paris during the eighteenth century (Place de l'Odéon) has been infused with a discreet Italian element which is apparent in the delicacy of the window frames and the single string course.

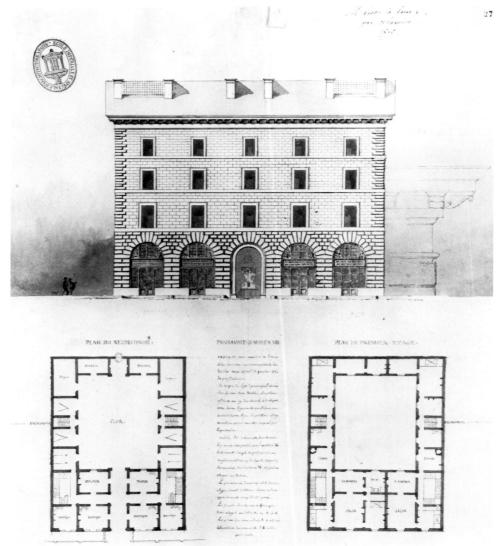

51 'Maison à louer', first prize at the École des Beaux-Arts; Jean Antoine Alavoine, 1805.
An academic exercise in the Italian style of the Cinquecento advocated by Percier and Fontaine; here the severity of the style has close affinities with the general values of neo-classicism.

ments civils, and was adopted in dozens of similar buildings. The anthology published by Gourlier, Biet and others, *Choix d'édifices publics projetés et construits en France depuis le commencement du XIXe siècle* (1825–36), played an indisputable part in its dissemination.

This return, over and beyond French models of the seventeenth and eighteenth centuries, to the Florentine *palazzi* of the Quattrocento and the Roman of the Cinquecento, inevitably calls to mind the Raphaelism and pre-Raphaelism evident in art history at the same period. There is more than coincidence in Quatremère de Quincy's publication of a *Histoire de la vie et des œuvres de Raphael Sanzio d'Urbin*, 1824, in which he eulogizes the nobility and purity of style in the Pandolfini Palace in Florence, and in the label 'Raphael of Architecture' which Caristie bestowed on his master Percier in 1840. There are also resemblances between this movement and neo-Palladianism: Percier, Fontaine and their emulators did for town architecture what Burlington and Kent had done for that of country houses eighty years previously. Neither this Palladianism, nor this 'Raphaelite classicism', if the appellation be allowed, are strictly speaking revivals; however, by isolating the type of the Palladian villa and that of the Florentine and Roman *palazzo* in the Renaissance tradition, they appear in retrospect to be the first manifestations of that tendency to a stylistic typology which was characteristic of the nineteenth century.

By reason of its characteristics and its open-mindedness to foreign influences German architecture reflected the diversity of European architectural culture during the first decades of the nineteenth century. Friedrich Weinbrenner (1766–1826) transformed Karlsruhe into a city of exemplary neo-classicism.

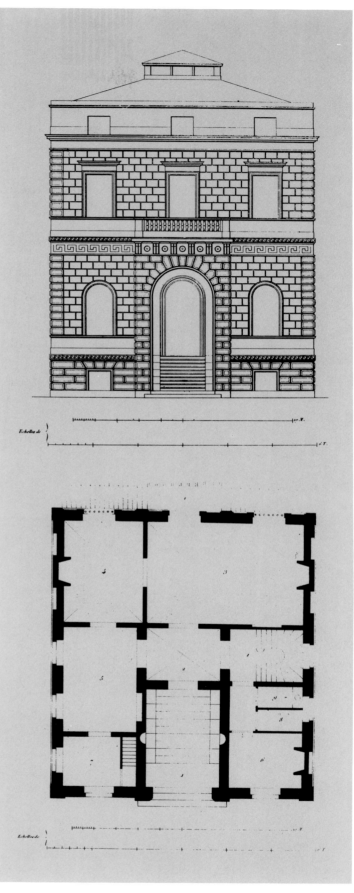

52 House at Poix, Somme, *c.* 1840. A typical example of Italianate neo-classicism.

53 House in the rue Las Cases, Paris 7: elevation and plan; Jean Constantin Protain, 1832. After L. M. Normand.

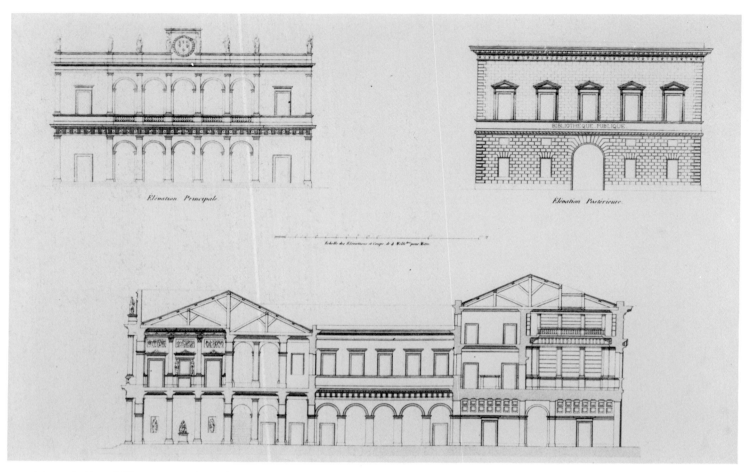

Élévation Principale.

Élévation Postérieure.

Echelle des Élévations et Coupe de 4 Mill.mes pour Mètre.

54   Town hall and library, Moulins, Allier; François Agnety,
1821. After Gourlier and others, 1825–36, vol. I, Pl. 39.

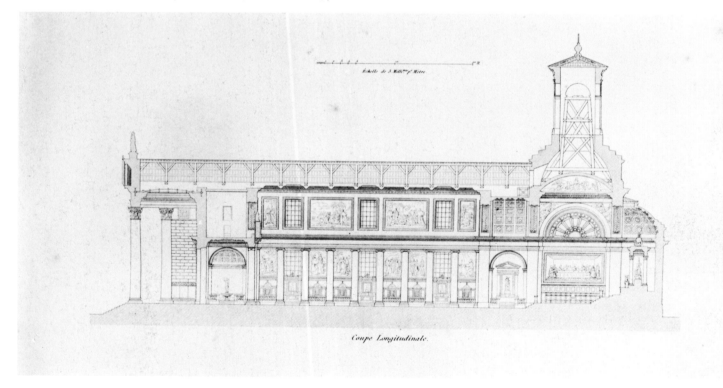

Echelle de 3 Mill.mes p.r Mètre.

Coupe Longitudinale.

55   Notre-Dame-de-Lorette, Paris: section; Louis Hippolyte Lebas, 1823–36. After Gourlier and others, 1825–36, vol. I, Pl. 117. 'When he (Lebas) gave serious thought to this work which was to become Notre-Dame-de-Lorette, he had continu- ally before him the memory of the gracious image of Santa Maria Maggiore' (Félix Pigeory, 1849, p. 147). The Early Christian basilicas of Rome remained the model of the neo-classical church until about 1840.

56 Notre-Dame-de-Lorette, Paris: front; Louis Hippolyte Lebas, 1823–36. The exterior with its somewhat severe majesty remains within the tradition of Jean-François-Thérèse Chalgrin's Saint-Philippe-du-Roule.

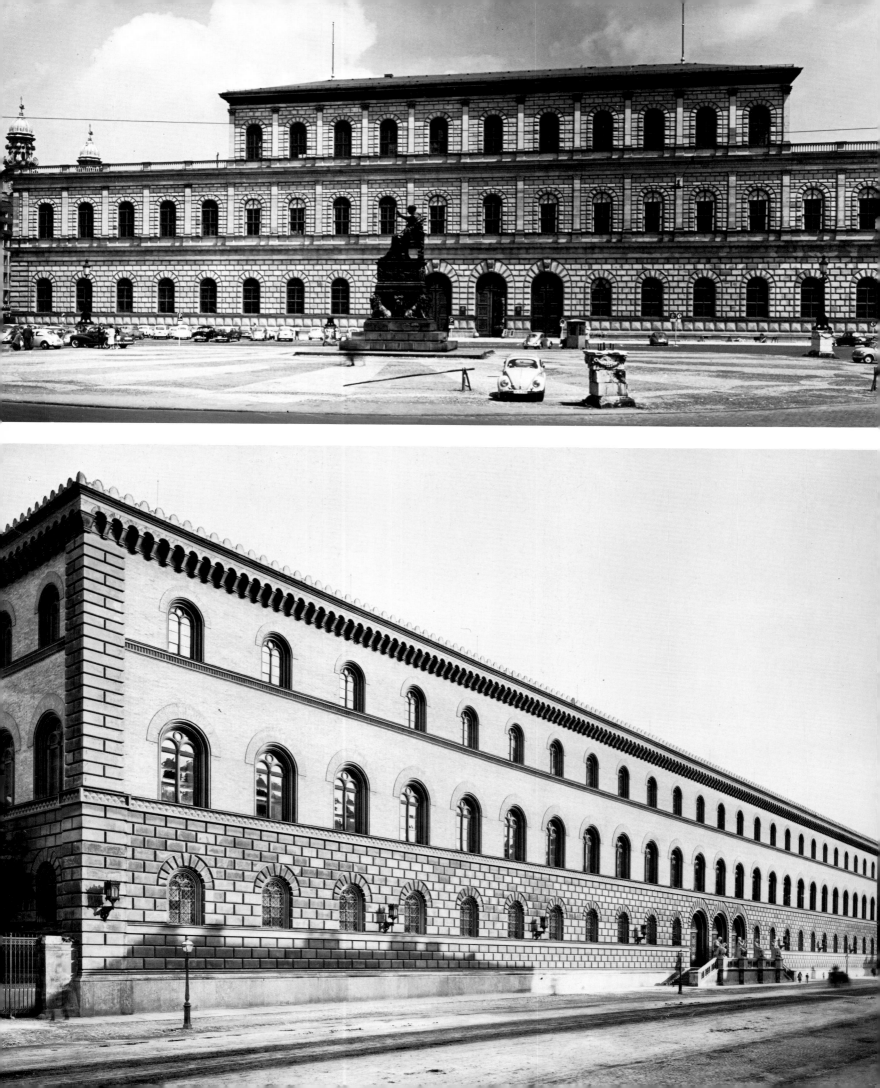

57 Königsbau, Munich: front facing the Max-Joseph Square; Leo von Klenze, 1826–33. The silhouette of the Palazzo Pitti, the general composition of the Palazzo Rucellai, and inside a free and asymmetrical layout.

58 Library (Staatsbibliothek), Munich; Friedrich von Gärtner, 1831–40. A subtle variation on the archetype of the Quattrocento Florentine *palazzo*.

59 Rosenstein Castle, Stuttgart; Giovanni Salucci, 1824–9. For the central portico, which is taller and juts out further, Ionic columns were used, but for the smaller ones on either side those of the Doric order were chosen.

60 Alte Post, Hamburg; Alexis de Chateauneuf.

61

62

63

64

65

61 Mausoleum for the royal family of Württemberg on the Rotenberg near Stuttgart by Giovanni Salucci, 1820–4. The exterior is a felicitous adaptation of the model of Palladio's Villa Rotonda at Vicenza. The interior is divided into a lower vault and an upper chapel.

62 Stock exchange, Hamburg; Carl Ludwig Wimmel and Gustav Joachim Forsmann, 1836–41. Extension by Lindsay after the fire of 1842.

63 Charlottenhof, Sans Souci Park, Potsdam, G.D.R.; Karl Friedrich Schinkel, 1826–9. The hierarchy of the buildings is clearly stated by the contrast between the Hellenized style of the castle of Charlottenhof and the rustic Italianate style of the gardener's house, but the picturesque asymmetry and the interplay of the pergolas brings unity to the whole.

64 The gardener's house, Sans Souci Park, Potsdam, G.D.R.; Karl Friedrich Schinkel, 1828–9. Here the gardener's house is treated like a rustic Italian pavilion.

65 Schauspielhaus, Berlin; Karl Friedrich Schinkel, designed 1818, executed 1819–21. The line drawing in hard pencil emphasized the reduction of the Greek vocabulary to almost abstract elements.

66 Academy of Architecture (Bauakademie), Berlin; Karl Friedrich Schinkel, 1831. The building is notable for terracottas of Italian inspiration, mouldings in the Greek spirit and yet a monumental 'neo-classical' simplicity; this was one of the first artistic uses of glazed brick in modern times.

67 Feilner House, Berlin: elevation and section of the façade, details of decoration; Karl Friedrich Schinkel, 1829. The extensive use of terracotta and the motifs of the bas-reliefs are adopted from the Italian Renaissance, but the proportions of the openings and the slenderness of the frames are in keeping with the Hellenizing tendency.

68 Bauakademie, Berlin: section of the façade; Karl Friedrich Schinkel, 1831.

69, 70 Bonifatius Basilica, Munich; Georg Friedrich Ziebland, 1835–50. One of the most ambitious basilicas in Europe in the revived Early Christian style.

In the Marktplatz he placed the frontispiece of the Protestant church (1806–17) opposite that of the town hall (1821–5). In Berlin Friedrich Gilly would have proceeded on similar lines but for his premature death. In Munich, Leo von Klenze, who had travelled in Italy and England and who was one day to succeed Grandjean de Montigny at the court of Westphalia, was, like his rival Friedrich von Gärtner (1792–1847), very open-minded in cultural matters. He handled the neo-classic idiom with ease (Glyptothek) and, like his Parisian master Percier, was responsive to the model of the Italian Renaissance *palazzo*. The Leuchtenberg Palace (1817) reflects his admiration for the Farnese *palazzo* but he often tends towards a more vigorous Florentine style. More than once he found inspiration in the silhouette of the Pitti *palazzo*, which he combined with a façade composition suggested by the Rucellai *palazzo* for the War Ministry (1824–6), and in that of the Quaratesi *palazzo* for the Royal Residence (Königsbau, 1826–33), where, however, he adapted it by dispensing with the ground-floor order so as to create a plinth effect which shows the *piano nobile* to greater advantage. His interest in the Tuscan forms of the Quattrocento and his pondering over the lessons of Durand on elementary forms led him to evolve a

successful style of simple forms punctuated by semi-circular arches. Two decades later it linked up with the reviving interest in Romanesque architecture to form what the Germans call *Rundbogenstil* (round arch style).

Karl Friedrich Schinkel, whose personality dominated the cultural life of Berlin directly and indirectly for almost a century, approached architecture with a much broader vision. He bestowed on the massing of his neo-classical buildings in Berlin (Schauspielhaus, 1819–21; Altes Museum, 1824–8) an impressive authority. At Potsdam, in the Charlottenhof (1826–9), he skilfully rang the changes on antique reminiscences and Italian picturesqueness in the landscape but, after 1828, he also experimented on an increasing scale with terracotta and brick. In this medium he was able to blend his admiration for the Renaissance architecture of Lombardy, his taste for 'Greek' forms of slender elegance, and his interest in technological experiments (Feilner house, 1829; Bauakademie, 1831). He was also interested in the possibility of producing Gothic arabesques in cast iron (Kreuzberg Memorial, 1818–21) and, like Goethe, was responsive to the sublimity of both the Greek temple and the Gothic cathedral.

The Gothic Foundation

'The peculiar charm of Gothic architecture is in its associations; they are delightful because they are historical, patriotic, local and intimately blended with early reminiscenses.'
(Report of the Commission for the Reconstruction of the Houses of Parliament in London, 1835)

Picturesque Gothic and Medieval Archeology

The interest in the Gothic style, which had survived on the fringes of the dominant classical culture, underwent a marked revival towards the end of the eighteenth century. In England and Germany, and later in France, there was a new sensitivity to the airy lightness of pointed arches, to the sublime effects of shadowed naves, to the picturesque outline of Gothic pinnacles and window tracery. Round this sensitivity was woven a whole texture of literary and historical associations, for example the development of the 'Gothick novel' and the new interest taken in national history. The analogy between the primal forest and ogival architecture provided a base as natural as that which antique architecture had acquired from the myth of Adam's hut in Paradise. Very soon each country claimed Gothic as its national architecture: in his essay *Von deutscher Baukunst*, published in Frankfurt in 1772, Goethe hailed Gothic architecture as 'the German architecture, our architecture', and in *The Ancient Architecture of England* (London, 1795–1814), John Carter (1748–1817), one of the English 'antiquaries', saw it as 'our national architecture', as he wrote.

At the same time Carter advanced another idea which was to be still more influential subsequently: the notion of a specific link between Gothic style and religious architecture. As he wrote in *The Builder's Magazine* (1774–8), 'Nothing can be more in character and better adapted to a place of worship than that awful style of building (i.e. Gothic) . . . Grecian and Roman architecture should be confined to mansions and other structures of ease and pleasure.' Thus we find set forth for the first time the principle which was to become one of the fundamental ideas of nineteenth-century architectural culture; namely, the use of different styles depending on the type of building – what might be called compendiously: typological eclecticism.

With Soufflot, Laugier, Avril, the French seemed more sensitive to the structural logic of the Gothic style; the Germans with Goethe, Herder and Forster to the sublimity of the lofty vaults; and the English with Walpole to the picturesque character of the forms; but at the dawn of the nineteenth century the overlapping was too great for any true frontiers to be drawn in the new awareness of the Gothic style.

In the famous chapter devoted to the Gothic cathedral in his *Génie du christianisme* (Paris, 1801, III, 1, 8), Chateaubriand skilfully interweaves these themes, the basis of the Gothic revival, which were spread throughout Europe by the brilliance of his style:

1. Gothic architecture is national architecture: Each thing must be in its proper place [...] The Greeks would have no more liked an Egyptian temple at Athens than the Egyptians a Greek one at Memphis. If these two monuments had changed places, they would have lost their chief beauty, that is, their relationship with the institutions and habits of the nations. For us this notion applies to the ancient monuments of Christianity.

2. It is better adapted than the antique style to Christian worship:
It would be vain to build elegant and light-filled Greek temples to bring together the good folk of

71   Imaginary design with an ancient basilica; Karl Friedrich Schinkel.

Saint Louis and to make them worship a metaphysical God; they would always miss their Notre-Dame of Rheims and Paris, these moss-grown basilicas filled with generations of departed ancestors and the souls of their fathers.

3. It is sublime and picturesque:

These vaults with their carved leafwork, these pillars which support the walls and end abruptly like broken tree-trunks, the coolness of the vaults, the shadows of the sanctuary, the dark wings – all these recreate the labyrinth of forests in the Gothic church while invoking religious awe, mystery and divinity. The two lofty towers at the entrance to the building out-top the elms and yews of the cemetery and make a picturesque effect against the blue of the sky.

In the early decades of the nineteenth century this new sensitivity to the visual qualities and the religious and national value of the Gothic style spread ever more widely. The political and industrial revolutions marking the end of the eighteenth century were conducive to a new vision of the medieval epoch; what

had been condemned at the Renaissance as an age of ignorance and obscurity was soon to become, as institutions and customs crumbled, a golden age. Aggravated by the Napoleonic wars, German nationalism turned towards the glorious past of the German Holy Roman Empire and identified the Gothic style with the national German style – the *Neudeutsche-religiös-patriotische Kunst*. In France the neo-royalists set against the rationalist ideology of the Enlightenment the myth of Christian kingship and the popularity of Saint Louis. In Great Britain the tensions of the Industrial Revolution fostered nostalgia for the verdant England of medieval times.

Gothic sublimity was not admired to the exclusion of all else: Gothic cathedrals and antique temples were set side by side, like Shakespeare and Sophocles. In parks crenellated towers and ruined chapels flanked Chinese pagodas and little Greek temples. However, appreciation of the logic of pointed arch construction was always accompanied by condemnation of the Gothic vocabulary. Conversely, the aesthetic of the picturesque singled out from the Gothic style only its detached motifs, its crenels and lancet arches, its turrets and bartizans. Before this picturesque Romantic Gothic could be transformed into the Gothic re-

72 Imaginary design with a medieval cathedral, a variation on the Duomo of Milan; Karl Friedrich Schinkel.

vival, the Middle Ages had to replace antiquity as the ideal term of reference and medieval archeology had to provide working instruments as refined as those of ancient archeology.

It was not until the first decades of the nineteenth century that this ideological revolution got under way, along with the gradual development of archeological research. Two phases can be clearly distinguished: in the first of these the Gothic style was at best an alternative to the ancient style and medieval motifs were retained for their symbolic value and picturesque qualities. In the second the Gothic style was claimed to be a substitute for the ancient style. This second phase, neo-Gothic in the strict sense of the term, began after 1830 when the progress made in archeology in each country enabled an architectural content to be given to medieval Romanticism. In this way the gap was between rational analysis of the structure and picturesque vision of details.

Between the one and the other there is notable contrast without any actual break, and, significantly enough, the two trends are often reflected in a concrete father-son relation. William Pearson published in 1807 two volumes of topographical views of old country churches and picturesque cottages, *Antiquities of Shropshire*, 'to record old buildings before their impending destruction'; his son, John Loughborough Pearson (1817–97), was one of the protagonists of the neo-Gothic movement. The same phenomenon is to be seen in Augustus Charles Pugin (1762–1832) and his son Augustus Welby Pugin (1812–52).

In Great Britain the first expressions of the picturesque were mingled with numerous forms in which the Gothic had survived. Throughout the seventeenth and the eighteenth centuries the colleges of the English universities remained true to the Gothic style. From the 'Tom' Tower at Christ Church (Oxford) by Sir Christopher Wren (1681–2) to the Gothic screen of King's College by William Wilkins and the New Court of St John's College at Cambridge by Thomas Rickman (1825–31), the continuity was unbroken.

From 1796 to 1807 James Wyatt was working at Fonthill Abbey, the most ambitious Romantic 'folly' in Europe. It was designed in accordance with the wishes of its proprietor, William Beckford, as 'an ancient ruined abbey with the chapel, dormitory and part of the cloister still standing', and had its asymmetrical buildings grouped round an octagonal tower, the design of which was inspired by engravings in a monograph on Ely Cathedral published in 1771 by James Bentham, one of the first detailed studies of medieval architecture. The tower collapsed in 1825 but Fonthill Abbey remains one of the most potent images of the reaction to the Palladian ideal and of the new Romantic sensibility.

The notion of building a medieval castle for symbolic reasons is virtually contemporaneous with the dissolution of feudal society. From the mid-eighteenth century onwards, Inveraray Castle in Scotland (1745) furnished a model of a medieval-looking castle – a rectangular structure confined by round crenellated towers. This model was an unquestionable success in the British Isles down to the first decades of the nineteenth century (Taymouth Castle, Perthshire, 1806; Lee Castle, Scotland, 1820, and others). The poetics of the picturesque were soon to give a new lease of life to this model which, with its symmetrical layout and simple forms, is clearly derived from neo-classical rationalism. In 1808 Wyatt built Ashridge Castle (Hertfordshire), which, with its symmetrical plan confined within crenellated walls, seems also to be part of tradition, as is Eastmore Castle by Robert Smirke, built in 1812. Gwrych Castle (1814–15), near Abergele, North Wales, however, represents an innovation: the massive crenellated towers and crude openings are reminiscent of this neo-classic Gothic, but the architect Charles Augustus Busby (1788–1834) shows a very modern sense of the picturesque by the off-centre arrangement of the masses in a steeply falling landscape.

Karl Friedrich Schinkel's Babelsberg is an echo of these modern English Gothic castles which he had visited in 1826; by and large, however, continental architects built on a more modest scale in this respect: garden pavilions like the Cappèlla dei Templari at the Vigodarzere Villa near Padua by Giuseppe Jappelli, 1817; hunting lodges like the Château de la Reine Blanche near the Étang de Commelles, Oise, by Victor Dubois, 1825; best of all, small follies like the house of the Marquis de Forbin-Janson at Mont Valérien, west of Paris, c. 1820. Everywhere the Gothic style is simply a patchwork of stereotyped motifs; everywhere it is nothing but a version of the picturesque; from modern cottage to extravagant folly, the owner makes his choice between exotic, rustic, Italian or Gothic styles. Everywhere the taste of the proprietor, usually an eccentric aristocrat or a Romantic writer, was the determining factor: the villa of the Vallée aux Loups at Chatenay-Malabry (Hauts-de-Seine) in 1808 for Chateaubriand; Abbotsford Castle near Melrose (Roxburghshire) in 1816–23 for Sir Walter Scott, whose historical novels were largely instrumental in making this romantic and picturesque Gothic style a success in Europe.

In France the Gothic picturesque style had monarchist overtones which are apparent in the pompous ceremonials designed by Jacques Ignace Hittorff (1792–1867) for the baptism of the Duke of Bordeaux and the coronation of Charles X at Rheims, or in the small Chapelle des Herbiers in Vendée for the Duchesse d'Angoulême. In Germany, where national ambitions were growing, the equating of Gothic and German style explains why there was some hesitation between a neo-classical temple and a neo-Gothic church for Valhalla near Regensburg (1830–42, Leo von Klenze), that monument to the glories of Germany, why it was decided to complete Cologne

73 Taymouth Castle, Perthshire, Scotland; Archibald Elliot, 1806. Subsequent additions to the left and right have given a somewhat more picturesque note to an oversimplified design consisting of a square block with round towers at its corners derived from Inverary Castle (1745).

74 Taymouth Castle, Perthshire, Scotland: interior; Archibald Elliot, 1806. The fan vaulting, usually in stucco, is one of the most frequently adopted treatments for British interiors in which a medieval spirit is sought.

75 St Peter's Church, Brighton, Sussex, England; Sir Charles Barry, 1822. One of the churches constructed with the funds of the Parliamentary Commissioners.

Cathedral after 1815, and why in 1819 Schinkel gave the war memorial on the Kreuzberg in Berlin the form of a Gothic shrine.

In a number of English, American and German churches, the Gothic style was an economical alternative to the prevalent neo-classical. The most elaborate of the English churches built from 1818 onwards with the subsidies of the Church Commissioners feature a steeple and a neo-Greek portico. However, the majority of them – 174 out of the 217 begun before 1829 – were in elementary Gothic style. This allowed the idea of a church to be evoked at little cost and saved expenditure on a portico with columns in the antique style. Edward Garbett drew his inspiration from Salisbury Cathedral for his church at Theale (1820–32); but the ribs of most of these churches, whether in stone or cast iron, have nothing archeological about their style and, with the exception of St Luke's in Chelsea by James Savage (1779–1852), the vaults are of laths and plaster. As Augustus Welby Pugin, one of the protagonists of the subsequent

phase, observed in 1836: 'In some cases the architect tried to give his work the appearance of an ancient church with pointed arches, but the moment one enters the illusion vanishes. What looks like an old Gothic church is no more than a modern house of prayer.' Similarly Viollet-le-Duc was to laugh at 'these microscopic castles which are like children's playthings with their towers where a dog would feel cramped and their crenellations made for the cats' (*Entretiens sur l'Architecture*, II, 1863–72, p. 368).

By insensible degrees the development of countries changed the image of medieval architecture. The first societies of antiquaries were formed in England from the end of the eighteenth century onwards. It was then that the first scientific studies appeared and the first polemics broke out over the correctness of restoration work. During the early decades of the nineteenth century this interest in archeology became a European phenomenon and grew in intensity. A close network of learned societies, both local and national, was formed; international contacts were maintained

77, 78   Two studies for the Friedrich-Werdersche Kirche, Berlin, in classical style (above) and Gothic style (below); Karl Friedrich Schinkel, 1822. The handling of space is virtually the same, the only difference being that the proportions are a little more slender in the Gothic version.

76   Friedrich-Werdersche Kirche, Berlin: Karl Friedrich Schinkel, 1825–8.

79 'Group of churches to illustrate different styles of architecture'; Joseph Michael Candy after John Soane. Romanesque, Doric and Gothic variations for the church of St Marylebone, London, 1822–4; in the background a design in Ionic style for St Peter's, Walworth, *c.* 1822 and a funerary chapel at Tyringham, *c.* 1800. Drawing exhibited at the Royal Academy Exhibition, 1825, No. 902.

and the national architectural heritage was studied with enthusiasm. A growing number of publications appeared containing picturesque illustrations and archeological accounts of medieval buildings. The first of these tutored public taste and the second provided architects with graphic material, the accuracy of which was in no way inferior to that found in works on ancient archeology.

In 1806 John Britton (1771–1857) began to publish *The Architectural Antiquities of Great Britain* (1806–14), the first illustrated chronological history of English medieval architecture. This was followed in 1814 by fifteen monographs on English cathedrals, entitled *The Cathedral Antiquities of Great Britain* (1814–35). In France Baron Isidore Taylor (1789–1879) and Charles Nodier (1780–1844) undertook the publication of their *Voyages pittoresques et romantiques dans l'ancienne France* (21 volumes, 1820–78) and Nicholas Joseph Chapuy that of *Cathédrales françaises* (1823–31). In Germany Georg Moller published his *Denkmäler der deutschen Baukunst* (1815–18, translated into English in 1834 and 1836),

which inspired a comparable venture in Vienna by Joseph Fischer, and Sulpiz Boisserée published his study of Cologne Cathedral, *Domwerk: Geschichte und Beschreibung des Doms* (1823). Similar works saw the light of day in Spain (*Recuerdo y bellezas de España*, 1839–65 in twelve volumes, and *España artistica y monumental*, 1842–50), and elsewhere. All these studies, as a critic wrote of Britton's publication in 1815, were 'scientific enough to interest the expert, and picturesque as well as varied enough to entertain splendidly the non-specialist reader'.

Stylistic distinctions began to be made. Thomas Rickman (1776–1841) in *An Attempt to Discriminate the Styles of English Architecture*, 1817, taught the English to distinguish between 'Early English' (to 1290), 'Decorated English' (1290–1350) and 'Perpendicular English' (1350–1560). Arcisse de Caumont (1802–73), in his *Essai sur l'Art du Moyen Age particulièrement en Normandie* (1824), and then in his *Cours d'antiquités monumentales* (1830–1) proposed the terms 'Romanesque', 'Pre-Romanesque', 'Secondary Romanesque', 'Primordial or Lancet Gothic', 'Secondary or Radiant Gothic' and 'Tertiary or Flamboyant Gothic'. Similarly in Germany, Christian Ludwig Stieglitz (1756–1836) presented the first history of medieval German architecture in his *Von Altdeutscher Baukunst*, Leipzig, 1810.

The antiquarians did not devote themselves exclusively to monuments, cathedrals and castles; peas-

80 Jumièges in Haute-Normandie: entrance to the former abbey. After Charles Nodier, Isidore Taylor and Alphonse de Cailleux, vol. I, Paris, 1820, Pl. 24.

81 'Antiquarians at work': reconstruction of a window of the Abbey of Saint-Wandrille in Normandy. After Charles Nodier, Isidore Taylor and Alphonse de Cailleux, vol. I, Paris, 1820, Pl. 6.

ant vernacular architecture also attracted their attention, this being the architectural side of a more general interest in popular arts and traditions which was conceived in the nineteenth century. The mountain chalet assumed something like the form of a national architecture in Switzerland, where in the 1840s it was studied with an almost archeological seriousness, without, however, losing its picturesque value internationally. Similarly, the Moorish style which, until the end of the century, held its place for exotic evocations, took on in Spain the nature of a national style.

There were kindred bonds between the national studies of archeology, the restoration of ancient buildings, and the neo-Gothic movement. Rickman intimated that his object was to 'transmit sufficiently clear notions of history so that the guardians of our churches may be able to do careful restoration work, and to help architects to choose components in Eng-

lish style when they design churches'. Through restorations which were initially clumsy and perfunctory modern architecture linked up with the architecture of the Middle Ages: there was no break in continuity from simple repairs to free re-creation.

The churches and the cathedrals neglected or damaged during the revolutionary crisis and the Napoleonic wars were repaired; the spires and the pinnacles that had fallen down in the eighteenth century were restored; buildings still unfinished were completed: Carlo Amati (1776–1852) worked on the façade of Milan Cathedral (1806–13) and H. Grégoire gave a western front to the church of Saint-Ouen in Rouen (1845–52). When in 1801 it was planned to demolish the unfinished cathedral of Cologne, a campaign for its completion was started by Sulpiz Boisserée and Georg Moller. To re-create the cathedral as it should have been, Boisserée turned himself from an antiquary into a 'neo-Gothic' architect before his

time. In 1823 he published his studies under the title *Domwerk*. Restoration work began in 1823, was continued in 1842 after a campaign for the completion of the cathedral, and was not finished until 1880.

Almost all the neo-Gothic architects carried out restorations, which were often the most important part of their work, and new constructions at the same time. Jean-Baptiste-Antoine Lassus (1807–57) learned his profession repairing the Sainte-Chapelle and Chartres, Eugène-Emmanuel Viollet-le-Duc (1814–79) restoring Vézelay and Notre-Dame de Paris, just as Sir George Gilbert Scott (1811–78) did on the sites at Ely and Westminster, and Friedrich von Schmidt (1825–91), the architect of the Vienna town hall, on that of Cologne. Experience acquired on restoration work began to determine and shape new constructions. It can often be seen how the solution to a technical or sculptural problem on a restoration site was embodied directly in a modern neo-Gothic building.

This identification of restoration with creation reached its apogee in 1845, when a new neo-Gothic church in Rheims was described by Didron, the editor of *Annales archéologiques*, as a 'rare opportunity to resuscitate on a small scale this admirable church of Saint-Nicaise which was sold as national property and razed to the ground'. This link was so natural that, in 1867, Anatole de Baudot (1834–1915) mixed Gothic and neo-Gothic edifices in his *Églises de bourg et de village*. He worked out estimates for small thirteenth-century churches as if they had been contemporary buildings, stressing conversely that contemporary buildings were 'a serious application of medieval principles to our needs and our tastes'.

Neo-Gothic Churches

In the first decades of the nineteenth century religious feeling underwent a marked development. In reaction to the rationalism of the Enlightenment, the post-revolutionary generation again gave emphasis to emotional values and the liturgy. A young English architect, Augustus Welby Pugin (1812–52) by name, a convert to Catholicism, and a group of ritualistic Cambridge Anglicans together with the French Catholics round Count Charles de Montalembert (1810–70) created an architectural expression for this Romantic Counter-Reformation.

In their eyes the model of the classical temple was the reflection of a faith led astray by reform and rationalism, and a return to Gothic architecture seemed to them the instrument for restoring true Catholicism. 'The cathedral of Vannes is worth a hundred of these Greek temples of modern architects which have no kinship with our Christian ideas, no shadow, no meditation, no mystery,' wrote Abbé Fournier of Nantes in 1833, clearly with a page of the *Génie du christianisme* in mind; in 1836 H. R. Cleveland similarly went on record in the *North American Review* with the statement that the Gothic style is a 'style of architecture peculiarly appropriate to Christianity'. The 'neo-Gothic' church – the term was used by Montalembert after 1834 – sprang from the union of this development in religious feeling and the progress achieved in national archeology.

In 1798, John Malton, one of the protagonists of the picturesque movement, in *An Essay on British Cottages*, had already lamented the absence of a religious character in neo-classical churches. 'Anyone who

83, 84 Cologne Cathedral 'as it should have been completed' according to Boisserée: exterior and interior view. Sulpiz Boisserée, Stuttgart, 1821.

85 All Souls Church, London: view of the interior; John Nash, 1822–4. An example of the prayer-house against which the Ecclesiologists were to react.

travels through our counties and sees for the first time one of these modern buildings that have been called churches would probably be embarrassed if he had to guess what they were for. They look more like an assembly hall or a theatre than a church.' He went on to suggest old parish churches as a model: 'The indestructibility and picturesque beauty of our old parish churches can and must be perceived by anyone with a taste for rural scenery. Why not choose the finest examples and, since architects seem to lack the necessary imagination, to create fine designs, build new churches from these models?'

Forty years later this idea was taken up again by Augustus Welby Pugin but, whereas the problems of the picturesque were still present to the architectural mind, return to Gothic formed part of a general plan to restore an idealized medieval society and became absolute. In 1836, in his *Contrasts*, Pugin compared medieval and modern buildings in a nostalgic and ironic strain. In a series of lectures given in Dublin in 1841, and published under the title *The Present State of Ecclesiastical Architecture in England* (1843), he pleaded for the 'revival of our ancient parochial church', which was better suited than cathedral architecture to the small Catholic communities which, in 1829, had been granted by the Relief Act the right to build new places of worship. To justify this radical architectural reform, he evoked the poetry of 'village steeples', 'old porches', 'venerable yews', 'old grey towers' and the picturesque diversity of Gothic façades. 'How much more gratifying it is to have two beautiful façades of different aspect to look at than to see the same thing repeated.' At the same time he stressed the appropriateness between the layout of medieval churches and the Catholic religion.

This original combination of liturgical rationalism and the visually picturesque gave rise to a series of recommendations. The church must be surrounded by the small parish graveyard, for 'nothing can better awake earnest feelings of devotion than passing through the place where the faithful sleep'. The choir should be clearly distinguished from the nave, externally by its form and internally by its décor. There should be a tower culminating in a steeple, 'the most characteristic feature of a church', set at the end of the nave, of a wing or at the intersection of the nave and transept; and a porch, necessary for the rites of baptism, built on to the south side. Pugin here defines a picturesque style of a rational character which differs as much from an abstract rationalism in search of expedients to conceal irregularities as from a gratuitously picturesque style which creates useless irregularities. The picturesque elevation is derived log-ically from the plan, from the articulation of the different parts of the church – nave, choir, porch, presbytery – and not from an arbitrary intent: 'a building which is arranged to look picturesque', he wrote, 'is sure to look like an artificial waterfall' (*The Present State of Ecclesiastical Architecture in England*, 1843, pp. 62-3).

In the case of Pugin, the return to Gothic was the expression of a militant Catholicism, but it was not long before Anglicans were defending similar notions. Indeed, from 1833 onwards, a group of Oxford theologians led by John Keble (1792–1866) and John Henry Newman (1801–90) were seeking to bring the official church closer to its Catholic past by publishing their *Tracts for the Times*. In Cambridge, after three years of informal activities, 'Tractarian' sympathizers set up in 1839 the Cambridge Camden Society, which in 1845 became the Ecclesiological Society. In their journal *The Ecclesiologist* (1841–68), and in countless small pamphlets published in their thousands and sold for a few pence (*A Few Words to Church Builders*, *A Few Words to Church Wardens*, etc.), they set about giving an architectural content to the new ritualistic aspirations. The rules they suggest hardly differ from those of Pugin: a return to medieval models, a departure from symmetry, and a clearly marked distinction between nave, choir and presbytery expressed in the roofs.

Proceeding on converging lines, Pugin's campaign and that of the Ecclesiologists rapidly brought about a new trend in both Anglican and Catholic building. The twenty or so churches that Pugin built are so many manifestos 'for the revival of Christian architecture in England', to echo the title of another of his books, *An Apology for the Revival of Christian Architecture in England* (1843). To begin with, he drew his inspiration from the Perpendicular of the fourteenth century (St Mary's, Derby, 1837) and then veered rather towards the Lancet style (St Wilfrid's, Hulme, Manchester, 1839–42) or the Decorated style of the thirteenth century (St Chad's Cathedral, Birmingham, 1839–41), in St Giles's at Cheadle, built for the Earl of Shrewsbury, who had estates there, the interior is richly decorated, whereas in St Augustine's at Ramsgate, Kent (1845–51), which he built independently, he shows a taste for greater sobriety. Sir George Gilbert Scott, who said reading Pugin's articles was like 'being awoken from a long feverish dream', joined the Cambridge Camden Society in spite of his evangelical origins.

He built twenty or so churches between 1839 and 1846 on the model of the 'old parish church'. It is significant that he should have sent his plans to the

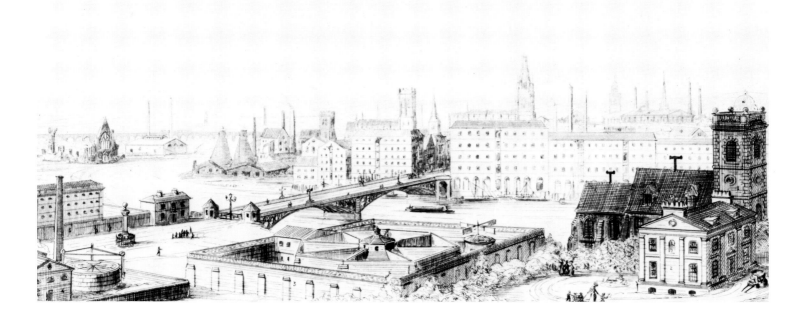

86   Contrast between a Catholic town in 1440 and the same city in 1840. After Augustus Welby Pugin's *Contrasts*, London, published 1841. The first view is notable not only for the ramparts and the picturesque pattern of spires but also for the contrast between the wealthy abbey on the left in Decorated Gothic style and the little parish church on the right in Early Gothic and the half-timbered houses in the Old English style in the foreground. In the modern city the spires have been replaced by factory chimneys and the walls by warehouses, while the prison with its panoptic plan and the foundry also figure prominently.

87 The Grange (1843–4) and St. Augustine's Church (1847–9), Ramsgate, Kent, England (Victoria and Albert Museum, London, No. D 124-1890): drawing; Augustus Welby Pugin revived a coherent medieval architectural landscape with church, vicarage and school (on the right) and his own residence, the Grange (on the left); the countryside with its workers in the fields and the burial in progress in the little parish cemetery endow the picture with social and religious overtones.

Camden Society for their criticism. The most interesting are undoubtedly St Giles's, Camberwell in South London (1842), St Mark's, Worsley near Manchester (1844), and SS. Simon and Jude's, Bradfield, Berkshire (1847). John Loughborough Pearson also subscribed to the aesthetics of Pugin from 1843 onwards and embodied them in Ellerker Chapel (1843–4) and then in All Saints, North Ferriby, Yorkshire (1846–8), the design of which attracted the interest of the review *The Builder*. But it was Richard Cromwell Carpenter (1812–55) who was during these years the favourite architect of the Ecclesiologists, who commissioned him to design St Paul's, Brighton (1846–8) and St Mary Magdalen's, Munster Square, London (1846–9). In all these churches there is a clearly marked choir, while the tower and porch are often placed symmetrically. Depending on the nature of the specifications, the style ranges from the most elaborate 'Decorated' style, for example All Souls, Haley Hill, Halifax, by Scott (1856–9), to the most crude 'Early English' at St Mary's, St Austell, Cornwall (1847), by George Edmund Street (1824–81): 'Let mean material appear mean', stated *The Ecclesiologist* in an article of 1843 entitled 'On Simplicity of Construction, especially in Churches of the Early English'.

The reform of religious architecture sought by English Ecclesiologists was very soon espoused by the whole English-speaking world. The Camden Society, which counted among its members several American, Australian and New Zealand bishops from 1839 to 1841, asserted its missionary vocation in the very first number of *The Ecclesiologist*. In a somewhat naïve manner, very typical of the nineteenth-century spirit, it sought to adjust its recommendations to what it considered to be local needs. On being asked for advice by the Bishop of Auckland, it suggested a Norman style as a model, rather than the 'Middle-Pointed' style which it recommended for England, 'because the work will be done mainly by local artists. It seems natural to teach them first this style, which was originally predominant in our country, because its roughness and massiveness and the primitive character of its sculpture will no doubt be easier for them to understand and appreciate.' Similarly, in 1845, *The Ecclesiologist* announced that the designs for three ancient churches had been chosen to serve as models for the colonies: it was the simplicity of their 'Early English' style that determined the choice. An American took back with him particulars of the little church of St Michael's, Longstaton, Cambridgeshire, and these served directly as models for St James the Less, Philadelphia (1846–50).

At Trinity Church, New York (1839–46) Richard Upjohn (1802–78) was close to the Pugin ideal, as was James Renwick (1818–95) at Grace Church on Broadway; and at St Mary's, Burlington, New Jersey (1846–8), he took his inspiration from the medieval church of St John's, Shottesbrook, Berkshire. Similarly, John Notman (1810–65) found his inspiration for Emmanuel Church, Cumberlands, Maryland (1850–1) in an engraving of St Paul's at Brighton by Carpenter which appeared in *The Ecclesiologist*.

It was not long before the New York Ecclesiological Society, modelled on the English society, was formed. It, too, published a journal, *The New York Ecclesiologist* (1848–53). Like its English counterpart, it sought to foster religious architecture of high qual-

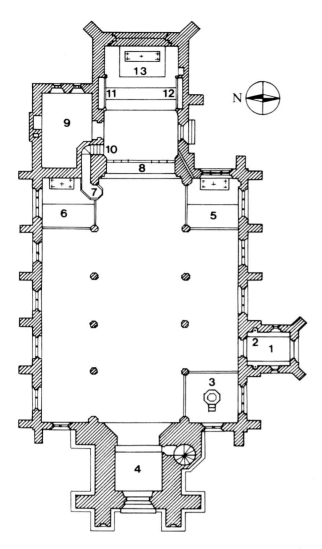

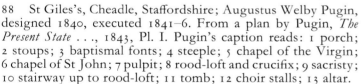

88 St Giles's, Cheadle, Staffordshire; Augustus Welby Pugin, designed 1840, executed 1841–6. From a plan by Pugin, *The Present State . . .*, 1843, Pl. I. Pugin's caption reads: 1 porch; 2 stoups; 3 baptismal fonts; 4 steeple; 5 chapel of the Virgin; 6 chapel of St John; 7 pulpit; 8 rood-loft and crucifix; 9 sacristy; 10 stairway up to rood-loft; 11 tomb; 12 choir stalls; 13 altar.

89 St Giles's, Cheadle, Staffordshire, England; Augustus Welby Pugin, designed 1840, executed 1841–6. The church was built at great expense for the Earl of Shrewsbury and is a striking design by reason of the rigid severity of the stonework and the Decorated style of the tracery.

ity by critical assessment of recent buildings and to suggest models which could readily be reproduced.

In France the channels through which this new architectural ideology was disseminated, i.e. the archeological societies and neo-Catholic circles, are less clearly defined or, rather, have been less closely studied.

One must distinguish chronologically between chapels and large churches, restorations and new buildings, definition of specification, preliminary plans, approval and execution of the project, for the time-lags from one to the other were sometimes considerable. The history of Saint-Nicolas, Nantes, which could have been the first large neo-Gothic church in France, is a good example in this respect. About 1823–4 the first reconstruction plans, put forward by Jean-Baptiste Ogée (c. 1760–c. 1845), architect and road surveyor in Nantes, was a variation in the spirit of Durand on Chalgrin's Saint-Philippe-du-Roule. From 1834 the new parish priest Fournier (1803–77), influenced by Hugues-Felicité-Robert de Lamennais and Philippe Joseph Benjamin Buchez,

90, 91 St Mary, St Austell, Cornwall, England: external view from the south-east and view of the interior; George Edmund Street, 1847. A typical example of the small neo-Gothic churches built in the English countryside. Surrounded by its small cemetery, the church has only one side-aisle because of the effort made to supply precisely the needs of the small community. Local materials, exposed beams, Early English (or 'lancet') style all play their part in creating a coherent impression of rusticity.

92 All Souls, Haley Hill, Halifax, West Yorkshire, England; Sir George Gilbert Scott, designed 1855, executed 1856–9. This is a building distinguished by the asymmetrical balance of its masses and the felicitous upscaling of the model of the parish church; moreover, it shows awareness of the problems defined by the English Ecclesiologists in the 1840s.

thought of rebuilding his church in the Gothic manner, the 'true Christian style'. In 1837 the architect Louis-Alexandre Piel (1808–41) was invited to draw up plans. He had chosen, he explained, 'the style of the thirteenth rather than the fourteenth century which is more deeply carved, more florid, more extravagant, and consequently more expensive' and 'took Notre-Dame in Paris as the model for the layout of the bays, the combination of the vaults, and the proportion and shape of the intersecting ribs'. After further vicissitudes a new project was drawn up by Lassus, but the work, begun in 1844, was not concluded until 1876, when the battle over neo-Gothic had long been won.

After 1840 the advocates of neo-Gothic stepped up their pressure. In 1844 they founded the *Annales archéologiques*, which was in close contact with its English and German equivalents, *The Ecclesiologist* and the *Kölner Domblatt*. This extremely active pressure group also elicited some lively opposition. This often involved considerations which were as much economic and technical as they were aesthetic, the com-

93 Emmanuel Church, Cumberland, Maryland; John Notman, 1850–1. John Notman, who in 1837 had built one of the first American Italianate villas at Burlington and, in 1845, the Athenaeum in Philadelphia, one of the first Italianate *palazzi*, had sought inspiration in 1847 for his St Mark's in Philadelphia by studying Richard Cromwell Carpenter's All Saints at Brighton; in this instance he made use of an illustration of St Paul's, another Brighton church also built by Carpenter and published in *The Ecclesiologist*.

94 Sainte-Clotilde, Paris; Franz-Christian Gau and Théodore Ballu, 1846–57. This was the first neo-Gothic church to be built in Paris and its erection was a public intimation that the model of the Early Christian basilica had been abandoned.

petence sometimes being vested rather in the neo-classical than in the neo-Gothic party. The arguments that broke out in 1846 round Franz Christian Gau's (1790–1853) Gothic design for Sainte-Clothilde in Paris simply brought into the public arena a controversy that since 1837 had caused neo-Catholic church councils to clash with the Orleanist and neo-classical Council of Civil Building. In 1845 the *sous-préfet* of Loudhéac in the Côtes-du-Nord announced his intention of subscribing to the forthcoming publication of 'Parallèle des projets d'église en style ogival du XIIIᵉ siècle' by Hippolyte Louis Durand. He favoured adoption of Gothic for the next series of works to be carried out by his department, where three churches already under construction were in

antique style (*Annales archéologiques*, 1845, p. 511). In 1852 Didron counted two hundred Gothic churches under construction (*Annales archéologiques*, 1852, p. 164), and in 1855, when the Bishop of Amiens succeeded in pushing through thirteenth-century Gothic style for three churches in his diocese, Antoine, the town architect who had designed a neo-classical project, decided to hand in his resignation.

In Germany, on the site of Cologne Cathedral, which was the focus of the new neo-medieval culture, the transition from Romantic musings on the Gothic-cum-national-German style to archeological neo-Gothic was accomplished smoothly between 1815 and 1842, the date of the cathedral's official opening.

95 Saint-Nicolas, Nantes, Loire-Atlantique; Jean-Baptiste Lassus, 1844–76. The final designs were not adopted until 1850; a preliminary design by Lassus had been published in the *Annales archéologiques* in 1844 as 'plan of a church in the style of the thirteenth century'.

96 Mariahilfkirche, Au, suburb of Munich; Joseph Daniel Ohlmüller, finished by Georg Friedrich Ziebland, 1831–9. It took the form, traditional in Germany, of a hall church, i.e. one with nave and aisles of equal height. The gables and sculptured pinnacles cannot disguise the squat proportions, classical rather than medieval, and the isolated position on an open square is characteristic of the nineteenth century.

As in France and England, the number of new churches went on increasing, particularly after 1840: Mariahilfkirche (1831–9), near Munich, where Daniel Ohlmüller (1791–1839) adopted the traditional form of the hall church (1839), St Apollinarius Church (1839–43) at Remagen by Ernst Friedrich Zwirner (1802–61), a Catholic church at Leipzig (1845–7) by Carl Alexander von Heideloff, etc. . . . 'We must reject all pseudo-classicism and return to Gothic, our true, glorious and traditional art', August Reichensperger (1808–95) asserted in a text which runs parallel to Pugin, *Die christlich-germanische Baukunst,* Trier, 1845.

The convergence of all these research efforts did not escape the notice of contemporaries. In 1834 Boisserée was elected a member of the Société Française d'Archéologie and, if Montalembert refused to join the heretical English Camden Society, Pugin visited the Sainte-Chapelle in 1844 with Didron, who had attended the inauguration of St Giles's at Cheadle.

Differences were nevertheless perceptible. Pugin and Viollet-le-Duc both proposed a rational analysis of the Gothic style, but the former, aware of the absence of character in Protestant meeting-houses, sought to give the plan a liturgical articulation and this led logically to the picturesque silhouette; the latter, on the defensive against academic criticism, upheld the rational logic of Gothic buildings by arguing from the structural form of the vaults. In England

97 Petrikirche, Hamburg; Alexis de Chateauneuf and Hermann Peter Fersenfeldt, 1843–9. Neither Romantic nor archeological, this is one of the 'modern Gothic' churches. It was built in red brick and was destined to attract the attention of English architects face to face with the problem of the urban church.

98 Apollinariskirche, near Remagen, W. Germany; Ernst Friedrich Zwirner, 1839–43.

in the 1840s the model remained the parish church of the fourteenth century, in France the cathedral of the thirteenth century; whereas in Germany recourse was had to the models provided by local hall churches.

About 1850 this phase of the first Gothic revival was complete. Medievalist architects could now handle Gothic techniques and outlines with the same skill as the antique style, and in 1902 Hermann Muthesius (1861–1927), a keen German observer of English architectural culture, wrote that Holy Trinity, Bessborough Gardens, at Westminster, built in 1849–50 by John Loughborough Pearson, could be taken for an old church.

Romantic Castles

In religious architecture the confrontation between the two models for churches, the Early Christian basilica and the medieval church, is necessarily glaring and public, insofar as a domain is involved where there is large-scale architecture and in which public institutions (church councils, ministries of education and cultural affairs) have a right to be consulted. In secular architecture, where the free taste of the owner, like the poetics of the picturesque, give rein structurally to every kind of fancifulness, the gradations are naturally more discreet. In the years from 1830 to 1840 the eccentric taste of clients and picturesque and historical associations remained determinative, but the new scale of architecture and the number of buildings erected show that a new phase was also starting.

Conventional picturesque Gothic was replaced by archeologically accurate motifs. But in this field the rediscovery of the Gothic style was naturally more extensive in its scope. The Elizabethan style in England and the style of the Early Renaissance in France and Germany were, needless to say, rehabilitated to indulge the picturesque imagination and the national taste which had condemned them in the classical aesthetic. Their jagged outline and their overloaded ornamentation had the same charm as those of medieval architecture, but these models appeared to be better suited to secular architecture.

Between 1830 and 1840 a dozen or so volumes devoted to Elizabethan architecture were published in England. The dramatic silhouette, the large glazed oriels, and the great hall of these houses could not fail to appeal to a milieu which had a nostalgic yearning for the English hospitality of yore.

Anthony Salvin (1799–1881) rang the changes on different styles, depending on the inspiration of the site and the tastes of the owner, with an archeological skill acquired while restoring old castles (Brancepeth Castle at Durham, 1829). After building at Mamhead, Devon (1827) and Morby (1827–33) two houses in the Gothic Tudor style, he raised at Harlaxton, on a site where an old Elizabethan manor was falling into decay, one of the most stunning of neo-Elizabethan houses. Gregory Gregory, the proprietor, was one of that eccentric group of aristocratic building fanatics who, from Lord Burlington to Lord Bute, gave English architectural culture its special features. Harlaxton Manor is a personal fantasy and the crystallization of eager architectural studies which, after the traditional 'grand tour', had turned towards the Elizabethan age, which Walter Scott's *Kenilworth* had begun to popularize.

For Lord Tollemarche, a great landowner who ran his huge estates of 26,000 acres on modern paternalistic lines, he built a castle in the style of the thirteenth century. Peckforton Castle was one of the most ambitious efforts to bring medieval secular architecture back to life; the asymmetry of the courtyard enabled him to produce a felicitous reconciliation of the picturesque with the functional layout. The same desire to recreate an authentic medieval house had already taken a systematic turn at Scarisbrick Hall, which Pugin remodelled between 1837 and 1884. As in his churches Pugin gave expression to his ideal of picturesque functionalism. The silhouette is a reflection of the layout: small hall, great hall with its oriel and own roof, porch, tower and kitchen.

It was not long before similar buildings began to appear in Austria, Germany and Switzerland in increasing numbers.

In France the not very numerous buildings prior to 1830 began to multiply as the generation of *émigrés* faithful to the neo-classical style gave way to that of the young 'ultras' whose taste, after the Revolution, was formed by reading Chateaubriand and Joseph de Maistre, and who, on coming into their inheritance, liked to build neo-Gothic residences. It was no longer the practice to build solely small follies and country seats (like the Marquis de Forbin-Janson's house at Mont Valérien, c. 1820, the 'castel' of the Comte de l'Escalopier in Montmartre, 1835, or the Beauchêne manor in the Bois de Boulogne, 1835, near Paris) but large castles, like those of René Hodé in Anjou or of Châtaignier in Touraine. After 1830 the Gothic style began to be the rallying sign of the Legitimist nobles, and the neo-Gothic castles which they built on their estates when they withdrew there in the 1840s, convinced they could return to power only after winning back the peasantry, expressed their nostalgia for a popular feudalism.

99 Harlaxton Manor, Grantham, Lincolnshire, England: view from the south; Anthony Salvin, 1831–7, completed by William Burn, 1838–44, for Gregory Gregory.

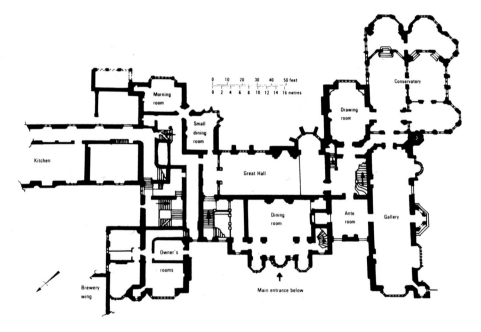

100 Harlaxton Manor, Grantham, Lincolnshire, England: plan of the first upper storey of the main building; Anthony Salvin, 1831–7.

However, the contrast between the plans of French and British neo-Gothic castles remains striking. The latter were marked by an asymmetric balancing of the masses reflecting in the elevation a pattern of layout which grew by flexible accretion, whereas in the French castles Gothic contours, flamboyant gables and François I pilasters took the place of classical contours, but there were still the symmetrical massed plans and the ternary compositions featuring the *avant-corps* and the pavilions of the French classical tradition.

These buildings might also serve to emphasize the attributes of a dynasty. The king of Prussia, Frederick William IV, had a whole series of medieval castles in the Rhine valley rebuilt (Rheinstein (1825–9) by Johann Claudius von Lassaulx (1781–1848); Stolzenfels (1836) begun by Schinkel and the castle chapel by Anton Schnitzler (1843) – schemes which were more modest but also earlier than those of Queen Victoria's Balmoral Castle (1853–5) by William Smith or of Napoleon III's Pierrefonds (1858–61) by Viollet-le-Duc.

After the fire in October 1834 it was decided to reconstruct the Houses of Parliament at Westminster, London, in the Perpendicular or Elizabethan style. This showed a traditional concern with historical continuity combined with a taste for the picturesque, along with a more archeological approach to details.

101 Harlaxton Manor, Grantham, Lincolnshire, England; Anthony Salvin, 1831–7. Picturesque Elizabethan style.

102 Scarisbrick Hall, Lancashire, England; Augustus Welby Pugin, 1837–45. Pugin wanted to revive the 'old English Catholic mansion'. The various kinds of accommodation are 'not masked or concealed under a monotonous front but by their variety of form and outline increase the effect of the building'. The original tower was replaced by a more imposing bell-tower designed by Edward Pugin, the son of Augustus Welby.

103   Scarisbrick Hall, Lancashire, England: great hall; Augustus Welby Pugin, 1837–45.

104   Study for the kitchen at Scarisbrick Hall; Augustus Welby Pugin. The intention was to recreate the atmosphere of medieval life as an integral whole. The kitchen was finally built on a more complex octagonal plan but also with exposed beams.

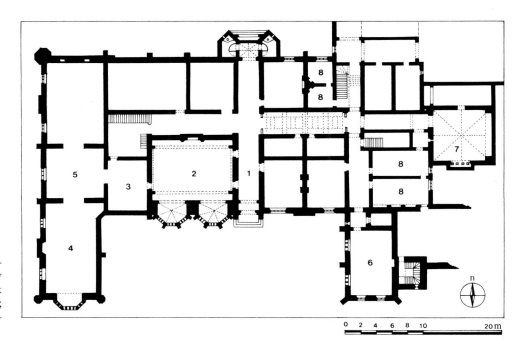

105   Scarisbrick Hall, Lancashire, England: plan (from an original drawing by Pugin): 1 corridor; 2 grand hall; 3 oak room; 4 red room; 5 King's room; 6 study; 7 kitchen; 8 rooms of the steward and butler.

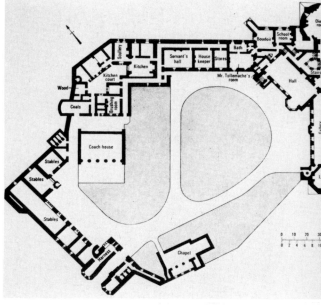

106 Peckforton Castle, Cheshire, England; Anthony Salvin, 1844–50, for Lord Tollemarche. Salvin had restored a number of medieval castles, including the Tower of London; in this instance he combined the picturesque grouping of the masses of his master Nash with his own archeological experience.

107 Peckforton Castle, Cheshire, England: ground-floor plan; Anthony Salvin, 1844–50.

108 Anif Castle, near Salzburg, Austria, 1838–48, for the Count of Arco-Steppberg after a drawing by Georg Pezolt. The sixteenth-century core of the castle was rebuilt in English neo-Gothic style.

109 Schwerin Castle, G.D.R.; Georg Adolph Demmler, completed by Friedrich August Stüler, designed from 1840 onwards, executed 1843–57. The overall outline is reminiscent of the castles of the Loire.

111 Schadau Castle, near Thun, Switzerland: designed by Pierre-Charles Dusillon, built by Ludwig von Rütte, 1849–54. In place of a previous medieval building the castle was erected for Denis Alfred de Rougemont-de Pourtalès, modelled on English manor-houses and castles of the Loire.

110 Schwerin Castle, G.D.R.: detail of façade; Georg Adolph Demmler and Friedrich August Stüler, 1843–57. The use of Italianate terracotta reliefs and busts gives this building an Italian cachet.

112 Schadau Castle, near Thun, Switzerland: spiral staircase; Pierre-Charles Dusillon, 1849–54.

113 Marienburg near Nordstemmen, Lower Saxony; designed by Conrad Wilhelm Hase, executed by Edwin Oppler, 1858–67. The building, begun under Georg V of Hanover, was only partially completed in 1867, when work was stopped.

114 Château de Comacre, Sainte-Catherine-de-Fierbois, Indre-et-Loire; Châtaignier for the Marquis de Lussac, 1845–8 (destroyed in 1962). The outline is of the French type but the architect has conjoined French Flamboyant details with English features such as the bow window, with a small balcony.

115   Château de Challain-La-Potherie, Maine-et-Loire; René
Hodé, designed 1846, executed 1847–54. Built for Count Albert
de La Rochefoucauld-Bayers on an estate of 1500 acres, it is one
of the first and largest of French neo-Gothic castles and seeks in
its style to recall the Flamboyant castles of the Loire valley.

116 Stolzenfels Castle, on the Rhine, view from the north; Karl Friedrich Schinkel, begun 1836 for Frederick William IV. Like the castle of Rheinstein, built for Prince Frederick of Prussia, it is a reconstruction of a medieval castle on the Rhine.

117 Stolzenfels Castle, on the Rhine: knights' hall; Karl Friedrich Schinkel.

118 Houses of Parliament in London: general view; Sir Charles Barry, assisted by Augustus Welby Pugin, designed 1836, executed 1840–67. In front of Westminster Hall and the cloisters of St Stephen's Chapel, which had escaped the fire of 1832, the new parliamentary building is arranged regularly on two axes which cross at the central hall, which is surmounted by a central spire. The Victoria Tower, on the left, which stands over the royal entrance, and the clock tower, 'Big Ben', on the right break up the severe symmetry.

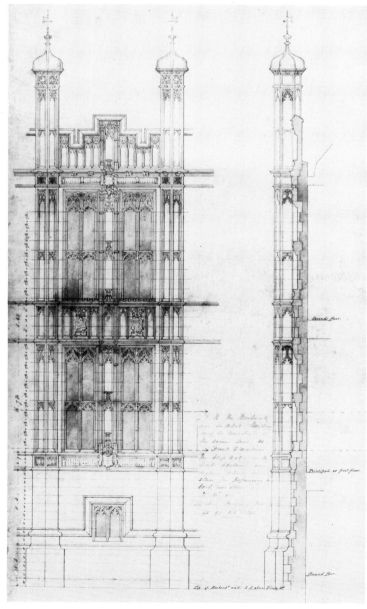

119 Working drawing for a bay of the north wing of the new Houses of Parliament; Sir Charles Barry.

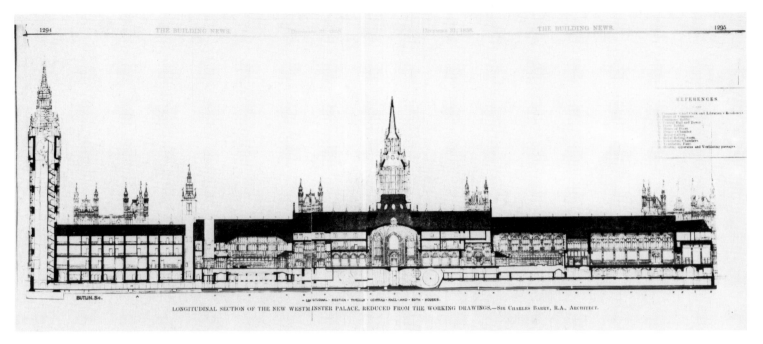

LONGITUDINAL SECTION OF THE NEW WESTMINSTER PALACE, REDUCED FROM THE WORKING DRAWINGS.—Sir Charles Barry, R.A., Architect.

120   Houses of Parliament, London: longitudinal section; Sir Charles Barry, 1836–67.

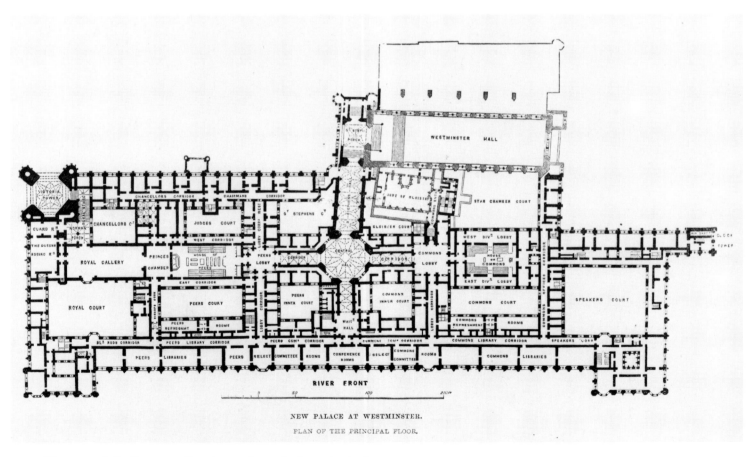

NEW PALACE AT WESTMINSTER.

PLAN OF THE PRINCIPAL FLOOR.

121   Houses of Parliament, London: plan of the principal floor; Sir Charles Barry, 1836–67.

122 Royal chapel of Saint-Louis, tomb of the Orléans family; Dreux, Eure-et-Loir; rebuilt by Pierre Bernard Lefranc, 1839. The neo-classical rotunda was built in 1816–22 by Cramail.

The idea of Gothic as the national style was modern. The central octagonal tower, at the crossing point of the long corridors, recalls Fonthill Abbey, the most sumptuous of the eccentric country houses in picturesque Gothic. This point impressed the French neo-Gothic architect Lassus, who saw in it 'a marvel from the Thousand and One Nights' (*The Ecclesiologist*, 1853, p. 47). The intervention of Pugin, one of the main protagonists of the second phase, gave the details a quite novel authenticity.

In France, Louis-Philippe was responsible for the restoration of the Château de Versailles and the completion of the Arc de Triomphe. He had the Orléans family mausoleum at Dreux, which had been begun in 1822 as a neo-classical temple, restyled in the Gothic manner. There is an obvious political aspect to this architectural eclecticism, which reflected the desire of the regime of the *juste milieu* to base its legitimacy on the whole of the national past. It was also indicative of profound shifts in French architectural culture.

The Quest for a Nineteenth-Century Style

'It is said that everything has already been invented, that the age of invention is over, and that all that art can do is to choose and copy.'
(James Savage, *Observation on Style in Architecture*, London, 1836)

The Revival of Neo-Classicism

About 1830 the approach to the classical tradition underwent a renewal. In England and the United States, where attitudes towards an excessively monotonous Hellenic classicism began to cool, this renewal took the form of a return to the national classical tradition. In France it was reflected in a more concrete approach to the forms of antiquity, and before long the residents of the Académie de France in Rome were to wish they could go to Greece. The itineraries were reversed but they distilled down to the same reaction to an overly abstract style. There was the same discovery of a concrete classical tradition with its historical vicissitudes and in all its diversity.

As early as 1823 Cockerell noted in his diary his opposition to the professors . . . 'who disparage Palladio, Jones and Wren,' and in 1839 he presented his 'Tribute to Sir Christopher Wren' to the Royal Academy, where, significantly enough, he succeeded William Wilkins, one of the major proponents of the Hellenic Renaissance.

The discovery of the dramatic site of the Acropolis with its contrasting masses of sculpture and its asymmetrical balance had been partly instrumental in releasing the English imagination from the shackles of Roman and French formalism. The Hellenic forms found favour by reason of their elegant novelty. Cockerell noted in 1821 that he had used in the Hanover Chapel an Asiatic Ionic that had not yet been seen, the capital of Sardis, the pilaster of Miletus; and that the motifs of Athena Niké and the Erechtheon, used to excess, were becoming wearisome clichés. The designs he proposed for the Royal Exchange in London and especially for the Ashmolean Museum in Oxford testify to a return to the Roman tradition and a quest for a more pronounced plastic articulation. Thomas L. Donaldson (1795–1855), Sir Charles Barry (1795–1860), Decimus Burton (1800–81), James Pennethorne (1801–71) and others proceeded along similar lines.

In America Arthur Gilman wrote in 1844 in *The North American Review* that the introduction of Grecian architecture had been a great mistake. He proposed to return to the style of Bramante, Palladio and Michelangelo: 'The *palazzi* Riccardi, Piccolomini, Strozzi and Gondi in Florence, the famous Farnese, magnificent Massimo in Rome, Piccolomini in Siena, display a true greatness of manner.' He stressed the growing taste for the '*palazzo* style', quoting the Travellers' Club and the Reform Club in London.

In England the diffusion of the modern 'Italian' style had its impact on the very specific design of clubs. If Burton's Athenaeum (1829–30) is more Palladian than Roman in tone, the Travellers' Club (1829–31) and especially the Reform Club (1837–41) by Sir Charles Barry in Pall Mall in London, like the Athenaeum he designed in Manchester (1837–9), have about them a distinctly Roman air, which was soon to be found in America (Athenaeum in Philadelphia, by John Notman). It was not long before banks, insurance companies and office blocks, which sprang up in increasing numbers during this very decade, also adopted this style, as did apartment blocks and large private town houses.

123 Ashmolean Museum and Taylorian Institute, Oxford:
façade; Charles Robert Cockerell, 1839–41.

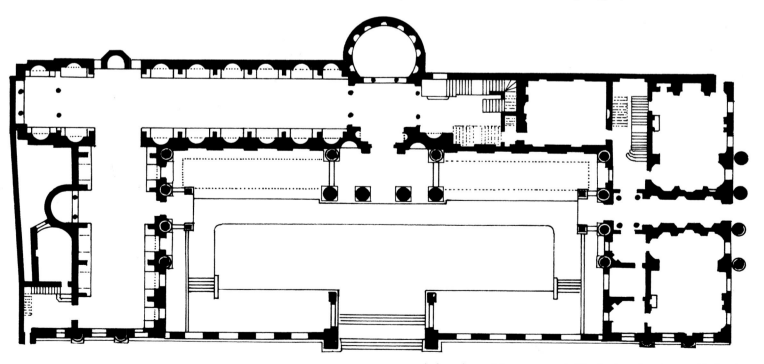

124 Ashmolean Museum and Taylorian Institute, Oxford:
plan; Charles Robert Cockerell, 1839–41.

125   Reform Club, Pall Mall, London: façade; Sir Charles
Barry, 1837–41. On the left can be seen part of the Travellers'
Club (1829–32).

126   Reform Club, Pall Mall, London: plan; Sir Charles Barry,
1837–41. After *Revue générale de l'architecture*, 1837, Pl. 37.

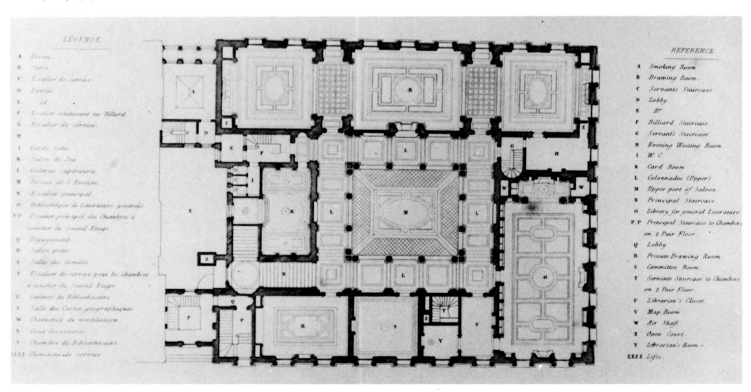

127 Temple of the Lycaonian Jupiter, restoration of the Isola Tiberina in Rome, fol. 12. Work submitted to Paris in the fourth year by Marie-Antoine Delannoy, a boarder at the Académie de France at Rome, 1832.

The monumental publication by the French author Paul Letarouilly (1795–1855), *Édifices de la Rome Moderne* (1840–57), was the instrument of this revival of Italian style, to borrow from the title of an opuscule by W. H. Leeds, published in 1839 *(An Essay on the Present State of Architectural Study and the Revival of the Italian Style)*.

However, in France, under the vigilant supervision of Quatremère de Quincy (1755–1849), permanent secretary of the Academy from 1816 to his death in 1849, the old generation preserved an ideal image of antiquity. While compatible with the 'modern' Italian style, this image suffered a severe blow from the polychrome reconstructions and the excavation of real buildings proposed by a new generation.

The publications on the *Jupiter olympien* by Quatremère de Quincy in 1815, and on the *Antiquités nubiennes* by Franz Christian Gau in 1822, had emphasized the importance of polychromy in the archaic art of antiquity, and this was quickly confirmed by Corneto's study of Etruscan tombs in 1827. In 1822–4 Hittorff made a long journey in Italy. In Rome he kept company with Bertel Thorvaldsen (1770–1844), the great Danish sculptor, and, hearing from the English architect Thomas L. Donaldson of the discoveries made at Aegina by C. R. Cockerell, James Woods and Sir Charles Barry, he set off with Ludwig von Zanth (1796–1857) as his companion to examine the traces of painted stucco on the Sicilian temples, in which Leo von Klenze soon also became interested. On his return to Paris, he defended before the Académie the hypothesis that the ancients were in the habit of 'using colour and painted ornaments to enhance not only the interior of their temples but also the external walls of the cella, the columns, architraves, metopes, cornices and pediments and even the roof tiles'. In 1827 he published together with Zanth and presented to the salon of 1831 polychrome restorations of the temples of Selinunte and Agrigento. The richness of the colours, blue, yellow and red, and their application to the whole surface of the architecture proposed by

Hittorff, led to lively adverse criticism. But, from 1828 onwards, members of the Académie de France resident at the Villa Medici in Rome, Félix Louis Jacques Duban (1797–1870) and the brothers, Henri (1801–75) and Théodore (1799–1885) Labrouste, being won over to these ideas, investigated the matter and, in the 1830s, the idea that ancient temples, if not painted all over, were at least enhanced with touches of colour, gained acceptance by a cosmopolitan circle and sparked off an international debate which continued into the 1850s.

It would seem that Hittorff, von Klenze, Semper and some others hoped that by this brilliant polychromy the architectural culture of the classical world would be revived, just as it had been half a century earlier by the discovery of archaic Greek art, and sought to apply this system to contemporary buildings but without great success. Of the many projects proposed to this end, only a few designs conceived under the aegis of the picturesque in archeology came to fruition, such as two modest works in Munich by von Klenze, the restoration of the frontispiece of a temple in the hall of the Glyptothek where the reliefs of Aegina were exhibited (1823–30), and the monopteral tempietto of the English Garden (1836). In festival buildings like the summer Olympic Circus or the Parisian cafés built by Hittorff in 1838–42, the Napoleon amphitheatre or the winter amphitheatre in 1852, in the polychromy is clearly more restrained than it is in the projects drawn up in 1834 for the Champs-Elysées. Similarly, after suggesting in 1837 for the Thorvaldsens Museum in Copenhagen a blue and red colonnade, which was a polychrome variant on Karl Friedrich Schinkel's Berlin Museum, Gottlieb Bindesbøll (1800–56) adopted a quieter 'Etruscan' polychromy of yellow and green (1839–48).

This polychromy, or lithochromy, to use Klenze's term, was less important for its immediate effects, which were not great, than for its repercussions. These took the form of an interest in the techniques of enamelled lava, which was invented in 1827 and appealed to Hittorff, who hoped it might provide a solution to the fragility of painted colours, and then, in the 1840s, in the technique of glazed brick on the one hand, and in medieval and Arabic polychromies and the general theory of colour, which engaged the attention of Owen Jones and Gottfried Semper, on the other. If the analogy which contemporaries saw between this polychromy and Romanticism is far-fetched, this very fact spelt the end of the simplicity of contrasting light and shade in neo-classical buildings; the Greek temple of ideal whiteness became a material object once again and the dispute over polychromy became part of a wider debate in which the last proponents of the aesthetics of sublime beauty were ranged against those whom contemporaries would call, somewhat improperly, the neo-Greeks.

In France the first sign of this revival was intimated by the story of the conflict between a hard-working and hard-headed pupil of the École des Beaux-Arts, Henri Labrouste (1801–75), and his teachers – a conflict that was exacerbated by the political undercurrents of the July revolution in 1830 and the quarrel over Romanticism. The winner of the Grand Prix de Rome in 1824, Labrouste, found Blouet, Émile Jacques Gilbert (1793–1874) and Duban at the Villa Medici and began to study ancient architecture not as an interplay of forms and volumes but as a real structure that had actually been built. A draughtsman of greater authority than Blouet, he sought to unite the two separate schools of teaching at the École des Beaux-Arts: Rondelet's tradition of construction and Percier's graphic archeology.

The reports Labrouste sent from Rome astonished everyone; their tenor was unexpected. While the style of presentation remained discreet, there were liberties which were greatly at variance with common practice. Things were to be discovered which had no sanctioned place in documents drawn up according to the Academy. In his observations he neglected nothing, noted everything, he wrote about everything including the bonds and introduced them in his renderings. In them can be felt a second-order rhythm sustaining the principal rhythm of the forms.

The linear elegance with which Percier and his imitators treated modern Italian style could be smoothly absorbed into the neo-classical aesthetic. The new generation remained faithful to this style which, in the Hôtel Pourtalès, is to be seen in one of its most refined versions but, following a quest for more solid effects, is generally given rather more body.

There were the materials there for a quiet renewal within the classical tradition. To the very end Labrouste remained faithful to this approach, by which he sought to solve the problem of integrating modern materials and which was also borrowed by Duban, Joseph Louis Duc (1802–79) and some others. However, just at the very moment when the progress of

128   Design approved for the Thorvaldsens Museum, Copenhagen; Gottlieb Bindesbøll, 1839.

129   Cirque d'Hiver, boulevard du Temple, Paris; Jacques Ignace Hittorff, 1850.

130 Hôtel Pourtalès (today head office of the Mutuelle Générale Française), Paris; Félix Louis Jacques Duban, 1836. The finest example of the Italianate style in the tradition of Percier, it has no discernible model.

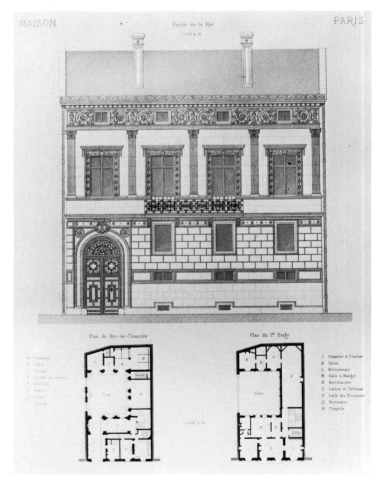

national archeology allowed the logic of the structural lines to be rediscovered behind the flamboyant arabesques, ancient sublimity and medieval picturesqueness, after following two similar routes, met on the ground of constructive rationalism. Conversely, by a curious paradox, the development of archeology, the taste for historical and psychological associations, the selection of certain models (Palladian villa, Roman *palazzo*) from the historical tradition, and the dissociation effected by Durand between syntax and vocabulary, which had developed without tension within the neo-classic aesthetic, prepared the way for historicism.

In this respect the Sainte-Geneviève Library is a perfect epitome of the unobtrusive but decisive shifts taking place in architectural culture during the first half of the century. A living archeological culture and the new basic contributions of modern industry combined harmoniously and without any apparent strain to satisfy, with discreet symbolism, the requirements of a very specific design. The quality of the building is due in very great measure to the care with which Labrouste supervised its construction. He kept a day-to-day watch on the least details from 1843 until its completion in 1850. The striking and deliberate contrast between the austerity of the external block of masonry and the light-filled airiness of the aisles in the reading-room springs from the execution of a specific programme and is peculiarly felicitous in its effect.

From Romanticism to Eclecticism

However, between 1830 and 1850 the joint effects of the poetics of the picturesque and the progress of national archeologies, and also of the bibliographic revolution and the neo-Gothic quarrel, led to a marked broadening of the cultural horizon.

The interest taken by Owen Jones (1809–74) in antique polychromy was extended in its scope by his study of the Alhambra Palace at Granada, on which he published in 1836–45 a monumental work notable for its colour lithographs. In 1837–41 von Zanth, who accompanied Hittorff on his travels in Sicily, built the Villa Wilhelma near Stuttgart. The outside

131 Hôtel Pourtalès, Paris: elevation and plans; Félix Louis Jacques Duban, 1836.

132 House and studio for the painter Jules Jolivet, 11 Cité Malesherbes, Paris; André Jal, 1856. Archeology and modern industry: an attempt to revive classicism by the use of glazed lava.

133   Palais des Études, École des Beaux-Arts, Paris; Félix Louis Jacques Duban, designed 1832–4, executed 1834–9. As in the Hôtel Pourtalès, with which it is almost contemporary, Duban was generally inspired by Italian architecture of the Cinquecento.

134   Bibliothèque Sainte-Geneviève, Paris; Henri Labrouste, designed 1842, executed 1843–50. The general composition recalls the Palais des Études de l'École des Beaux-Arts, but the decorative vocabulary is more original in its detail.

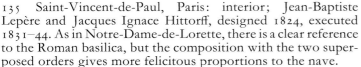
135 Saint-Vincent-de-Paul, Paris: interior; Jean-Baptiste Lepère and Jacques Ignace Hittorff, designed 1824, executed 1831–44. As in Notre-Dame-de-Lorette, there is a clear reference to the Roman basilica, but the composition with the two superposed orders gives more felicitous proportions to the nave.

136 Saint-Vincent-de-Paul, Paris: façade; Jean-Baptiste Lepère and Jacques Ignace Hittorff, designed 1824, executed 1831–44. A kind of Hellenized version of the church of Trinità dei Monti in Rome.

is remarkable for its vivid structural polychromy, which strikes an Italian rather than an antique note with its alternating horizontal bands of white stone and red brick. The inside is remarkable for a suite of Arab salons, which underlines its character as an exotic 'folly'.

The revived interest in Gothic, to which a natural extension is formed by the rediscovery of the picturesque styles of the Early Renaissance in its different national versions (Elizabethan and Jacobean; François I, Henri IV and Louis XIII in France; Flemish Mannerism in northern Europe), soon gave additional impetus to the national classical traditions. Still severe in its judgment of the *grand style* of Louis XIV, the new Romantic generation yielded to the charm of the picturesque polychromy of these styles for the very reasons which caused *le grand goût* to condemn it. Like the flamboyant gables and the candelabra of the Early Renaissance, the ringed columns and the broken pediments of Nordic Mannerism are a remedy against neo-classical monotony. Brick and stone poly-

chromy appeared as the national version of neo-classical lithochromy, and the Louis XIII or Jacobean style as a happy medium between classical aridity and Gothic fantasy.

In interior architecture the palette of styles was broadened ever more. At Harlaxton Salvin built the hall and dining-room in Elizabethan style, whereas the entrance hall, staircase and drawing-room are Baroque (1831–7). Admittedly, this was a piece of architectural fantasy. But between 1840 and 1850 it became increasingly common to find a deliberate contrast in the stylistic treatment of the different rooms – a Gothic hall, a Louis XIII dining-room, a Louis XIV drawing-room, a Louis XV boudoir, and an Arab smoking room – on a scale that foreshadowed the typological and stylistic eclecticism that became general in the 1850s.

It was quite natural that the rediscovery of the Gothic style should extend farther back in history, to the Romanesque style. A number of Romanesque buildings are illustrated in the *Denkmäler der deutschen*

137 Ludwigskirche, Munich; Friedrich von Gärtner, 1830–44. In the eyes of contemporaries the building summoned up Italian religious architecture of the fourteenth century.

Baukunst of Georg Moller in 1815–21, and Heinrich Hübsch (1795–1863), who published in 1828 a book with the significant title *In welchem Style sollen wir bauen?* (In what Style are we to Build?). He proposed a return to the Romanesque style, which significantly enough he compared to pre-Raphaelite painting. In 1836, in his *Designs for Rural Churches*, G. E. Hamilton showed his interest in the 'Norman' style, and in 1844, in its first number, the *Annales archéologiques* announced, after a model of a parish church in 'ogival' style, another 'with round arches in pure Romanesque style'.

This return to Romanesque style, which was in most cases presented as an economical alternative to the Gothic style, was less spectacular than the Gothic revival. This neo-Romanesque sprang up amidst an Italianizing Romanesque, which was a natural extension of the interest taken in the model of the Early Christian basilica and in the Florentine culture of the Quattrocento.

The ambiguity is particularly apparent in Germany. In the Ludwigskirche in Munich (1830–44), von Gärtner drew his inspiration very freely from fourteenth-century Lombardian architecture, but in the Protestant church at Kissingen in 1827 he drew closer again to the local Romanesque forms. Heinrich Hübsch, who in 1828 had pleaded for a modern style derived from Romanesque *(Rundbogenstil)*, built three churches in the Romanesque style of the abbeys of Southern Germany between 1840 and 1850 at Freiburg im Breisgau and Rottenburg. In its plan the Friedenskirche by Ludwig Persius (1803–45) at Potsdam (1843–8) recalls San Clemente in Rome, but the campanile is obviously derived from that of Santa Maria in Cosmedin. The gallery with small columns in the apse was modified by Persius in the course of execution to give an archeological flavour.

The early interest shown by the Germans for Florentine and particularly Lombardian architecture

138 St Matthäuskirche, Berlin, 1844–6, as the model of a church to seat 1,500, by Friedrich August Stüler. Copy dated 1854 by C. Niermann, after Stüler, 1846, Pl. 1.

90

KIRCHE MIT 1500 SITZEN

139, 140 Friedenskirche, Potsdam, G.D.R.; Ludwig Persius, designed 1843, executed 1844–8. The plan and the interior elevation are inspired by the composition of San Clemente in Rome; the bell-tower, which is similar to that of Santa Maria in Cosmedin – one of the first examples of the fascination exerted by the Italian campanile – gives it an appearance which is at once more Romanesque and more picturesque.

141 Saint-Paul, Nîmes, Gard; Charles Auguste Questel, designed 1835, executed 1838–50. A little earlier than St Mary's, Wilton, Wiltshire, England (1840–6) and the Friedenskirche, Potsdam (1844–8), this church shows the same shift from Early Christian to Romanesque models; but whereas in England and Germany the models were Italian, in this case they were French, i.e. national in character.

of the Trecento and Quattrocento, with its bonded polychrome bricks and its terracottas, broadened still further the scope of cultural reference, as may be clearly seen in a series of churches in Berlin (Johanneskirche by Schinkel, 1832–4, and Friedrich August Stüler (1800–65), 1844–56; St Matthäus in the Tiergarten, 1844–6, by Stüler).

In England J. L. Petit (1801–68), who had drawn the church of San Michele in Pavia and the cathedral in Worms, proposed a revived Roman, Lombardian or Italian style. In France Baron Isidore Taylor took an equally favourable view of a return to the Romanesque, so that in both countries similar phenomena and the same conflicts can be observed. The church of Saint-Paul (1840–9) at Nîmes by Charles Auguste Questel (1807–88) is frankly French Romanesque in tone, whereas Christ Church at Streatham, London (1840–2), by James William Wild (1814–92) and more especially St Mary's (1840–6) at Wilton, Wiltshire, by Thomas Henry Wyatt (1807–80) and David Brandon, designed at the express wish of the principals in imita-

tion of San Zeno in Verona, are imbued with the same Italophilic spirit as the clubs and private houses in the manner of Italian Renaissance *palazzi*. They could be regarded as the religious pendant of the '*palazzo* style'.

The competition held for the construction of the Lutheran St Nikolaikirche in Hamburg in 1844 shows how closely-knit the international neo-Gothic movement was and at the same time reflects the new diversity of architectural culture: the church council preferred the neo-Gothic design of the English architect Sir George Gilbert Scott, who drew his inspiration from both French and German medieval models, but the jury gave their votes to Gottfried Semper's 'Romanesque' design. If the controversy raging round the return to the Gothic style has made special claims on our attention, as it did on that of contemporaries, neo-Gothic is only the most conspicuous sign of a more general shift in architectural culture: it was an experience nourished by all the architectural images derived from history and it had

142, 143 Christ Church, Streatham Hill, London: exterior and interior; James William Wild, 1840–2. Like St Mary's, Wilton, Wiltshire, but with fewer resources at its disposal – which explains the lack of exterior ornamentation – it represents an attempt to produce a variant of the Italian medieval models (it had no successors in Great Britain); it is contemporary with Saint-Paul at Nîmes and the Friedenskirche in Potsdam.

to be provided with theoretical foundations differing from the beauty of nature in the antique world.

From the time of the Renaissance, the practice of European architects was based on the myth that there was an identity between the antique tradition and nature; by claiming that the place of the antique temple had been taken by the medieval church as the sole model, neo-Catholics and Ecclesiologists invited general reflection on this imitation. In France, where decisions were more centralized, the quarrel, which involved more especially Raoul Rochette for the Academy and Jean-Baptiste Lassus and Viollet-le-Duc for the neo-Gothics, erupted in 1846. The neo-Gothics criticized the pagan temple on the grounds that it was unsuitable for our habits, for the Christian religion, and for the modern way of life, to which the neo-classicists retorted that they were not imitating the Greek temple but that they merely sought inspiration from the eternal principles of beauty it embodied and that Gothic churches, being designed for the men of the thirteenth century, were no more suited than antique temples to the needs of the nineteenth century. Taking up a new position, the neo-Gothics replied that they did not want merely to repeat the

144 St Nikolaikirche, Hamburg; Sir George Gilbert Scott, designed 1844, executed 1845–80 (partly destroyed in 1944). The church was built in yellow brick and stone at a cost of £180,000. It was consecrated in 1863 although construction was not completed until 1878–80, when the baptistery was finished (it can be seen on the right).

145 Second design for the St Nikolaikirche, Hamburg in 'Roman style'; Gottfried Semper, 1844. Awarded first prize, the design was rejected by the church council which, after consulting Sulpiz Boisserée and Ernst Friedrich Zwirner, gave preference to that of Sir George Gilbert Scott.

Gothic forms but rather derive from them principles of construction for designing a building in accord with our habits and our age and that, by reason of its structural rationality, the Gothic style was the best suited to modern developments.

Taking advantage of the shift the argument had produced in the positions of the neo-Gothics, the Academy maintained that since there was no question of imitating the Gothic style but simply of enriching modern practice with experience garnered from the past, there was no reason to impose a veto. Paradoxically, through an inversion of the original terms, the

quarrel ended with the crystallization of a classical eclectic aesthetic and a neo-Gothic rationalist theory: Gothic, which had entered the cultural field through the picturesque, established itself by eschewing it in favour of a liturgical rationalism (Pugin) or a structural rationalism (Viollet-le-Duc). The quarrel over neo-Gothicism paved the way to eclecticism, whereas it was precisely a dogmatic rejection of the antique temple as a model that had given birth to neo-Gothicism.

'The devotee of the arts ranges through the world, stuffs his album with tracings of all kinds, carefully

146 Pompeianum, Aschaffenburg: the side overlooking the river; Friedrich von Gärtner, 1842–9. Built by Ludwig I of Bavaria on the model of the Castor and Pollux house at Pompeii. It is one of the most successful of the archeological follies which were so numerous in the nineteenth century. Bulwer-Lytton's novel *The Last Days of Pompeii*, 1834, no doubt crystallized an interest that had long been taken in this type of architecture.

147 Pompeianum, Aschaffenburg: atrium; Friedrich von Gärtner, 1842–9. As in the Roman villas of the Renaissance, the interior décor is a mixture of pastiches (mural paintings) and authentic collector's pieces (mosaics, bronzes and pottery).

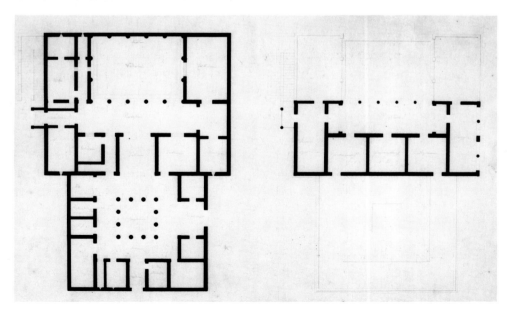

148 Pompeianum, Aschaffenburg: plan; Friedrich von Gärtner, 1842–9.

149 Villa Wilhelma, Bad Cannstatt, Stuttgart; Ludwig von Zanth, 1837–41. This pleasure pavilion, together with greenhouses in the middle of a park, now a zoological garden, was part of a folly in the Moorish style built for Wilhelm I of Württemberg.

150, 151 Konversationshaus, Baden-Baden: Louis XIV hall (above) and Pompadour salon in Louis XV style (below). Analytical eclecticism began with the interior décor: pompous Louis XIV style for a large hall and more gracious Louis XV for the small salon.

stuck in, and returns home, perfectly happy, cheerfully waiting to be asked to build a Valhalla in Parthenon style, a basilica in Monreale style, a boudoir à la Pompeii, a palace in Pitti style, a Byzantine church or perhaps even a bazaar in the Turkish manner', wrote Gottfried Semper somewhat facetiously in 1834, with his rival von Klenze in mind. 'Love of the Byzantine has been followed in ascending chronological order by the passion for Gothic, Moorish and the Renaissance. Starting with François I, architectural art has conjured up in turn the reign of the Medi-

cis, Louis XIV, Louis XV, and curiously enough, we are about to enter the style of Louis XVI', the Belgian Jobard commented in 1849 (*Revue générale de l'architecture*, 1849, p. 27).

In twenty years the circle of imitation had expanded to include the whole domain of architectural history. The Greek, Pompeian, Italian, Byzantine and medieval 'courses' arranged by Sir Joseph Paxton (1801–65) in the Crystal Palace at Sydenham from 1852 to 1854 with an obvious educational intent is clear evidence of this broadening of cultural horizons.

152 'The Architect's Dream'; Thomas Cole (1801–48), 1840. The Toledo Museum of Art, Toledo, Ohio. The architect's dream combines antique sublimity (pyramid and Egyptian temple, Doric and Ionic Greek temples, tholos and arcades of Roman brickwork) and Gothic picturesque: the epitome of Romantic classicism.

The Greek style is no longer *the* style but *a* style. 'There is no style which does not have its particular beauties; there is no fixed style now prevalent; we are wandering in a labyrinth of experiments', wrote Donaldson in 1842. The normative idealist aesthetic of neo-classicism was replaced by a relativist historical aesthetic.

This crucial cultural shift took place by stealth in as much as historical relativism was formed within the classical culture and Gothic was first introduced through the back door of the picturesque. The first turning-point is to be located about 1770, when the birth of scientific archeology and the discovery of real Greece transformed antiquity into history. The second came about 1840, when the proponents of neo-Gothic claimed that they were replacing the model of antiquity by that of the Middle Ages and this brought about a medieval revival, in truth a counter-Renaissance, without winning an affirmative vote from all contemporaries. But the natural link between antiquity and history was also broken symbolically by the French revolution and the Napoleonic empire. Contemporaries felt keenly the importance of this brutal incursion of history: 'Since the Napoleonic campaigns, the battles of the Greeks and Romans no longer seem so splendid.' From this point of view, the nineteenth century really does begin about 1800, but it was not until about 1860 that contemporaries felt that they had truly broken with the preceding century. The virtually simultaneous appearance of the expressions 'Victorian architecture' in *Building News* in 1858, and 'style Napoleon III', attributed to Charles Garnier, are clear testimony to the originality of these new developments in both classical and Gothic style.

Greeks and Goths

'We do not believe that the restoration of Gothic art is possible, or even desirable, we prefer to have ideas revived . . . . We hope that a style will emerge which will be partly new and partly a medieval revival.' (Karl Schnaase, *Annales archéologiques*, 1851)

The Idiom of Eclecticism

The years 1840–50 ushered in the most controversial phase in the history of European architecture – the period which by common consent is known as eclectic. The cacophony was the upshot of three phenomena becoming superimposed: the spread of the aesthetic of the picturesque, a Gothic revival which ultimately assumed the form of neo-Gothic, and the new life given to classicism by a more liberal use of the whole vocabulary of the Graeco-Roman tradition.

Imitation was widespread but in reality it embraced rather widely varying practices. Architects were at one in condemning pastiche but all of them subscribed to the idea that it was not a question of imitating the past but solely of seeking inspiration in its principles and experience in order to envision the style of the nineteenth century; everyone practised quotation, the pleasure of which ultimately derived from a development of the picturesque aesthetic.

From this past, to whose diversity and historic depth they were becoming increasingly and more discriminatingly sensitive, architects picked out sometimes a structural principle, sometimes an archetypal form, sometimes a layout, sometimes a motif, and these they adapted to the needs and resources of modern times. There was nothing new about this phenomenon, it must be said, for Renaissance architects were doing precisely the same thing when they adapted the superposed orders of the Colosseum to

traditional Venetian *palazzi* and French châteaux, but now these loans were made from every period of architectural history – from the Egyptian period to the town mansion à la Louis XVI.

The *ne plus ultra* of these contrasting effects is to be found on the Ring in Vienna, where, within a regular and well-balanced plan, a neo-classical Parliament building stands side by side with a neo-Gothic Town Hall, a University in the style of Louis XIV, and a theatre designed in Italianate Baroque.

But this diversity, which reflects the scope of the imaginary architectural museum of nineteenth-century architects and their clients, must not be allowed to delude us. The coexistence of different styles is confusing only for us, who no longer know how to read the code. The disconcerting juxtaposition of several styles was one of the means of expression open to nineteenth-century architects.

The term eclecticism encompasses two different phenomena: on the one hand what might be called a typological eclecticism: depending on the specifications, on the character he wishes to give to his design, the architect turns to one model or another in the past, which he adapts and modifies to meet his needs; on the other hand, a synthetic eclecticism: here the architect has recourse to past architectural experience in order to combine in a novel manner the principles, solutions and motifs of different periods. And this synthesis can take a field of greater or lesser extent for its operation.

We have seen that, as long ago as 1798, John Malton had already emphasized that classical style was particularly well suited to public buildings and Gothic style to religious buildings. This idea constantly recurred throughout the century – in New York in 1841, in Hamburg in 1845, and in Madrid in 1905. 'In the minds of many', as a Spanish critic writes, 'it is

153 Aerial view of the Ringstrasse in Vienna. Left fore-ground: the Houses of Parliament in neo-classical style, Theophil von Hansen, 1873; left centre: the Town Hall in Gothic style, Friedrich von Schmidt, 1872–83; opposite on the right: the Burgtheater in Italian style, Gottfried Semper and Karl von Hasenauer, 1874–88; background: the New Univer-sity in the grand French academic style, Heinrich von Ferstel, 1873–4; right foreground: the Theseion, Pietro Nobile, 1821–3, a scaled-down version of the Hephaisteum of Athens; back-ground, behind the University: the Votivkirche in fourteenth-century Gothic style, Heinrich von Ferstel, 1856–79 (Pl. 198).

clear that classical architecture is the most appropriate for public buildings such as museums and law courts, medieval architecture for religious buildings such as churches and mausoleums, and Arab architecture for recreational buildings.'

There was a kind of distribution according to types and styles: greenhouses, covered markets and halls, exhibition pavilions, passages and utility buildings were built in a modern iron or steel style; churches and vicarages in a medieval, Byzantine, Roman or Gothic style; public buildings and apartment blocks in a classical, Italian or French style.

This typological eclecticism is based most often on the fascination exercised by an archetype – the thirteenth-century cathedral, the small medieval par-ish church, the Italian *palazzo*, the Netherlands town hall – but also by a form or motif – the oriental salon, the Italian campanile, the Italian belvedere, the im-perial dome of Jacques Lemercier's (1585–1654) Pavillon de l'Horloge at the Louvre. Here again, the novelty does not reside in the phenomenon itself (the design of the Pantheon or the triumphal arch was exhausted in a similar way in the Renaissance) but in the extreme diversity of these suggestions. The medieval fortress inspired a whole series of American barracks, the first of which was the impressive Seventh Regiment Armory in New York (1878), whereas the Florentine *palazzo* with bossed stone-work (recalling the Medicis) proved particularly sug-gestive for savings and commercial banks. It was al-ready a tenet of classical aesthetics that the formal treatment of a building should be in harmony with its specification but that only the choice of orders and the patterning of the mouldings could determine its character. The scope of the imaginary museum of

154 Houses of Parliament, Ringstrasse, Vienna; Theophil von Hansen, 1873 (photograph taken in 1898).

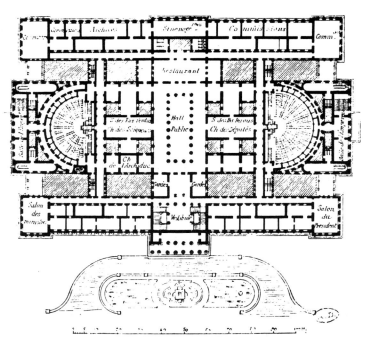

155 Houses of Parliament, Ringstrasse, Vienna: plan; Theophil von Hansen, 1873. In spite of the difference in style of the elevations, the layout resembles that of the Houses of Parliament in London.

nineteenth-century architects and their clients made it possible for this expressive palette to be enriched without limit. The classical range of orders (Doric, simple; Ionic, graceful; Corinthian, majestic) was replaced by a range of styles (Greek, simple; Renaissance, graceful; Louis XIV, majestic; Louis XV, elegant; etc. . . .).

In suburban villas and apartment blocks the variety of the styles used is part of a generalized picturesqueness, but the stylistic variety in buildings of a more elaborate type is a conscious, significant variety. Whether more picturesque or grandiose, more majestic or elegant, the different styles are modes in the grammatical or musical sense of the term. Law courts evoke more sobriety and severity, a theatre more colour and gaiety. Furthermore, the architectural composition will be different, more picturesque for a repertory theatre, more sumptuous for a large operahouse. If the façades of the two Châtelet theatres in Paris lack the brilliance of that of the Opéra, this is no doubt due to the somewhat bland manner of their architect, Gabriel Davioud (1823–81), but also to the character of the building: a municipal theatre cannot display the pomp and circumstance of the imperial Opéra.

In a still more subtle and exceptional manner, these different historical styles can serve to orchestrate the

156   Town Hall, Vienna; Friedrich von Schmidt, 1872–83. An effort has been made to achieve a 'modern' synthesis between the grand classical tradition and the Gothic style. It is easy to discern the tripartite composition (base, arcaded storey in the centre and attic) of the façade of Garnier's Paris Opéra.

157   Hermesvilla, Lainzer Tiergarten: front overlooking the garden, Vienna, 1898. An opulent-looking and clumsy instance of synthetic eclecticism: picturesque asymmetrical composition with the corner tower as in Italianate villas, an Early Renaissance style with coloured bricks; roofs in French style, and metal verandas with vaguely oriental associations.

158   The 'rue des Nations' at the Universal Exhibition in Paris in 1878. From left to right: the pavilion of Central and Southern America by Alfred Lambert Vaudoyer, inspired by a sixteenth-century palace at Lima; the Danish pavilion in a style inspired by Nordic Mannerism; and the Greek pavilion in a Hellenized neo-classical style. Here the style is intended to express the cultural tradition of each country: a somewhat dramatized version of typological eclecticism, i.e. the use of a different style depending on the purpose to be served (*The Builder*, July 1878, p. 778).

159   Truro Cathedral, Cornwall, England; John Lough-borough Pearson, 1880–1910. The archetype of a cathedral.

160   Biltmore Manor, near Asheville, North Carolina, U.S.A.; Richard Morris Hunt, built for a Vanderbilt, 1890–5. The spiral staircase, a variant of that at Blois, and the conservatory frame the central pavilion.

different parts of a composition. Charles Garnier's (1825–98) Opéra is exemplary in this respect. Garnier dips into the palette of styles as the classical architects did into that of orders: for the administrative buildings at the back, he uses a fairly sober Louis XIII style, for the rotundas of the Emperor and the season-ticket holders classical half-engaged columns, and on the main façade he lavishes all the resources of the colourful grand style of the Venetian Renaissance; inside, the white François I arabesques of the basement give way to the ornate Baroque of the main staircase.

In 1850, in his *Rudimentary Treatise on the Principles of Design in Architecture*, Edward Garbett divides the Italian Renaissance into three schools – Florentine, Roman and Venetian – and relates them to the Doric,

Ionic and Corinthian respectively. Abadie used the Romanesque style of the eleventh century for his village churches in the Dordogne and the Gironde, but thirteenth-century Gothic for his sub-prefectures at Bergerac or Lesparre-Médoc; and for the Sacré-Cœur in Paris (begun 1876), the metropolitan church of pilgrimage, a Byzantine style which was inspired by Saint-Front at Périgueux in the Dordogne. With a wider field of reference, Théodore Ballu (1817–85) proceeded on similar lines in his Paris churches: the contrast between the Romanesque style of Saint-Ambroise (1865) and the flamboyant Renaissance of the Trinité (1863–7) is due to the different character with which he wanted to endow these churches, each in its different quarter, one popular and the other a fashionable shopping area.

161   Neuschwanstein Castle, Bavaria, 1869–86. Designs by the court painter Christian Jank; built by Eduard Riedel who was succeeded by Georg von Dollmann in 1871.

162, 163   Church of Valeyrac, Gironde: views of the exterior and the interior; Paul Abadie, 1853. Romanesque style for a church in a small country market town.

164, 165   Church of Lesparre-Médoc, Gironde: views of exterior and interior; Paul Abadie, designed 1853, executed 1860–5. Gothic style for a church in a town that is a sub-prefecture.

The return to the grand Baroque style for official buildings, which partly reflects a shift of taste, is also a reflection of the endeavour to find in the range of historical styles the one most appropriate to a public building. The distinctions may be very fine: the adoption of Queen Anne in preference to Gothic style in schools built in England after the vote on the Education Act was intended to express the modernistic and enlightened ideals of the reformers. The contrast to be seen in Lille between the neo-classical Faculty of Letters of the State University and the neo-Gothic Catholic University is no less significant, as has already been observed. When Hittorff built the town hall of the 1st *arrondissement*, which forms a pendant to Saint-Germain-l'Auxerrois, he repeated the overall design of the church but adopted an 'early Renaissance' style rather than Gothic in order to give it a more 'secular' character.

Sometimes architects had a choice between several logical associations which occasionally contradicted one another. Thus, when in 1846 James William Wild, seeking local colour, designed oriental horseshoe arches for a church in Alexandria, *The Ecclesiologist* protested vehemently: 'to build a Christian church in a land where a false religion is predominant . . . in the style of that false religion is more than a solecism of taste, it is a gratuitous bruise to our religious feelings.'

The accent could be placed either on the function or on harmony with local culture: the town hall at Tourcoing (1863–5) is built in a grand showy national style, whereas that of Wambrechies (1868) is in a regional Flemish one.

A similar contrast can be seen in Algeria between the town hall of Biskra in 'Arab style' and that of Bône in a showy classical style. François I and Louis XIII styles added to the rich range of picturesque types suitable for suburban villas but as a national style also lent themselves to a town hall. The Moorish style lost nothing of its exotic value in France, Germany and England but in Spain it figured as the national style, as Hellenized neo-classicism did in Greece.

Conversely, the same style can appear in different buildings because of different mental associations. For example, the same style of oriental inspiration can be found in a synagogue, such as that in Berlin (1859), and in an eccentric dwelling house like the Victor Vaissier villa in Lille (1892), built in Moorish style.

166 Basilica of Sacré-Cœur, Paris; Paul Abadie, 1876–1919. Byzantine style for a metropolitan church of pilgrimage.

167 Saint-Ambroise, Paris; Théodore Ballu, 1865.

168 La Trinité, Paris; Théodore Ballu, 1861–7. The contrast between the Romanesque style of Saint-Ambroise and the florid Renaissance style of La Trinité is due less to shortage of funds than to the specific character which Ballu wanted to give to churches in different districts; one is located in an elegant commercial district, the other in a more popular one.

170 Town Hall, Wambrechies, Nord, 1868. The adoption of a regional style which antedates the developments of the following decade is to be explained in part by the fact that the town is a small one where a picturesque style is more acceptable.

169 Hotel-pension Müllberg, Mittelthurgau, Switzerland, 1854–74 (destroyed). Hotels, which grew in number with the development of middle-class railway tourism, naturally took over the rustic style (half-timbering and belvedere) of picturesque villas.

171 Town Hall, Tourcoing, Nord; Charles Maillard, 1863–5. By recalling the outline and forms of the Tuileries and the Nouveau Louvre of Napoléon III, Maillard underlines the character of this official building.

172 Synagogue, Orianenburgstrasse, Berlin; Eduard Knoblauch, 1859–66 (destroyed). The pattern of bricks and polychromic terracotta is in keeping with the Berlin tradition but the Romanesque style *(Rundbogenstil)* here produces oriental overtones for symbolic reasons.

173 Palais Vaissier, rue de Mouvaux, Tourcoing, Nord; Charles Dupire-Rozan, 1892 (destroyed in 1925) for Victor Vaissier, the inventor of 'Congo soap'. An 'oriental palace', whose histrionic character contrasts with the Royal Pavilion by John Nash or the Villa Wilhelma in Bad Cannstatt, Stuttgart, by Ludwig von Zanth.

174 Bull-fighting arena, Carretera de Aragón, Madrid; Emilio Rodriguez Ayuso, 1874 (destroyed in 1934). One of the most monumental constructions in the neo-Mudéjar style in Spain. The suggestion of the Moorish epoch is combined with the modernism of the metal grandstands.

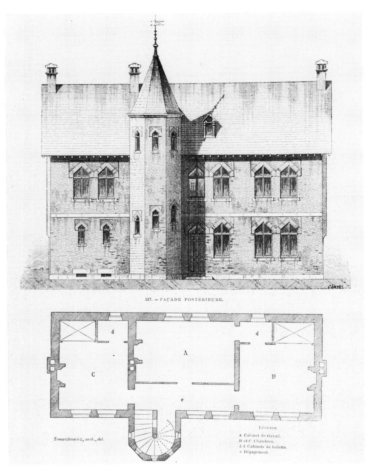

176 Priest's house, Masny, Nord: elevation and plan of upper storey; Émile Boeswilwald. After *Gazette des architectes et du bâtiment*, vol. 7, 1869–71, p. 196. 'This dwelling certainly has the simple and even austere character which is appropriate to it but, above all else, it is a house; moreover, it is not pretentiously gloomy and monumental, it is nothing else but the presbytery of a commune which has not the surplus funds to lavish on the ornamentation appropriate to such a building.'

175 Loggia dei Lanzi, Florence; Benci di Cione and Simone Talenti, 1376–82.

177 Feldherrnhalle, Munich; Friedrich von Gärtner, 1841–4. An almost literal copy of the Loggia dei Lanzi at Florence.

178 Porte Dauphine or Baptistery Gate, Château de Fontainebleau, Seine-et-Marne, 1600.

179 Château de Chantilly, Oise: entrance and chapel; Henri Daumet, 1875, for the Duc d'Aumale. The outline of the gate is derived from that of the baptistery at Fontainebleau, but Daumet replaced the bosses of his model by ringed columns as in the Tuileries, hollowed out the engaged piers of the gallery of niches as in the portico at Écouen, and arranged sarcophagi as amortizements as at Anet.

Like the iconological games of the Renaissance with their ingenuities and fakeries, these effects, which are sometimes artificial, are part and parcel of the architectural culture of the nineteenth century and the only clue in this labyrinth of styles, even if this logic of styles sometimes conflicts with that of the gratuitously picturesque, as well as with triumphant bad taste. Pugin was already poking fun at those who built Swiss chalets in flat countries, Italian villas in cold countries, and Greek temples in shopping streets. The neo-Gothic quarrel of the 1840s came to an end with a sort of inversion of the initial positions: the picturesque and religious neo-Gothic style became established as rational and sought sublimity in effects of massing and surface. Conversely, architects with a classical training, cutting their losses and recognizing the suitability of medieval styles for religious architecture, inserted into neo-Baroque compositions Early Renaissance pilasters or gable ends in the Mannerist style.

Thus architectural culture took its bearings from two poles, one modern Gothic, which was to achieve its most spectacular developments in the British Isles, and a revived classicism, which was to dominate on the Continent, with the contrast between Anglo-Saxon and French culture (already noted at the beginning of the century) still remaining palpable. America and Central Europe were drawn by these two centres and only Berlin, where the tradition of Schinkel was strong, retained its independence.

180 Hospice de Barbieux, Roubaix, Nord; Louis Barbotin, 1890–3. The motif of the portico at Fontainebleau is echoed here but with more bourgeois and regional overtones as befits the purpose of the building. The design of the dormers is derived from those of the Hôtel de Montescot, at Chartres (1614), published by Sauvageot in 1867.

181 Windows of the former Bourse at Lille, Nord, 1652.

182 Windows of an apartment house, rue des Manneliers, Lille, Nord. The taste for the Flemish Mannerist style is based on a local example.

183 Roundwyck House, Kirdford, Sussex, England; John Loughborough Pearson, 1868–70.

184 The Parliament of Glyndwr, Machynlleth, Wales, fifteenth century. One of the models for the Old English style.

185 St George's Church, Edinburgh, Scotland: design; Alexander Thomson.

186 St Vincent Street United Presbyterian Church, Glasgow, Scotland; Alexander Thomson, 1857–9. A picturesque mixture of Greek and Egyptian features.

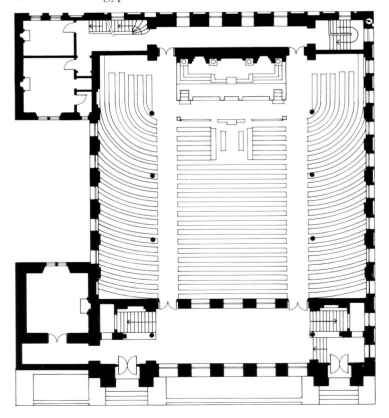

187 St Vincent Street Church, Glasgow, Scotland: plan; Alexander Thomson, 1857–9.

188 Holmwood, Netherlee Road, Cathcart, Glasgow, Scotland; Alexander Thomson. An original blend of the ancient tholos and the bow-window.

189 New Zealand Chambers, Leadenhall Street, London; Richard Norman Shaw, 1871–3 (destroyed during World War II). The first appearance of the Queen Anne style in a commercial building. One of the most successful examples of how an architectural idiom from the past can be reworked to suit modern needs. The façade is only a wall of glass to give the offices generous lighting.

190 Thomaskirche, Berlin: views of exterior and interior; Friedrich Adler, designed 1864, executed 1865–9. The synthesis of Romanesque and Renaissance styles is particularly apparent in the intersection of the transepts and nave.

191 Kreuzkirche, Berlin; Johannes Otzen, 1888. Gothic details are applied on an unusually compact building.

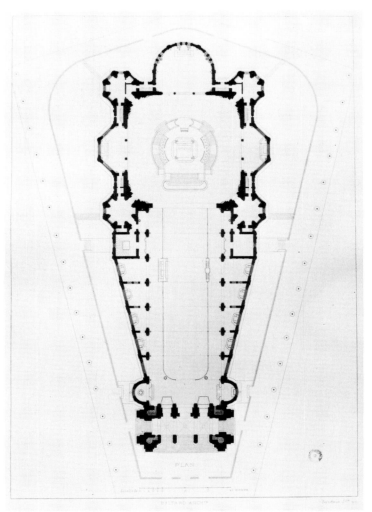

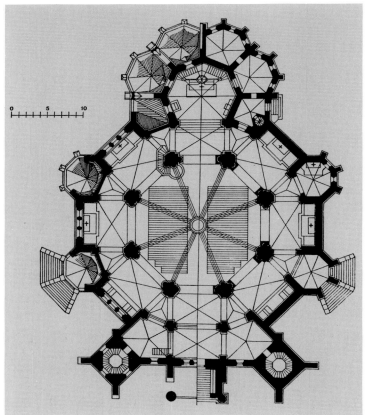

192 Saint-Augustin, Paris: plan; Victor Baltard, 1860–91. After Narjoux, 1880–3, vol. III.

193 Church of Maria vom Siege, Vienna: plan; Friedrich von Schmidt, 1868–75.

194 Saint-Augustin, Paris: view of the dome; Victor Baltard, 1860–91. The metal structure warrants an increase in the size of the nave.

195 Church of Maria vom Siege, Vienna; Friedrich von Schmidt, 1868–75. A successful eclectic synthesis between Gothic forms, a classical dome and the 'Baroque' design solution of steeples placed at an angle.

196 House of the printer Lorenz, Maximilianstrasse 30-34, Munich; Friedrich Bürklein, begun 1854. An attempt to create a new style.

From Archeological Accuracy to Neo-Gothic

About 1850, when its primary archeological and liturgical objectives were being attained, the neo-Gothic movement began to change its character. Its symbolic, religious, national and picturesque values, which had made possible the return to the Gothic style, did not disappear but became less influential than the values embodied in its structures, layouts and aesthetics; the culture inspired by the Middle Ages became diversified, more refined and more international; architects were freer vis-à-vis their medieval models and sought greater contrast in the treatment of their designs, from village church to metropolitan cathedral; finally the Gothic style was no longer the prerogative of religious buildings, of picturesque dwellings and of national and royal monuments. It became established as a universal style which was just as appropriate for public buildings (town halls, museums) and commercial buildings (banks, hotels) as it was for the new types of structure (stations, department stores). In short, it claimed the place of the classical and Italian styles whereas previously it had been complementary to them. Just as, after centuries of barbarism, the Italians of the Quattrocento had wanted to revive good classical architecture, so the new neo-Gothic generation wanted to pick up the thread that had been broken at the Renaissance and, by inversing the terms, aimed at a medieval revival.

'I shall make my pupils travel, but I shall limit them,' Pugin wrote in 1843, 'one to Durham, others to the steeples of Lincolnshire, others again to the spires of Northampton and the noble piles of Yorkshire . . . each county will be a school.' The first neo-Gothic churches in England all have a strong local flavour. After 1850 English architects continued to study local examples: this came to them all the more naturally in that they were engaged in restoration and new building work at the same time. They readily transferred technical and formal features from the one to the other, as did William Butterfield (1814–1900), who borrowed the motif of the buttress penetrating the window from the church he was restoring at Dorchester and embodied it in the new church of St Matthew at Stoke Newington. Their cultural horizon also broadened remarkably: through free cultural exchange and railway tourism, the English discovered the muscular Gothic of the French cathedrals and the highly coloured Italian Gothic.

Sir George Gilbert Scott, the English Viollet-le-Duc, who had discovered German Gothic at the time of the competition for the St Nikolaikirche in Hamburg, travelled in France in 1847, and in 1851 went on a 'grand tour' which took him as far as Italy, where he studied not the edifices of the Renaissance but Roman and Gothic architecture. His example was imitated by the majority of the architects of the new generation: William Burges (1827–81), after three tours in England between 1844 and 1849, spent eighteen months in France, Germany and Belgium in 1849–50 and returned to France and Italy in 1854; John Loughborough Pearson travelled in Belgium in 1853 and in France in 1855 and 1859; George Edmund Street went to France in 1850 and 1852, Germany in 1851, and North Italy in 1853, publishing two years later *Brick and Marble Architecture in North Italy* (1855), where he stressed the importance of 'the careful study of continental examples'. Alfred Waterhouse (1830–1905) travelled in France and Italy in 1853.

In the German-speaking countries, where it was now acknowledged that the Gothic style had developed in the Ile-de-France earlier than in Germany, there was no slackening of interest in Lombardian Romanesque architecture.

In France, 'the richest field for the study of Gothic art', interest in English and German Gothic, which was sustained by the fact that the neo-Gothic movement had started earlier in those countries, waned somewhat, but knowledge of the national architectural heritage continued to grow and become more finely differentiated. Viollet-le-Duc completed the publication of his monumental *Dictionnaire raisonné de*

197 Votivkirche, Vienna: design; Wilhelm Stier, 1853. Images of the ideal cathedral of Cologne, or even of Schinkel's cathedrals, have left their imprint on Stier's architectural imagination.

198 Votivkirche, Vienna; Heinrich von Ferstel, designed 1853, executed 1856–79. Comparison with the Mariahilfkirche in Munich shows the progress made by 'archeological Gothic' about 1850. Like the contemporary buildings of Scott and Lassus, its over-perfect stylistic unity is its sole modernity.

l'architecture française. He set about distilling rational principles of universal application from the analysis of medieval architecture, but he also paid due care to vernacular architecture, where structural procedures are more naïve and at the same time more apparent. After being focused exclusively on thirteenth-century Gothic, attention began to turn also towards Romano-Byzantine architecture (F. de Verneihl, *L'Architecture byzantine en France, Saint-Front de Périgueux et les églises à coupole de l'Aquitaine,* 1851) and during the last third of the century, as regionalism developed, towards more local manifestations such as the Romanesque style of the South of France (Revoil, *L'Architecture romane dans le Midi de la France,* 1861–7) or Breton Late Gothic. Sustained by travel, publications and the first collections of photographs (from 1871 onwards), the new medieval culture was handled

with ever greater freedom and only a few architects remained faithful to an archeological Gothic.

Lassus, who in 1856 produced his design for Notre-Dame de la Treille in Lille under the polemical motto 'eclecticism is the plague of art', was the leading representative in France of archeological purism. This was of a practical, academic kind which must be distinguished from 'municipal Gothic', where the effect of pastiche is the result rather of hastiness in design than of deliberate intent. Thoroughly versed in the 'principles' of medieval art, 'the true and only possible starting-point for modern art', he sought simply to perfect the art handed down to him without copying any particular product of that art. His designs (Saint-Nicholas at Nantes, 1850–76; Sacré-Cœur at Moulins, 1850–67; Saint-Pierre at Dijon, 1855–8; Saint-Jean-Baptiste at Belleville, 1853–9) de-

199   Saint-Jean-Baptiste, Belleville, Paris; designed 1853, executed 1854–9. 'Among the monuments of the capital, Saint-Jean-Baptiste is the pearl of what I would call the nineteenth-century Renaissance. . . . One would say it was a building dating from the time of St Louis, one of those pious edifices with which the saintly king was pleased to surround and fortify his goodly town' (Decloux/Noury, 1862, p. 111).

monstrate a cool and precise application of these principles. Viollet-le-Duc was not deceived and spoke of Saint-Jean-Baptiste at Belleville, a working-class district in Paris, as a 'learned pastiche' and as a 'full-scale study of thirteenth-century architecture' (*Paris-Guide*, vol. III, 1867, p. 727).

Rather than invent new forms in the medieval spirit, Lassus takes a matrix, which is almost always the overall design of the thirteenth-century cathedral, and reassembles on it a selection, borrowed from a stylistically coherent corpus, of the most felicitous answers found to architectural problems. The memorandum which accompanied his design for Notre-Dame de la Treille in Lille (1856) is illuminating in this respect. Just as Apelles made the most beautiful girls in Athens pose for his painting of Venus, he gave his cathedral the general dimensions of Laon, galleries of the same size as those of Notre-Dame at Châlons-sur-Marne; for the choir he sought inspiration in the 'admirable choir of the cathedral of Le Mans'; for the stalls he took those of Poitiers as his model; for the pavement he studied that of Amiens, 'a precious example of the system, displaying at one and the same time the greatest richness, variety and economy'. It was no longer to nature or the classical ideal that the architect went for inspiration but to the medieval past; the difference, however, was more superficial than profound.

During the 1850s in France, Hippolyte Louis Durand, who worked in the Basses-Pyrénées, Gustave Guérin (1814–81) in Tours, Paul Abadie (1812–84) in Angoulême, and many others, proceeded in like manner to build churches which were as correct as they were tedious. In every country it would be possible to name craftsmen in this archeological neo-Gothic style who worked on restorations at the same time as producing neo-medieval designs for new buildings: Louis de Custe (1817–91) in Belgium, Petrus Josephus Hubertus Cuijpers (1827–1921) in the Netherlands, Heinrich von Ferstel (1828–83) in Vienna and often even Sir George Gilbert Scott in England. However, Cuijpers displayed a sensitivity to textures not to be found among his French colleagues, and Scott, who sometimes, like Lassus, was very close to pastiche – as in Christ Church at Ealing, a literal imitation of Bloxham ('a very literal representation of Bloxham', *Ecclesiologist*, vol. VIII, p. 54) – never hesitated to introduce continental forms.

It was not very long before archeological propriety clashed with the desire to invent a modern Gothic style, and when Lassus disappeared from the scene in 1857 his anti-eclectic ideal was already superseded.

Proceeding from different and indeed opposed principles, John Ruskin (1819–1900) in England and Viollet-le-Duc in France played an essential part in giving the neo-Gothic movement a new direction.

Both of them brought the neo-Gothic movement out of its clerical and antiquarian ghetto and aimed at a Gothic revival; for both of them the Gothic style became the model for all architecture; but for Ruskin its universality rested on aesthetic and moral values, and for Viollet-le-Duc on structural and rational values. From Gothic architecture Ruskin singled out

200 St Willibrordus, Amsterdam; Petrus Josephus Hubertus Cuijpers, 1866. The ideal design for a cathedral.

visual emotion, Viollet-le-Duc structural logic; Ruskin looked at Italian architecture, Viollet-le-Duc at French. Ruskin's nostalgic aestheticism and his feeling for decoration no doubt had immediate effects which were more felicitous than the cold rationalism and dry design of Viollet-le-Duc; but the Frenchman's more abstract reading of Gothic cast his thinking in a more modernistic mould which made him one of the sources of the modernist movement.

Between one phase and the next there was no real break in continuity. Certainly, the major protagonists of the first phase left the scene, Pugin in 1852, Sulpiz Boisserée in 1854, Lassus in 1857; but Vinzenz Statz (1819–98), who built a number of neo-Gothic churches in the Rhineland in the second half of the century, and von Schmidt, the most important protagonist of Viennese neo-Gothic, learned their craft working on Cologne Cathedral; Viollet-le-Duc and Émile Boeswilwald (1815–96) could rely on

archeological experience acquired in the 1840s to lay the foundations for a modern Gothic under the Second Empire; Sir George Gilbert Scott, William Butterfield and John Loughborough Pearson received the imprint of Pugin before turning towards the more original expressions which the English-speaking countries refer to as Victorian Gothic.

The contrast between the memorial to Walter Scott (1832) in Edinburgh, which was built by George Meikle Kemp (1836, 1840–4), and those to Prince Albert, who died in 1861, designed by Thomas Worthington in Manchester in 1862–7 and by Scott in London in 1864–75, are good illustrations of the shifts that took place at the time. The Edinburgh monument was inspired by a flamboyant canopy at Melrose Abbey, the details of which Kemp reproduced on a bigger scale with archeological precision; the Victorian monuments to the prince consort were freely inspired by the Gothic tombs of Verona and bring into play a polychrome Anglo-Italian vocabulary in a rather free eclectic spirit.

John Ruskin expounded his views in two books, *The Seven Lamps of Architecture* (1849) and *The Stones*

of Venice (1851–3), and in some provocative lectures which he gave at Edinburgh, the 'Athens of the North', *Lectures on Architecture and Art* (1854). Often turgid, sometimes confused and contradictory, his architectural aesthetic is the retrospective rationalization of his personal likings: sensitivity to materials, textures and colours, a fascination for Italy and the light of Venice which, as in the case of Pugin, was inseparable from his ethical and social ideas: Greek architecture was condemned by reason of its bonds with slavery, that of the Renaissance because of its languid sensuality, and admiration for Gothic architecture was nourished by nostalgia for a Middle Ages of free craftsmen, the very opposite of mechanized civilization. Four styles seemed to him to be worthy of imitation: Pisan Romanesque, Early English Decorated, and particularly the Early Gothic of the Western Italian Republics and Venetian Gothic in its purest development. Giotto's campanile in Florence and the Doges' Palace in Venice were, for him, the models of all perfection. Ruskin brought about a double shift in contemporary sensibilities: by stressing decorative and visual values at the expense of symbolic and liturgical meanings, he secularized the neo-Gothic movement; by being more interested in Italian Gothic than in the English cathedral, he reconciled Gothic with Italophile dilettantism. But whereas the Ecclesiologists and Pugin sought to establish different styles for churches, public buildings and private houses, Ruskin, actuated by aestheticism, re-established a universal language in which a warehouse would be treated in the same idiom as a town hall. Ruskin undoubtedly played a role as an enlightener, but his feeling for coloured materials and for sculptured textures, as well as his fascination with Italian medieval architecture, both secular and religious, are common to all his generation.

Almost at the same time George Edmund Street and Sir George Gilbert Scott were defending similar ideas. In *A Plea for the Faithful Restoration of our Ancient Churches* (1850), and especially in *Remarks on Secular and Domestic Architecture, Present and Future* (1858), Scott, like Ruskin, emphasized that the Gothic style was appropriate not only for religious edifices and picturesque private houses but also for public and commercial buildings. Scott also shared Ruskin's interest in Italian Gothic, from which he took the struc-

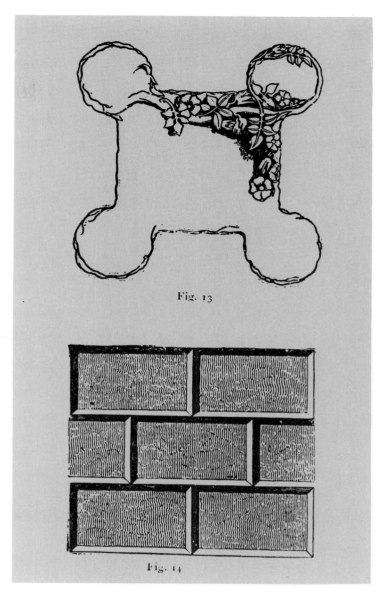

Fig. 13

Fig. 14

203   A Ruskinian contrast: a medieval and a classical carved surface. After Ruskin, 1854, p. 58, Pl. VIII.

tural polychromy, the simplicity of the masses and the regularity of the openings; but, being less dogmatic and less of an aesthete than Ruskin, he was more eclectic in his sources and also studied French and Nordic Gothic. He particularly recommended Netherlands and German Gothic for imitation; the cloth hall at Ypres seemed to him to be the archetype of modern secular Gothic. For him the Gothic system was only the nucleus of an open-ended research programme and he sought to adapt the pointed arch to the altered requirements of his own days by embracing every new material or system of construction. Thus, whereas Ruskin cared nothing for the creation of a new style, Scott hoped that, after a necessary phase of apprenticeship, a modern Gothic architecture would arise.

201   Sir Walter Scott Memorial, Edinburgh, Scotland; George Meikle Kemp, designed 1836, executed 1840–4.

202   Albert Memorial, Kensington Gardens, London; Sir George Gilbert Scott, designed 1862, executed 1864–75.

204, 205   All Saints, Margaret Street, Westminster, London: views of exterior and interior; William Butterfield, 1850–9.

Where small country churches were concerned, British architects remained faithful to the local style, but a very rich archeological culture in vernacular styles, a marked feeling for the picturesque qualities of materials, and an active and independent aristocratic patronage endowed these buildings with a refinement which had no equal on the Continent. Where city churches were concerned, a still greater degree of independence and freedom was displayed. A decisive broadening of the cultural horizon on the one hand and the desire to establish the characteristics of a modern Gothic style on the other were conducive to experiments of great diversity – and, it may be added, of great charm.

It was significant that the new Victorian style was first seen in the types of building for which Gothic was already accepted (churches and schools, university buildings) before it came to be adopted for civic and commercial purposes. The use of an Italian model appeared to provide a solution to the problem posed by the town church and school. The school of the Northern District at St Martin-in-the-Fields in London by Wild, built in 1849 and one of the first manifestations of secular Gothic in the Italian style, was in marked contrast to the small neo-Gothic country schools, just as All Saints, Margaret Street, London (1850–9) contrasted with the churches built in the 1840s.

Built by Butterfield for the Cambridge Camden movement, All Saints was deliberately designed as a practical example of constructional polychromy. The site was too small, and the church is remarkable for the brilliant and picturesque way in which its layout was contrived: it has a high dominating spire and particularly a pattern of black and red bricks arranged in horizontal and oblique bands. Inside, according to an expected progression, the chromatic effects are intensified. Red and black bricks, and terracotta enamelled green, yellow and grey, cover the floor and walls with flat geometric patterns. These are varia-

206   St James the Less, Westminster, London; George Edmund Street, 1859–61.

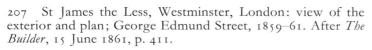

207 St James the Less, Westminster, London: view of the exterior and plan; George Edmund Street, 1859–61. After *The Builder*, 15 June 1861, p. 411.

208 St James the Less, Westminster, London: view of interior; George Edmund Street, 1859–61.

209 St Saviour's, Islington, London: view of choir; William White, 1865–6.

210, 211 St Martin's, Camden, London: views of interior and exterior; Edward B. Lamb, 1862–5. Of almost the same generation as Pugin, Lamb remained faithful to the more visual than archeological picturesqueness of J. C. Loudon.

212,213 Church of Christ the Consoler, Skelton-on-Ure, near Ripon, England: views of exterior and interior; William Burges, designed 1870, executed 1871–7. The church was built on a pastoral site by the Marquess of Ripon in memory of his brother-in-law who was murdered by Greek bandits. French features have been grafted on to English stock here and there, but what is impressive about the building as a whole is the full-bodied quality of the design, characteristic of all Burges's buildings.

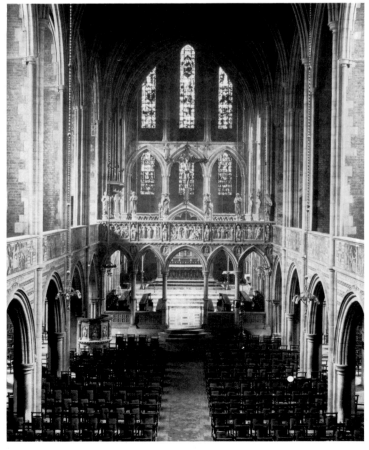

tions on the Cosmatesque patterns published in 1849 by Matthew Digby Wyatt (1820–77) in his *Specimens of the Geometrical Designs of the Middle Ages*, but the capitals and mouldings kept the English spirit. After building a dozen or so country churches in the following years, Butterfield returned to a more vivid polychromy, which explodes with particular force in St Augustine's, Penarch, Glamorgan, 1864; All Saints, Babbacombe, Devon, 1865; Keble College Chapel, Oxford, 1867; Rugby School Chapel, 1870–2, etc.

This jarring polychromy may have shocked his contemporaries, but in abandoning the impersonal ideal of archeological exactitude for artistic eclecticism, Butterfield made 'Gothic Revival step down from its pedestal of erudition' and opened up a new avenue which was to be explored also by George Edmund Street, William White (1825–1900) and others.

In St James the Less (1859–61) Street detached his steeple like an Italian campanile; he seems to have had in mind the spire of Sant'Agostino at Genoa, the gemel window of the campanile of Sant'Andrea of Mantua, and the apse of the Abbey of Bonport; inside there again appears the polychromy which was one of the recurrent features of Victorian Gothic. At Holy Saviour, Aberdeen Park (1865–6) White sought effects of colour saturation close to Byzantine mosaic. Edward B. Lamb (1805–69), who worked for the Low Church, remained faithful to a 'pre-Ecclesiologist' Gothic, which was picturesque rather than archeological, and created timber roof frameworks of extreme complexity (St Martin, Gospel Oak, London, 1862–5). James Brooks (1825–1901), on the other hand, worked in large surfaces of red brick and high airy naves with no decoration in his churches in the East End of London: St Columba, Kingsland Road (1867) and St Chad, Haggerston (1868–9); the Ascension, Lavender Hill (1876); the Transfiguration

214 St Augustine's, London: external view. The spire recalls that of Saint-Étienne at Caen in Normandy, the wide arch of the gable end that of Peterborough Cathedral, and the small narthex with its sloping roof that of Byland Abbey; but these are not so much quotations as free play with medieval architectural forms.

215 St Augustine's, London: view of the nave looking towards the chancel; John Loughborough Pearson, designed 1870, executed 1871–98. The church, which is almost cathedral-like in scale, is built in a thirteenth-century Gothic style which is more French than English. The handling of space, with interior buttresses, as in the cathedral of Albi (of which Pearson had a photograph), and galleries astride the transepts, is particularly elegant. The choir, with sculptures and stained glass forms a contrast to the nave where brick walls are only partially decorated with paintings.

at Lewisham (1880–6) and others. He followed the path pioneered by Pearson at St Peter's, Vauxhall, London (1863–5).

The building of the University Museum at Oxford (1855–60) by Sir Thomas Deane (1792–1871) and Benjamin Woodward, with the backing of Ruskin, was a brilliant statement of the universal ambitions of the neo-Gothic movement. Having already introduced Italianate details at Trinity College in Dublin in 1853, Woodward gave a marked Italian flavour to the main building, which is organized round a courtyard covered by a glass roof borne by cast-iron columns; but the principal roofs are Nordic and the laboratory building was inspired by the kitchens at Glastonbury in Somerset. To meet the wishes of Ruskin, two Irish sculptors, the O'Shea brothers, were called to the site to give each capital a different design.

This Italianate Gothic style, following a suggestion by Street, was also soon used for commercial façades: the Crown Life Assurance office in London by Woodward, in 1855 (destroyed), which was the first application of Ruskin's principles in London; the Fryer & Bynion warehouse, in 1856, a variation on the Doges' Palace, and the Royal Insurance Building, in 1861 (destroyed), in Manchester, by Alfred Waterhouse; offices at 59-61 Mark Lane, in London, by George Aitchison (1825–1910), in 1864; General Credit and Discount Company, 7 Lothbury, London, in 1866–8, by George Somers Clarke the Elder (1825–82), the windows of which were inspired by examples published by Ruskin in *Stones of Venice*.

Opposition to the use of neo-Gothic for public buildings grew stronger. Scott was unsuccessful in his Gothic designs for the town hall at Hamburg in 1854–5, for that of Halifax, and for government offices in Whitehall, London, in 1857. The design for Hamburg won a prize but was not carried out. At Halifax preference was given to a design by Sir

216 University Museum, Oxford; Sir Thomas Deane and Benjamin Woodward, 1855–60 (state before alterations were made to the laboratory pavilion on the right).

217 University Museum, Oxford: covered interior court; Sir Thomas Deane and Benjamin Woodward, 1855–60. The 'Gothic' metal arches with their rather naive ornamental work may be compared with those of the Sainte-Geneviève Library in Paris and the Natural History Museum in London.

218 University Museum, Oxford: plan, 1893. A medicine, B chemistry, C zoology, D geology, E anthropology (Pitt Rivers Museum), F anatomy, G physiology, H morphology, I Clarendon physics laboratory, J curator's dwelling; 1 entrance hall, 2 porter's lodge, 3 rooms and offices, 4 laboratories, 5 assembly halls.

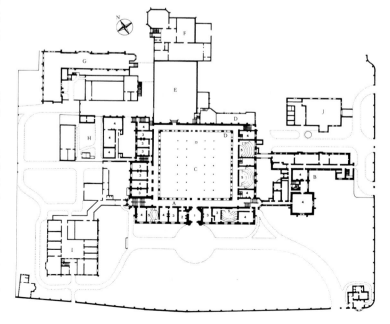

Charles Barry in an eclectic classicistic style. As to the Whitehall ministries, three designs in Italian style were at first awarded prizes; in 1858, taking advantage of the fall of Palmerston, and with the support of the new Tory prime minister, Scott took charge; when Palmerston, who was hostile to Tory neo-Gothic symbolism, returned to power in 1859, Scott had no alternative, if he wanted to remain in charge, but to produce a design in Italian style, after suggesting a middle-of-the-road solution in Byzantine. This battle of styles, which persisted for five years and in which political intrigues and administrative machinations were involved, bears witness to the lasting nature of the symbolic values attached to such matters but also to the ultimately secondary character of the stylistic elements at stake. Forced to work in the Italian style of the Renaissance, Scott, as he relates, bought expensive books and worked on the elevations of the Louvre in the same serious archeological spirit that he had previously brought to bear in his studies of English cathedrals. In actual fact changes of style had few repercussions on layouts, and contemporaries compared this quarrel, not without humour, to that between the big-enders and the little-enders in Jonathan Swift's *Gulliver's Travels*.

Scott failed because he could not completely free his Gothic design from the politico-religious symbolism which had spelled success for the first applications of this style, when, in the 1860s, there was a reversal of the trend. In 1859, while R.J. Withers built the modest municipal complex at Cardigan, Alfred Waterhouse won the competition organized for the Assize Courts in Manchester (1859–64, destroyed) with a design in which the Italian and English idiom was mixed eclectically. In 1861, against the advice of William Tite (1798–1873), the technical adviser to the municipality, who favoured a design in Italian style, Edward William Godwin (1833–86) won the competition for the town hall in Northampton with a thirteenth-century continental Gothic style. This was the first time that a Gothic style with a distinctly continental accent and the stamp of Ruskin's aesthetics on it was accepted for a public civic building in preference to an Italian or English Gothic composition. In the years that followed town halls of this type proliferated: at Preston in Lancashire, by Scott in 1862 (destroyed), in Chester by Lynn (1829–1915) in 1864, at Congleton, Cheshire by Godwin in 1864, in Manchester by Waterhouse in 1868–77, at Bradford by Lockwood and Mawson (1869–73), and at Rochdale in Lancashire by Crossland (1866–71).

Since the architectural imagination of the nineteenth century operated mainly in terms of arche-types, the particular success of this modern Gothic for town halls will occasion no surprise: the Broletto in Como and the Palazzo Publico in Siena on the one hand and the town halls of the Netherlands, of Ypres, Louvain and Ghent, and the archbishop's palace at Sens on the other, were just so many themes to be exploited.

The competition for the Law Courts in London, organized in 1866 ten years after that for the government offices, marks the climax of this movement: whereas in 1856 only eighteen designs out of 218 were in Gothic style, on this occasion all those submitted were. Street's design was the winner, and the construction, which did not begin until 1874, continued until 1882. The neo-Gothic style used for museums (Bristol City Museum, by Foster and Ponton, 1866–71, now the university), hospitals (Leeds Infirmary, 1864–8, by Scott; the Royal Infirmary at Edinburgh by David Bryce, 1870–9), universities (University of Glasgow, by Scott, 1866–71), hotels (Midland Grand Hotel at St Pancras, London, 1868–74), clubs (Manchester Reform Club, by Edward Salomons, 1870) and schools did indeed take on the appearance of a universal style. As Mark Girouard pointed out, the construction of the Natural History Museum in London (1873–81) was a repetition of that of the government offices, except that the roles were reversed. Called upon to execute the Italianate design of Captain Fowke (1864), Waterhouse produced a medieval version in German Romanesque style (1868–71), which was more acceptable to a classicist than the Gothic style. The compromise was similar to the one which Scott had sought in vain when he had suggested a Byzantine design for the ministries of Whitehall. However, the adoption of a Romanesque style was also symptomatic of a kind of regression in the Gothic movement which was apparent in the 1870s. In spite of some latter-day projects like the town halls of Barrow-in-Furness, Lancashire (1878–87), by W.H. Lynn, or Middlesbrough (1883–9), by G.O. Hoskins, branch offices of the Prudential Assurance Company in London and Liverpool (1878–86), by Waterhouse, or the import-

219 Foreign and India Offices, London: design in Gothic style; Sir George Gilbert Scott, about 1859 (R.I.B.A., London, *Scott*, No. 84, 10).

220 Foreign and India Offices, London: design in Italian style; Sir George Gilbert Scott, about 1860–3 (R.I.B.A., London, *Scott*, No. 84, 34).

221 Town Hall of Northampton, England: section and elevation of rear façade, competitive design; Edward William Godwin, 1861. (Victoria and Albert Museum, London, E. 579-1963.)

222 New Town Hall, Manchester; Alfred Waterhouse, 1868–77. Waterhouse studied Nordic models (Ypres Cloth Hall) rather than Italian ones but used bow-windows to give his design a more English and picturesque appearance.

223 New Town Hall, Manchester: design; Alfred Waterhouse, 1868.

ant series of schools built in Manchester (1873–98) by John Henry Chamberlain and Martin, the Gothic style began to go out of fashion. Instead architects turned to new 'Queen Anne' or neo-Baroque forms.

The Continent also had some buildings to show which recall Victorian developments. In the Imperial Chapel at Biarritz Émile Boeswilwald produced a polychromy no less strident than that of William Butterfield, but the brickwork is merely painted. In his suburban churches in Paris, Claude Naissant sought an effect of purification and geometrical abstraction which was partly imposed by a modest budget but is similar to the work of James Brooks (1825–1901), although the idiom is Romanesque and not Gothic. It is as if French and German architects were overawed by the medieval tradition or anxious to find a compromise with the ancient Roman tradition. Nevertheless, just as Street and Burges in England had started with Gothic material, so Joseph Auguste Émile Vaudremer (1829–1914) was successful in creating a modern Romanesque church at Saint-Pierre-de-Montrouge in Paris. Into a difficult triangular site,

bounded by two broad avenues, he confidently inserted a steeple, nave and large apse and ambulatory rising with contrasted masses in pyramidal forms and affording oblique views. In his modest work as a church builder, Viollet-le-Duc, like his English contemporaries, freely drew his matter from a capacious visual memory: at Aillant-sur-Tholon the steeple porch is turned to the side to face the town hall, and at Saint-Denis-de-l'Estrée he mingles Romanesque and Gothic forms to distinguish the nave and axial chapel. In his writings and oral teaching, however, Viollet-le-Duc gave the French neo-Gothic movement a direction which was more constructive and rationalist than aesthetic.

Several architects close to him – Anatole de Baudot, Boeswilwald, Jules Désiré Bourdais and Eugène Louis Millet (1819–79), whose *Gazette des architectes et du bâtiment* published their works – followed this line. Their works are characterized by a rational and methodical approach to layout, a structure which is clearly exposed both inside and outside, and the use of local materials as well as those of modern type.

224 Natural History Museum, London; Alfred Waterhouse, designed 1872, executed 1873–80.

At Masny, Boeswilwald caused arches of brick-work, the traditional material of the north, to rest on cast-iron columns and, the decoration being simply the result of the pronounced bonding, seemed to be seeking a deliberately abstract simplification of Goth-ic forms.

When, in 1869, Bourdais expounded 'the general ideas governing the design of the Protestant church at Nègrepelisse', he explained that, since the church ordinarily had to contain 800 seats, and 1,000 if re-quired at great festivals, and the cost was not to ex-ceed 50,000 francs, he needed 270 square metres of space (a square with a side of 16.5 m) and, in order to have an acceptable relationship between width and height, he had to make his buildings at least 12 metres high: 'in order to be able to dispense with weighty buttresses, I thought of making the angles re-entrant so as to provide four very rigid points of support on which I could rest two diagonal trusses without ties and, so as to make the thrust of the framework im-pinge as near as possible to the foot of the walls taking it, I unhesitatingly adopted a design with stays, partly exposed to view, which do the duty of oblique sup-porting columns shored one against the other by a horizontal tie-beam.' The original solution is present-ed as the logical answer to a structural problem; sty-

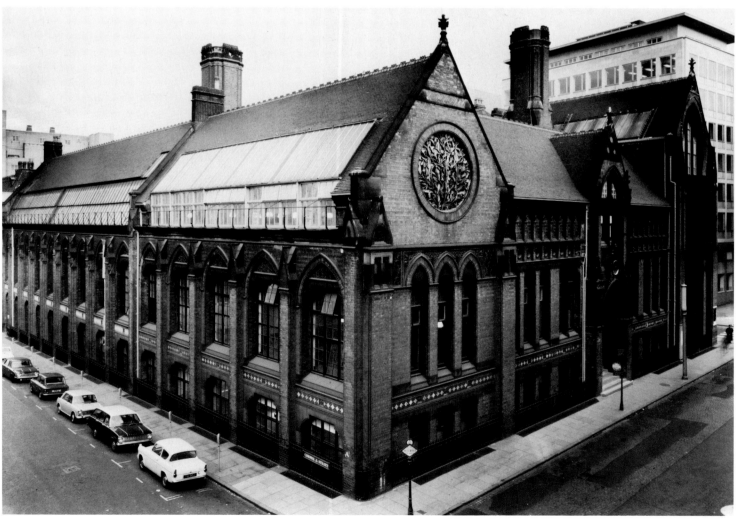

225 Natural History Museum, London: central hall; Alfred Waterhouse, designed 1872, executed 1873–80. The metal framework is clad, both inside and outside, with polychrome terracotta as both ornamentation and fire protection but is clearly exposed in the partially glazed ceiling.

226 College of Arts and Crafts, Birmingham; John Henry Chamberlain & Martin, 1881–5. A deliberate asymmetry of the façade, bas-reliefs and polychrome designs: the whole gamut of Ruskinian poetry is combined here, but the slightly abstract accentuation of the lines is a harbinger of new trends.

227 Imperial Chapel, Biarritz, Pyrénées-Atlantiques; Émile Boeswilwald, 1877. The chapel is still in existence but the Victorian polychromy has disappeared from its exterior. After *Revue générale de l'architecture*, 1877, Pl. 3.

228 Saint-Pierre, Charenton; Claude Naissant, 1857–9. The reduction of the historical vocabulary to near-abstract forms is reminiscent of Jean Nicolas Louis Durand's educational models and also of James Brooks's contemporary London churches. Similar circumstances – construction of a suburban church with limited funds led to comparable effects, even though in England the basic style is Gothic. In this case it is Romanesque, interspersed with Renaissance elements.

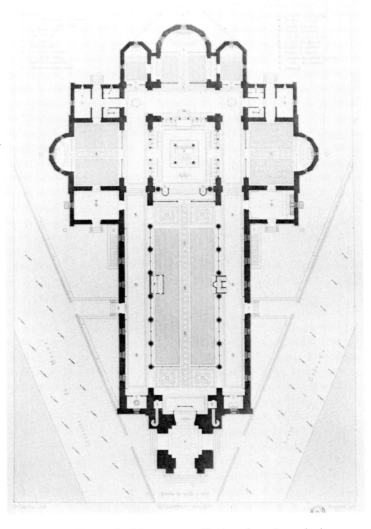

229 Saint-Pierrre-de-Montrouge, Paris; Joseph Auguste Émile Vaudremer, 1864–70. Situated on a city site comparable to that of Saint-Augustin, this church is more homogeneous than Saint-Augustin and more original than Saint-Ambroise; it is the only real success achieved by Parisian ecclesiastical architecture in the second half of the nineteenth century.

230 Saint-Pierre-de-Montrouge, Paris: plan; Joseph Auguste Émile Vaudremer, 1864–70. After Narjoux, 1880–3, vol. III.

listic considerations are left out of account and the façade is distinguished solely by its simplicity and the bold statement of its local materials.

In North America, even if it had to contend with competition from the 'French style', Victorian secular Gothic found expression in a number of structures. In Canada, as a natural consequence of the unity of the British Empire, Fuller and Jones adopted a Gothic design for the Parliament buildings in Ottawa (1859), which was fairly close to that proposed by Scott for the government offices in London.

On the Continent, on the other hand, the idea of a secular neo-Gothic style met with lively resistance. For the Berlin Reichstag in 1872 preference was given to Ludwig Franz Karl Bohnstedt's (1822–85) classical design over the neo-Gothic alternative. For the Palais de Justice (1857–68) in Paris Joseph Louis Duc studied projects in Gothic style so as to harmonize his façade with what remained of the medieval building and the Sainte-Chapelle, but finally decided in favour of a grand classical façade.

In German-speaking countries there are a number of fine neo-Gothic town halls, the most spectacular being that in Vienna, but the fact that a neo-classical design was adopted at the same time for the Parliament building shows that the choice was an eclectic one, made in the interests of variety, rather than one imposed by strict adherence to a coherent neo-Gothic system. The most attractive design was that of Imre Steindl (1839–1902) for the Parliament building in Budapest (1882–1902). There are perceptible reminiscences of the Houses of Parliament in London and

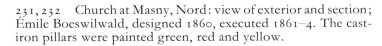

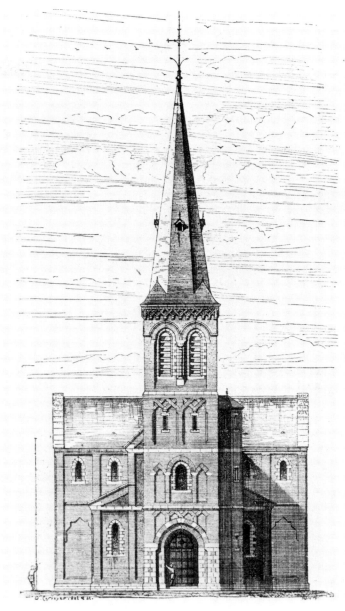

231, 232 Church at Masny, Nord: view of exterior and section;
Émile Boeswilwald, designed 1860, executed 1861–4. The cast-
iron pillars were painted green, red and yellow.

particularly of Scott's project for the Reichstag, and
the Gothicized dome recalls that of the Fünfhaus-
kirche in Vienna. Occupying a splendid site on the
banks of the Danube, Imre Steindl's Parliament
building shows authority in the organization of its
masses while there is a felicitous touch in the interplay
of roofs, buttresses and pinnacles.

In France the classical bent of the teaching at the
École des Beaux-Arts explains why public buildings
in medieval style are so rare. Viollet-le-Duc knew that
young architects came up against a block in their
training. He took advantage of his political connections (he was very close to the Imperial couple) and,
in 1863, pleaded for a reform at the École des Beaux-
Arts. Failure to carry out this reform against the opposition of the students tolled the knell of a Gothic

revival and ensured that an eclectic classicism, which
was no less original, won the day.

Eclecticism or Late Neo-Classicism

In spite of its variegated history, the classical tradition
had been sustained by the fiction of a timeless beauty.
The new and penetrating insight obtained into the
way its forms changed according to time and place
had spelled the liquidation of this ideal. The normative aesthetic of neo-classicism was replaced by a
historical and relativistic reading of the whole classical tradition, which historians and architects learned
to classify in styles and the typical features of which
were used to enrich the palette of the creators. As the

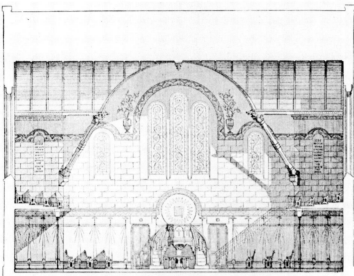

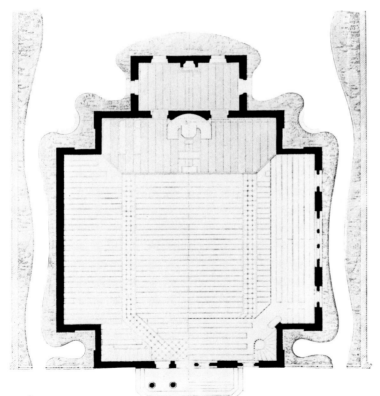

three variant designs put forward by Leo von Klenze for the Glyptothek of Munich showed, three different styles – Greek, Roman and Italian – had already been accepted for public architecture. After 1850 they still continued in use but none of them retained a place in the new cultural context except as one of the modes of the new implicit formal system which could be called eclectic classicism, the last re-appearance of the classical tradition.

As a result of the broadening spectrum of cultural reference, and as a reaction to the elegant but slightly bald and excessively international style of Italianate and Hellenized classicism, it was only natural that around 1850 there should appear forms which were more opulent, picturesque and national. Architects reacted to the double process of purification carried out by academic classicism on the one hand and neo-classicism on the other by reviving the whole gamut of traditional classical forms with their national in-flexions – those of the first Italian and French Renais-sance as well as those of Nordic Mannerism, those of the Italian, French or English *grand style*, of Bernini, Mansart or Wren and those of French or German Rococo.

The contrasts between Louis Tullius Joachim Vis-conti's (1791–1853) Molière fountain (1841–4) and Gabriel Davioud's (1823–81) Saint-Michel fountain (1856–60), between St George's Hall in Liverpool (1841–56) and the town hall in Leeds (1871–8), and between William Strickland's Tennessee capitol at Nashville (1845–59) and Arthur Gilman's and Gried-ley Bryant's town hall (1861–5) at Boston are good illustrations of the shifts that took place between 1850 and 1860 in the way the *grand style* was envisaged. Dissociating themselves from the heroic severity of neo-classicism and from the gracious elegance of the Italian style of the Cinquecento, architects showed a marked taste for more loaded sculptural effects, for what we today might call (quite improperly) some-thing more Baroque. Instead of simple volumes, predominantly horizontal compositions with regular colonnades and vast stretches of unadorned wall, they preferred stepped compositions rising in a pyramid, with pilasters and columns and a multitude of ex-uberant and often polychromic ornamentation.

233, 234, 235   Protestant church at Nègrepelisse, Tarn-et-Garonne: elevation, section and plan; Jules Désiré Bourdais, 1869. 'What is striking in this design is the simplicity of the composition and the system of construction and the frankness with which the latter is expressed.' (*Gazette des architectes et du bâtiment*, 1869, p. 82.)

236 Central Post Office, Aachen, 1889.
An example of neo-Romanesque administrative style.

237 Town Hall, Hamburg; Martin
Haller, in collaboration with other architects, 1886–97.

238 Parliament House, Budapest: grand staircase; Imre Steindl, 1882–1902.

239 Parliament House, Budapest: the Chamber of Deputies; Imre Steindl, 1882–1902.

240 Parliament House, Budapest; Imre Steindl, 1882–1902.

241 Parliament House, Budapest: plan; Imre Steindl, 1882–1902.

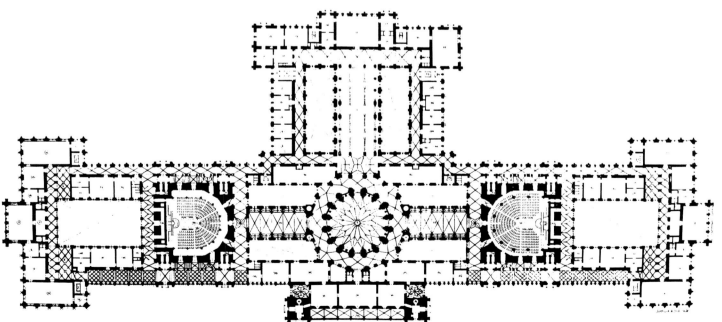

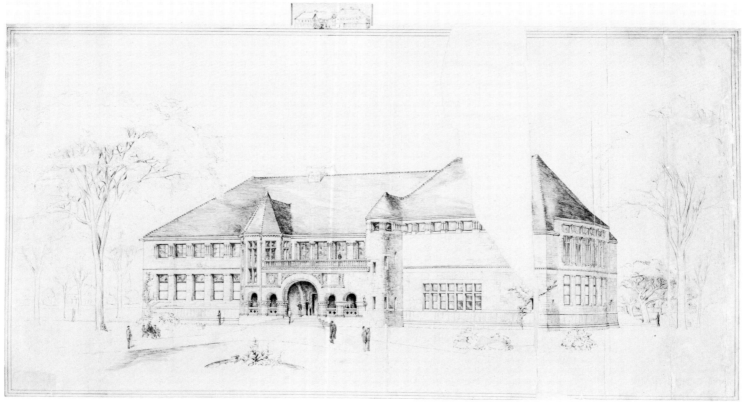

242 Winn Memorial Library, Woburn, Mass.; Henry Hobson Richardson, 1877–8. The first of an important series of university libraries and buildings. Through the interplay of the picturesque masses, the number of colonnettes, and rich polychromy, Richardson produced a slightly strident effect which he was able to tone down some months later in the Ames Memorial Library at North Easton, where he found the measured classical rhythm of his modern Romanesque.

243 Austin Hall, Cambridge, Mass.: first design, office of Henry Richardson, 1881. The design is more ambitious than that for the Crane Memorial Library at Quincy, 1880–3, and shows the same felicitious touch in producing an asymmetrical balance. One should not be misled by the label Romanesque given to Richardson's works by his contemporaries: points to note are the Elizabethan bow-windows, the Syrian-influenced arch of the portal, and the band of windows in the attic like those in neoclassical style by Schinkel in Berlin.

244 Crane Memorial Library, Quincy, Mass.; Henry Hobson Richardson, 1880–3. He plays on the contrast between Milford granite and Longmeadow stone, the asymmetrical balance of the masses and openings, various historical reminiscences (Syrian arch, Romanesque openings, Elizabethan windows) and displays that coherence of architectural language which is his hallmark.

245 Trinity Church, Boston, Mass.: first design; Henry Hobson Richardson, 1873. The transepts and apse were changed later. The tower is in the style of the cathedral of Salamanca. The motif of the large rose window clearly standing out in the wall of the gable is echoed by William A. Potter in the New South Church at Springfield.

246 Trinity Church, Boston, Mass.: plan; 1 church; 2 chapel; 3 vestibule; 4 vestry; 5 organ.

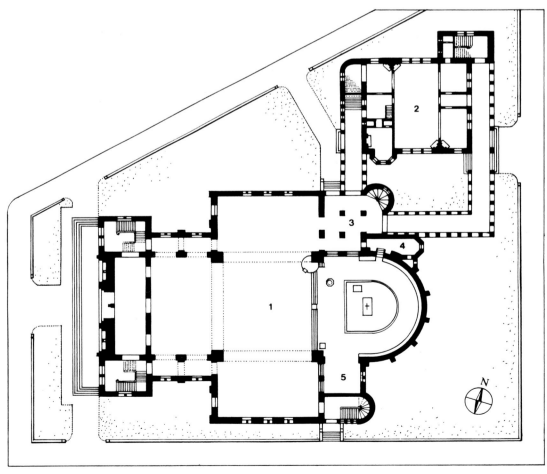

247   Trinity Church, Boston, Mass.: view looking from the
south-east about 1880; Henry Hobson Richardson, designed
1873, executed 1874–7. The porch and the east towers, executed
by Shepley, Rutan & Coolidge, are later.

Napoleon III or Second Empire style in France, General Grant or French style in the United States, Umberto I or neo-Baroque style in Italy – by their very variety these designations stress not only the official character of the style but also the French origin and, at the same time, the national colouring of the movement, but they conceal the international scope of the phenomenon. The influence of the École des Beaux-Arts and the prestige of the 'new Paris' of Napoleon III certainly played a part in its success in England, the United States, Germany and Austria, but the shift towards a more picturesque and orotund style began a little time before the establishment of the Second Empire. Certain European developments ran parallel to the Parisian development without there being any direct link between them. A movement rather than a style, like neo-classicism, eclectic classicism was not merely a late classicism, even though one isolated work or another might create this impression. By setting to work openly with modern materials and by solving entirely novel problems of layout on the one hand, and on the other by producing one variation, interpolation or even formal invention after another within the classical tradition, and by deliberately exploiting its historical depth in order to create significant contrasts, the architects who embarked on this course attempted to define a modern classicism – and sometimes succeeded.

Just as there was a contrast between Lassus and Scott, who remained faithful to a more archeological approach, and the new neo-Gothic generation (Street, Butterfield and others), which was much freer in its approach to the Gothic revival, the architects trained in the 1820s such as Semper, Labrouste or Sir Charles Barry were often content to make a simple switch in the classical tradition, from the Cinquecento to the Seicento, to obtain the more orotund effects called for by the new taste. The most eloquent contrast is no doubt that which exists between the two opera-houses at Dresden, designed thirty years apart (a boon for the historian) by the same architect, Gottfried Semper. The façades of the first one (1838–41) display a sober Italianate composition in which reminiscences of the Colosseum and the palace courtyard are almost too obvious. After a fire in 1869 the opera-

248 Town Hall, Albany, New York; office of Henry Hobson Richardson, 1880. The belfry makes an effective hinge at the corner of the two little squares overlooked by the town hall.

249 New South Church, Springfield, Mass.: design; William A. Potter, 1876. After *American Architect and Building News*, 2 December 1876.

house was rebuilt between 1871 and 1878 to a new design in which the sculptural effects and the syntactical articulation are clearly accentuated (rusticated basement, paired columns in the *avant-corps*, statues as crowning features).

Like Semper, James Fergusson (1808–86) stressed in his *History of Modern Styles in Architecture* (1862) that 'within the limits of Italian Renaissance, progress seems possible'. Certain works, particularly in Italy, where the Renaissance style figured as the national style, bore brilliant testimony to this contention, just as in Greece, for the same reason, the neo-classical Hellenized style experienced a late flowering of great merit (Zappeion and library at Athens; Corfu museum, etc.).

Similarly, Labrouste, who had used an Italianate style for the façade of the library of Sainte-Geneviève (1843–50), proposed for the front of the Bibliothèque nationale (1854–75) a composition frankly located within the classical French tradition, whereas Duban and Duc, in their late works, suggested the possibility of a discreet revival of the classical tradition with no perceptible pastiche, which gave the lie to any idea of progress in art. Jens Vilhelm Dahlerup (1836–1907) at Copenhagen, like Martin Philipp Gropius (1824–80) and Friedrich Hitzig (1811–81) in Berlin, provided brilliant confirmation of this initial move.

However, other architects handled this broadened classical culture with more freedom. Within the widened range of a classical tradition, they succeeded with more or less felicity, and sometimes a certain vulgarity, in producing a multiplicity of variant detail and in grafting motifs of varied origin on to neo-Baroque compositions.

In France the birth of the new style appeared, at least on the first analysis, to be connected with the completion of the Louvre. Between the restoration of the old Louvre, which was partly a recomposition and partly a reconstruction under Duban, and the new Louvre on which Visconti and Hector Lefuel (1810–80) worked in succession, there was a relationship rather akin to that existing between cathedral restorations and neo-Gothic; in both cases the restoration work was a school for style. But this is not in itself enough to explain why, while Visconti in 1852

250 Molière Fountain, rue Richelieu, Paris; Louis Tullius Joachim Visconti, 1841–4. One of the first manifestations of a return to the 'national' classical tradition, a choice which was no doubt partly determined by the iconography of the fountain.

251 Saint-Michel Fountain, Paris; Gabriel Davioud, 1856–60.

freed from extraneities the silhouette of the Pavillon de l'Horloge, with which his composition had to harmonize, Lefuel loaded it with exuberant ornaments and lent emphasis to the sculptural effects. In abandoning the linear and international ideal of neo-classicism, and even the purity of Italian Raphaelism, for a style that was more ostentatious (and also more French), Lefuel showed the way which was to be followed by a new generation of architects: Auguste Bailly (1810–92), Ballu, Davioud, Garnier, Auguste Joseph Magne (1816–85), Antoine Gaétan Guérinot (1820–91), Henri Espérandieu (1829–74), and others.

As if seeking a middle way between neo-classical spareness and Gothic profusion, they proposed something like a classical version of the silhouette and picturesque motifs of Gothic along with their imperial domes and shaft-ringed columns. With a very modern sense of freedom, they interpolated the polychromy of the Venetian Renaissance or of the Louis XIII style, the picturesque motifs of the first French Renaissance or of Nordic Mannerism into neo-Baroque compositions. This integration was made possible by an analytical breakdown of styles into motifs which were detached from their context and substituted for the classical orders, window-frames and crownings, and by a disjunction between architectural syntax and vocabulary which is characteristic of eclecticism. The Doric column was replaced by the François I pilaster or the shaft-ringed column in the style of Philibert de l'Orme, and the classical window-frames by Gothic pointed arches or Louis XIII dog-tooth ornament. As César Daly observed mischievously, 'the eclectic school treats the past as a kind of furniture depository, taking from it as occasion arises and as need or fancy requires everything that seems to be useful or attractive. For the eclectics the past is a storehouse of motifs.'

The strange impression created by those 'classical' buildings of the nineteenth century which are in appearance the most *correct* is often due to the sense of visual confusion induced by these barely perceptible shifts of scale and outline and these hybridizations of Early Renaissance or Mannerist motifs with compositions whose syntax is that of academic *grand style*.

In their quest for ideal beauty, aristocratic elegance and pleasing variety, neo-classicism, neo-Palladianism and picturesque Romanticism drew on a universal aesthetic and made use of an international idiom. The development of a national history of art (and not simply a medieval one) – a European phenomenon associated with the rise of national feeling, whose importance in the political and cultural history of the nineteenth century is well known – gave this new eclectic architectural culture a palpable national dimension.

However, even though this eclectic classicism assumed here and there a significant national colouring, the international influence of the École des Beaux-Arts and the prestige of Napoleon III's 'new Paris' effaced these differences, and eclectic French classicism tended to become a new international style. The mansard roof and in particular the imperial dome of the Pavillon de l'Horloge, the joint-lined basement façades and the *avant-corps* in the grand style of Louis XIV appeared everywhere as clichés.

Parallel developments were to be seen in England. St George's Hall in Liverpool, which Elmes began to build in 1841, was the last major neo-classical building in England: the simplicity of its massing in spite of a complex layout (concert hall, public hall and assize court) and the spare severity of its lines still recall the poetics of Schinkel, whose Berlin buildings Elmes had studied. Twelve years later, in the town hall of Leeds (1853–8), Cuthbert Brodrick shed this heroic severity for a more orotund style. This is also to be found in the interior of St George's Hall, completed in 1856 by Charles Robert Cockerell, and in the town hall (1859) of Halifax by Sir Charles Barry and Edward Middleton Barry (1830–80). In Leeds the colossal order has reminiscences of St George's Hall, but the two lateral projections and the pyramidal composition, together with the heavy ornamentation of the campanile, are clear evidence that another feeling for form has emerged: 'Baroque' rhetoric has replaced Greek purity and the elegance of the Italian Cinquecento style.

There is often a clear link with the new departures in France, as in the designs presented by Sir Charles Barry, Henry Garling and Henry Edward Coe (1826–85) for the new Whitehall ministries in 1856, which might have served as half-way stations between the Paris models and certain English provincial or American designs.

In London, in 1863, Prosper Mérimée, the author and also an inspector of historical monuments, wrote to Viollet-le-Duc that a large number of huge hotels were being built there in 'the Louvre style'. Rather as in the 1960s Le Corbusier's *cité radieuse* served as a model for hotels of the international class, so Lefuel's

252   First opera-house, Dresden, G.D.R.: south façade; Gottfried Semper, 1838–41 (burned down in 1869).

253   New opera-house, Dresden, G.D.R.; Gottfried Semper, 1871–8 (destroyed in 1945).

254 Art Gallery, Dresden, G.D.R.: façade facing the Elbe; Gottfried Semper, 1847–54. The Italian Renaissance style seemed to contemporaries to be that best suited to an art gallery.

255 Zappeion, Athens: view of the peristyle; François Boulanger and Théophil von Hansen, 1874–88.

256 Kunsthalle, Hamburg; Hermann von der Hude and Georg Theodor Schirrmacher, 1863–9.

257 Palazzo Ceriana, Piazza Solferino, Turin; Carlo Ceppi, 1878. A work within the classical tradition which attains an unobtrusive perfection in which familiarity and originality are felicitously united.

258 Palais de Justice, Paris: façade overlooking the place Dauphine; Louis Joseph Duc, 1857–68. According to the architect Paul Sédille, the general idea for the façade came from a palace of Dendera but the feature of the triglyph consoles is borrowed from the Veronese *palazzi* of Michele Sanmicheli and the capitals are copies of those of Stratonikeia in Asia Minor.

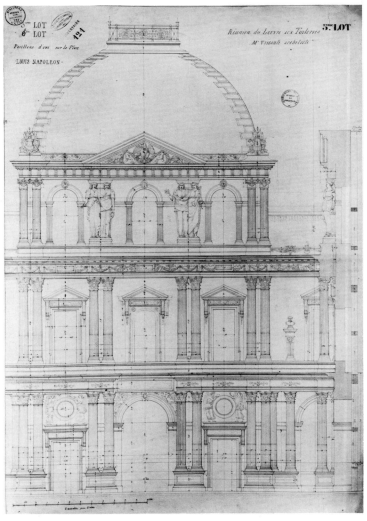

259 École des Beaux-Arts, Paris: façade on the quai Mala-quais; Félix Duban, 1860–2. The unexpected widening of the openings and the oculi, which were necessary to ensure good lighting in the exhibition halls of the new building, were the novel features of this façade. Its precise design and delicate shadows were designated 'neo-Greek' by contemporaries who, as may be seen, were referring to a tonality rather than a style.

260 Nouveau Louvre, Paris: design for a pavilion; Louis Tullius Joachim Visconti, 1852–3. By returning to the elegant French classic style of Lescot, Visconti found a national equiv-alent to the refined and linear Italianate style of his master Per-cier.

261 Lemercier's Pavillon de l'Horloge, Paris: study for a new west façade; Hector Lefuel, about 1854. An arranger of 'mediocre' ability according to Delacroix's severe but just ver-dict, Lefuel gives evidence here to a new taste for luxuriant and superabundant ornamentation which is the outcome of aban-doning the taut linear design of the preceding generation for the somewhat smudged effect of a wash drawing.

262 Mairie, 1st arrondissement, Paris; Jacques Ignace Hittorff, 1857–61. In conformity with Haussmann's wish the façade reflects the distribution of the masses in Saint-Germain-l'Auxerrois, which is located nearby; a rose window echoes the church, but the other elements shift from the Flamboyant to-wards the more 'secular' style of the early Italian Renaissance.

263 Mairie, 1st arrondissement, Paris; Jacques Ignace Hittorff, 1857–61. Eclecticism of the details: the columns are classical, the openings are somewhat reminiscent of Lombardian architecture at the end of the Quattrocento, and the balustrades have a 'Gothic' semblance.

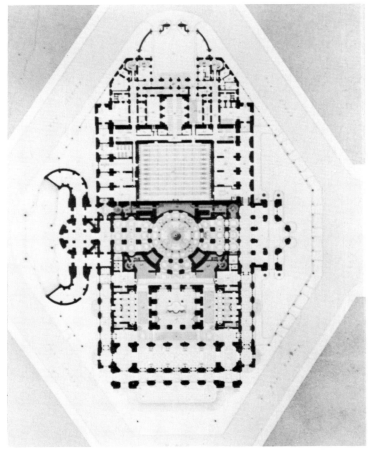

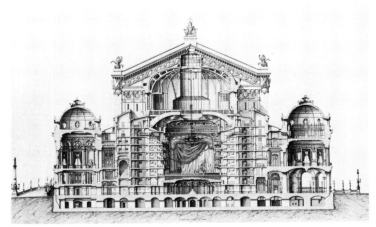

264 Grand Opéra, Paris: façade looking towards Place de l'Opéra; Charles Garnier, 1860–74.

265 Grand Opéra, Paris: plan of the ground floor; Charles Garnier, 1860–74.

266 Grand Opéra, Paris: section; Charles Garnier, 1860–74.

267 Grand Opéra, Paris: grand staircase; Charles Garnier, 1860–74.

new Louvre became the cultural point of reference for the hotel boom of the years 1850 to 1880, which was nurtured by the growth of middle-class railway tourism – even though Sir George Gilbert Scott adopted the Gothic style for the Midland Grand Hotel of St Pancras station and, for mountain and seaside resorts, architects liked to find their models in rustic and regional styles. In 1851–3, as contemporaries noted, Philip Charles Hardwick adopted a Louis XIV style for the Great Western Hotel at Paddington Station in London, and in 1863–5 Cuthbert Brodrick topped his Grand Hotel at Scarborough, Yorkshire, with mansard roofs.

In the United States the name 'French style', which came into common use, was an open acknowledgment of this relationship. When, in 1860, a competition was held for the new town hall in Boston, the report concluded by adopting Bryant's design and was quite explicit: 'this style is exemplified in the new portions of the Louvre at Paris, at once the most extensive and elegant of the public works with which the genius of the present emperor has enriched that attractive city. From the great intrinsic beauty of this style not less than from its extreme readiness of adaptation to the wants and uses of the present day it has

268 Palais de Longchamp, Marseilles; Henri Espérandieu, 1862. The Musée des Beaux-Arts and the Musée d'Histoire Naturelle are linked by a gallery to a water-tower.

269 Town Hall, Leeds, Yorkshire, England; Cuthbert Brodrick, 1853–8.

270 City Hall, Boston, Mass.; Arthur Gilman and Griedley Bryant, designed 1860, executed 1861–5. A slightly chilly late classicism recalling the outline of the Pavillon de l'Horloge by Jacques Lemercier at the Louvre and the Gaston d'Orléans wing at Blois by François Mansart.

attained universal popularity in Europe and in the chief cities of our own country.' (Report of the Committee on Public Buildings, City Document No. 44, Boston 1880, pp. 15–16.)

Alfred B. Mullet (1834–90), who in 1865 became chief architect for the Federal government, adopted this style for the innumerable official buildings erected during the presidency of General Grant. The New York central post office (1869–75), that of St Louis, Missouri (1873–5), and the Executive Office Building in Washington (1871–5) are the most characteristic structures in this undistinguished administrative style. This shift is very noticeable in the design of the capitols of New Hampshire (1864) and New York at Albany (1869) by Thomas Fuller, and of Springfield, Illinois (1867) by Cochrane, of Lansing, Michigan (1871), and others, where neo-Greek compositions were discarded for vast, pompous structures rising like a pyramid to a neo-Baroque dome.

The Law Courts of Brussels, like those of Rome, also bear witness to the development of this megalomaniac classicism, which is much indebted to the example of the grandiose designs upon which the École des Beaux-Arts in Paris conferred its prizes.

The battle of the neo-classical and neo-Gothic styles struck contemporaries, but whereas examples of clashes between the styles are numerous, actual cleavages are less conspicuous. In both parties there were over-learned architects like Lassus or Christian Frederik Hansen, imaginative architects like Garnier or Street, and decorators who were rather insignificant. Some of them were successful in creating their own sense of poetry and hall-marked their works by the personal note they were able to impart to Hellenized neo-classicism (Thomson, 1817–75), Romanesque (Henry Hobson Richardson), neo-Gothic (Burges) or Queen Anne style (Richard Norman Shaw, 1831–1912).

Alexander Thomson, with a twinkle in his eye, stressed that Scott's design for Glasgow University (1866) was not neo-Gothic but neo-classical, and indeed many of his Greek designs are more picturesque than many a neo-Gothic building on the Continent.

Two systems of design remained competitors until the end of the century: the classical system with its regular patterns, its axes of symmetry and its gradated and pyramidal compositions, and the picturesque system with its asymmetrical balances, its bays of various shapes and its jagged outline. Whereas at the beginning of the century they had been complementary to each other, they had now become rivals. First the prerogative of factories, colleges and eccentric follies, the picturesque design saw its field of application extend naturally to middle-class villas and seaside houses, to castles, then to churches about 1840, and blocks of town apartments and public buildings after 1850. It was English in origin and made little headway on the Continent except for villas and castles.

Another cleavage, with wider repercussions than that between styles, was to be found in the opposition between two entirely different conceptions of architecture, one more artistic and decorative and the other more constructive and rational. In the one case it was impossible to change the style without destroying the very form of the building; in the second the form was an ornament and the transition from one vocabulary to another remained a possibility.

271 City Post Office, New York; Alfred B. Mullett, 1869–75 (destroyed). Superimposed orders and square-domed pavilions, in Imperial style, are features of stereotyped classicism (*The Builder*, 25 November 1871, p. 927).

272 Palais de Justice, Brussels; Joseph Polaert, designed 1861–3, executed 1866–83. 'These sweeping architectural lines, these Babylonian colonnades, these grandiose vestibules and staircases which, in their layout, recall the famous labyrinth of Egypt, this dome which will dominate the whole town and its environs, this enormous cornice one kilometre long will certainly contribute very little to the ends for which this building was erected. The monument will be first and foremost a statement of our pride as a young nation' (*Rapport parlementaire* by Le Hardy de Beaulieu, 1879).

273 Palais de Justice, Brussels: vestibule; Joseph Polaert, designed 1861–3, executed 1866–83. 'The city is committed to one sixth; I want this sixth to cost it as dear as possible so that the law courts are worthy of their purpose and the city where they will be erected' (speech by mayor Jules Anpasch to the city council, October 1874).

274 Kunstgewerbemuseum, Berlin: design for the façade; Martin Gropius and Heino Schmieden, 1875. Built between 1877 and 1881, this museum with its polychrome bricks and its elegant Hellenism testifies to the strength of the Schinkel tradition in Berlin.

275 Polytechnical College, Aachen; Robert Cremer, 1865–70 (left) and chemistry laboratory by Franz Everbeck, 1875–9 (right). The Italian style maintained its popularity.

276 Municipal theatre, Augsburg; Ferdinand Fellner and Hermann Helmer, 1876–7. Built by two German architects specializing in theatre design, this is one of the many variants on the type of open loggia superimposed on arcades to be found in many countries, the masterpiece of the genre being Garnier's Opéra. Fellner and Helmer built the Volkstheater, Vienna, 1888–9 and the Stadttheater, Zurich, 1890–1.

277 Kaisergalerie, Friedrichstrasse-Behrensstrasse, Berlin; Kyllmann & Heyden, 1871–7 (destroyed in 1944). A typical example of eclecticism which owed more to France than to Italy. Early Renaissance motifs mingle with dormers flanked by caryatids (recalling the Louvre), while octagonal turrets underline the picturesque element of the outline.

278 Stock exchange, Berlin; Friedrich Hitzig, 1859–63; expansion after plans by Hitzig, 1880–3.

279 Reichstag, Berlin; Paul Wallot, 1889–98. The modernity of the large metal dome in the centre cannot gloss over the banality of the Baroque rhetoric displayed here.

280 Law courts, Munich; Friedrich von Thiersch, 1887–97.

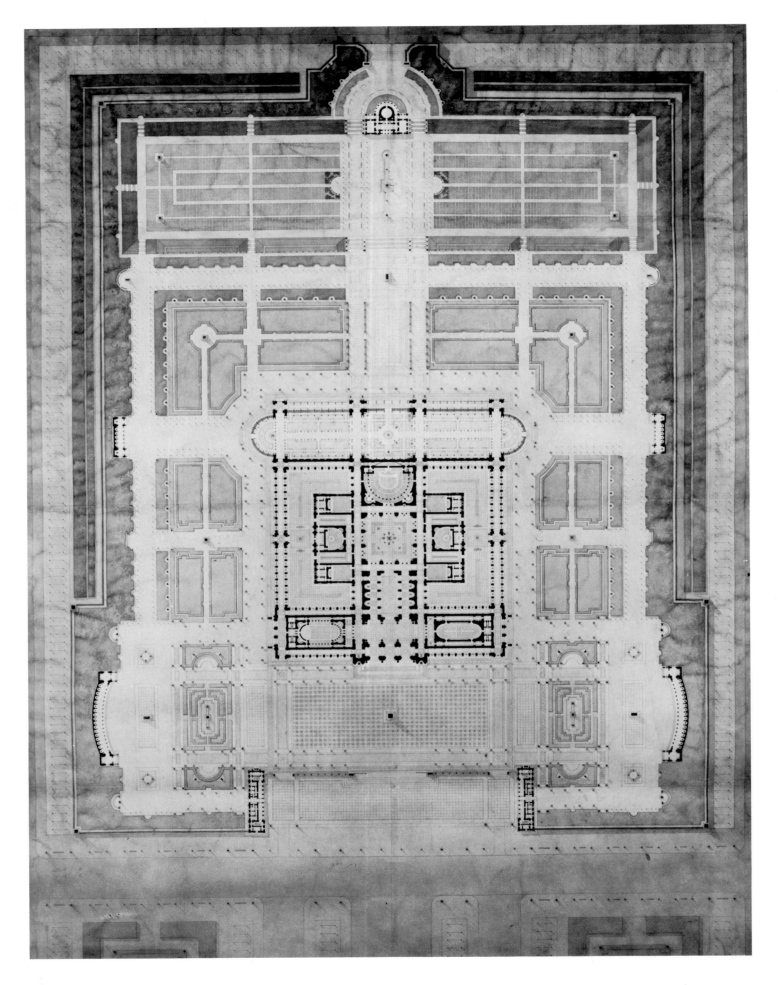

282 Ny Carlsberg Glyptotek, Copenhagen: design; Jens Vil-helm Dahlerup, designed 1888, executed 1893–5. With its black marble columns and red brickwork, Italianate vocabulary and balanced composition, this gallery is one of the successes of late classicism.

281 Athenaeum for a capital city: general plan; Paul Henri Nénot, 1877.

The Germans seem to have been the first to be interested in the aesthetic effects of bonding in brick-work and terracotta. This was connected with the revival of interest in vernacular architecture and the discovery of Islamic abstract polychromy. In England Victorian Gothic was to follow a similar course. In France the stress on structure which Labrouse and Viollet-le-Duc were able to inculcate in their pupils became one of the keys to architectural aesthetics, and the expression 'accentuate the materials' recurred like a leitmotiv. The use of enamelled bricks, the introduction of iron girders as lintels, iron columns as mullions, timber as weatherboards or in roof overhangs, and glazed roofs made it possible to produce variety and multiply effects while still remaining true to the materials. Viollet-le-Duc and his emulators thus defined a simple modern style which was to be found in schools, hospitals and working-class housing. Its brilliant polychromy sometimes attained astonishing saturation effects, as in the trade school at Armentières.

This architectural culture, which was already extremely rich at mid-century, continued to take on different shades and forms until the end of the century. Regularly architects suggested new models to their colleagues, drawing attention to the interest inherent in one period or another. Thus, about

284 Town Hall, Vienna: grand staircase; Friedrich von Schmidt, 1872–83. Whatever the style selected, the staircases of public buildings are often notable for their vast dimensions.

283 Foreign Office, Westminster, London: staircase; Sir George Gilbert Scott, 1863–8. The layout of the Ambassadors' Staircase at Versailles, the coffered ceiling of the Basilica of Maxentius in Rome, a dome on a 'Byzantine' pendentive – all represent a historicizing synthesis which seeks to create an imposing effect.

1865–70, a group of English architects developed the flexible and picturesque Queen Anne style (1702–14), which seemed to them better fitted to modern needs; the equivalent in France was the style of Louis XIII. At the same time the Belgians, Dutch and Germans turned to Flemish Mannerist architecture; about 1870–5 the Americans studied their colonial architecture. But there was no linear succession of styles because each type of building called for a certain style and, to take an example, the return to the *grand style* of Wren, apparent in the 1890s in a series of official English buildings, was contemporary with research carried on into domestic vernacular architecture.

Engineering: Architecture of the Future?

'The time is probably near when a new system of architectural laws will be developed, adapted entirely to metallic construction.'
(John Ruskin, *The Seven Lamps of Architecture*, London, vol. II, 1849.)

First Experiments

As long as iron ore was smelted with charcoal and hand-worked at the forge, cast and wrought iron found only a limited use in architecture, exemplified by, say, the chains used to ring domes (Saint Peter's in Rome; Saint Paul's in London) or reinforce lintels of exceptional span (colonnade of the Louvre; Panthéon in Paris). The widespread adoption of coke smelting (invented in 1709) during the second half of the eighteenth century and then, about 1820, the increasing use of the puddling process (perfected in 1784) opened up new fields of application for these materials, which could be produced at ever decreasing cost.

It is only when seen in retrospect that the extensive use of cast and wrought iron can be recognized as marking a revolution. All the building treatises of the first half of the century, the *Traité théorique et pratique de l'art de bâtir* by Jean-Baptiste Rondelet (1802–17), the *Etudes relatives à l'art de construction* by Louis Clémentin Bruyère (1823–8), and the *Supplément à Rondelet* by Abel Blouet (1847), contain studies of iron used side by side with stone and timber. They present the latest French and English structures, showing for every kind of innovation a curiosity typical of the Age of Enlightenment and the nineteenth century. There may have been a battle of styles, but there was no war of materials – or rather it was one waged in economic rather than aesthetic terms. In 1828 Bruyère emphasized the advantages of 'pillars of cast iron and arches of the same material', which he would have recommended for more general use 'if the price were not, unfortunately, a little high'.

Cast iron was, of course, used earlier in the industrial regions where it cost less; it was restricted to certain specific applications in which its particular qualities (fireproofness, resistance to compression, and casting properties) justified the extra outlay, which was still considerable.

The increasing number of disastrous fires in the big multi-storey spinning mills in the Midlands (five within 50 miles of Derby in 1791 alone) fostered the adoption of a mode of construction consisting of an all-metal framework with posts and lintels of cast iron and vaults of brick. The first example was apparently the linen mill built in 1796 near Shrewsbury (12 miles from Coalbrookdale, notable for its cast-iron bridge of 1777–9, the first of its kind), by Charles Bage (1752–1822). Another early specimen was the cotton mill at Salford near Manchester, by Matthew Boulton (1728–1809) and James Watt (1736–1819), the inventors of the modern steam engine, for Philips & Lee (William Fairbairn, in his work *On the Application of Cast and Wrought Iron to Building Purposes*, published in London in 1854 and in Paris in 1856, wrongly quotes this as the first). The North Mill at Belper, built in 1786 with wooden floors, burned down in 1803 and was rebuilt on the new system in 1803–4. By 1807 at least seven English mills had a frame entirely of metal.

285 Spinning Mill (now a malt-house, The Maltings), Shrewsbury: section and plan of the second storey; Charles Bage, 1796–7. For the first time wood was completely dispensed with and even the window frames were of metal.

286 Albert Dock, Merseyside, Liverpool; Jesse Hartley, 1845. The air raids of the last war have laid bare the structure.

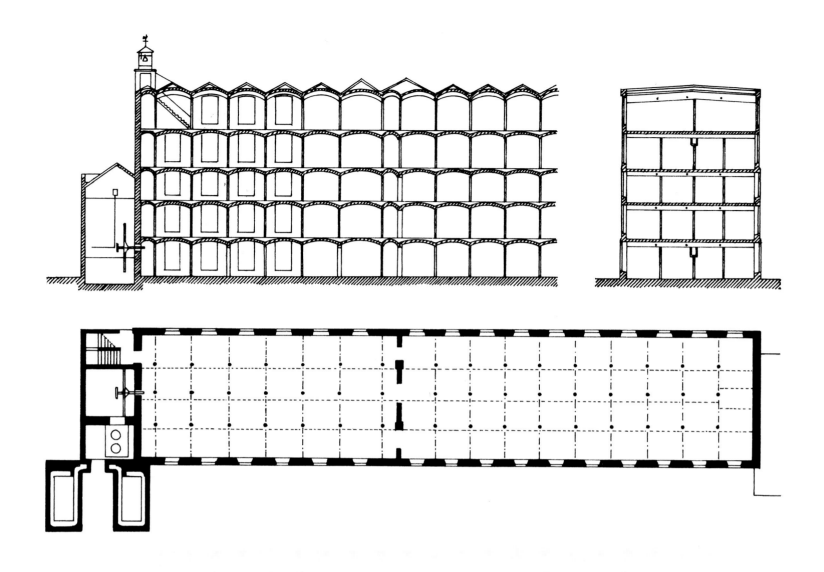

287 Halle au blé (Corn Market; Produce Exchange since 1889), Paris: view of interior; François Joseph Bélanger and F. Brunet, 1806–11. A similar design is to be found at the Coal Exchange in London (1846–9), by James Bunston Bunning, and at the Corn Exchange (1860) in Leeds, by Cuthbert Brodrick. The roof structure was originally covered with copper sheeting, apart from one or two skylights in the dome; the copper was replaced by glass when the Corn Market was transformed into the Produce Exchange in 1888–9.

After some improvements in points of detail had been made, this system was soon adopted for all kinds of industrial constructions: for example, St Katherine's Dock (1825) in London by Thomas Telford (1757–1834) and Philip Hardwick; the warehouse of the Lion Brewery (1836; destroyed in 1949), London, notable also for its great Palladian façade, by Francis Edwards; municipal warehouses (1842–5) in Brussels; Albert Dock (1845), Liverpool, by Jesse Hartley; Portsmouth docks (1843–9), etc.

In France a number of experiments were also made with metal floors and frames during the closing decades of the eighteenth century. The adoption of these new techniques was often hastened by the psychological shock following a conflagration: after the Palais Royal opera had burned down in 1781,

Victor Louis (1731–1800) roofed the new theatre (Théâtre Français) with an iron framework in 1786. In 1811 François Joseph Bélanger (1744–1818) replaced the timber framework of the Halle au Blé, which had burned down in 1802, by a huge dome comprising fifty-one trusses cast at the foundry of Creusot and covered with copper plates. In 1823 Jean Antoine Alavoine (1776/8–1834) began to rebuild the spire of Rouen Cathedral in cast iron; and in 1837–8 Edmond Baron made use of cast-iron trusses in Chartres Cathedral. This technique had already been employed in Southwark Cathedral in London in 1822. About 1830 these metal frameworks became a general practice in theatres where the lighting of huge chandeliers was always a ticklish problem. As François Thiollet (1782–1859) noted in 1837, the same desire to limit the risk of fire explains the replacement of timber by iron in 'general stores and shopping arcades', and

288 Cast-iron roof of Chartres Cathedral: design; Leture, 1836.

289 Rotunda with metal columns and dome: design; 1844–5. Concours d'émulation de Serrurerie, École des Beaux-Arts, Paris.

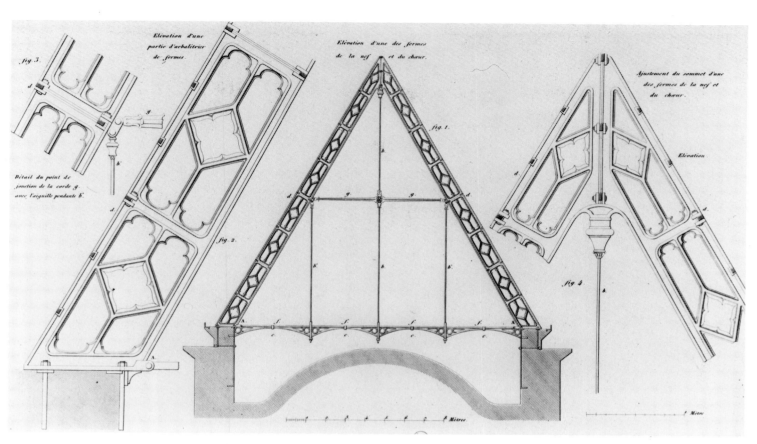

Elévation d'une partie d'arbalétrier de fermes.

Elévation d'une des fermes de la nef et du chœur.

Ajustement du sommet d'une des fermes de la nef et du chœur.

fig. 3.

Détail du point de jonction de la corde g avec l'aiguille pendante b.

fig. 2.

fig. 1.

Elévation.

fig. 4.

5 Mètres

1 Mètre

Iʳᵉ F.EUILLE

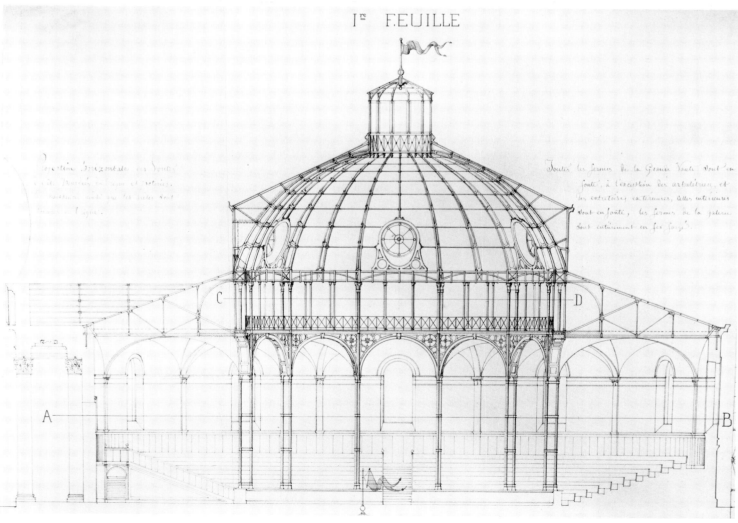

A   B

C   D

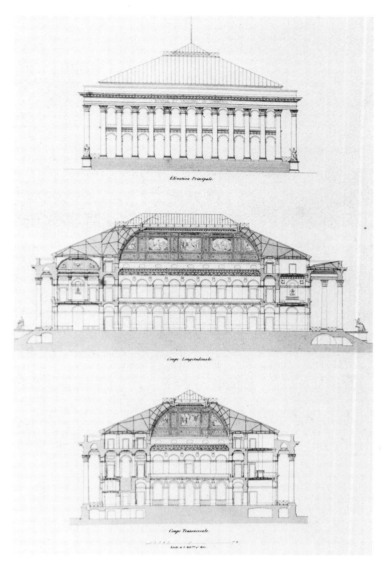

290 Bourse, Paris: elevation and sections; Alexandre Théodore Brongniart and Étienne Éloy de Labarre, 1808–15 (enlarged in 1902–3). After the precedent set by the Halle au blé (Corn Market), courtyards covered with a stucco-encased metal structure became very common in France.

Labrouste's choice of a metal structure for the new Sainte-Geneviève Library (1842). The use of cast iron was in no way irreconcilable with the most rigorous neo-classicism, and the Madeleine in Paris, no less than the Valhalla in Regensburg, had a roof of cast iron. These were the first hints of that marriage of modern technology with a sense of history that was characteristic of the whole of the nineteenth century.

Similarly metal frames of a lighter kind seemed to become mandatory for structures, particularly conservatories, where the maximum amount of light was required. Examples include those in the Nymphenburg Park, Munich (1807 and 1816, by Friedrich Ludwig von Sckell, 1750–1823); Jardin des Plantes, Paris (1833, by Rohault de Fleury, 1801–75); Kew Gardens, London (1845–7, by Decimus Burton and Rich-

ard Turner). Because of their strength and slender proportions they were also suitable as supports for the galleries in Protestant churches, where they did not impede the view (All Saints, Wellington, 1785; St Chad's, Shrewsbury, 1792). They were likewise employed for the same purpose in university auditoria (Royal High School, Edinburgh, 1825) or theatres (Walnut Street Theatre, Philadelphia, 1827–8), and for light roofing in verandas (Naval Hospital, Port Nelson, Virginia, 1826) and markets (Hungerford Market, London, by C. Fowler and Madeleine Market, Paris, by G. Veugny; both built after 1835 and since destroyed).

The possibilities inherent in the casting of iron also attracted attention. Foundries soon began to market cast-iron architectural features produced in series. One might also point to the first cast-iron staircase in the palace of Prince Albert of Prussia (1818), and the staircase at the Royal Pavilion at Brighton (John Nash, 1825), and the Galerie d'Orléans in Paris (1829). Everywhere balconies and handrails of cast iron were replacing those of wrought iron. In Paris Hittorff used cast-iron mouldings for gutters in the church of Saint-Vincent-de-Paul, 'in place of the marble or terracotta used by the ancients'. This had 'the advantage of saving the moulding in hard stone and the considerable price of sculptured ornaments'. Labrouste used the same technique in the Sainte-Geneviève Library. In the United States in 1829–30 John Haviland (1792–1852), who built the Miners' Bank at Pottsville, Pennsylvania, used painted and sanded cast-iron plates affixed to a brick façade to imitate carved stone bosses on the façade. The idea soon became generally adopted. In 1842 Gabriel Davioud, who was trained at the École des Beaux-Arts in Paris, submitted an entry in an ironwork competition in which he proposed a lighthouse with a façade of cast iron. Bridges nevertheless accounted for 'by far the largest part of iron constructions', as Molinos and Pronnier noted in their *Traité théorique et pratique de la construction des ponts métalliques* (1857). If the English were the creators of this new technique with the Coalbrookdale bridge over the Severn in

291 Greenhouse, Nymphenburg Park, Munich; Friedrich Ludwig von Sckell, 1807.

292 Palm House, Royal Botanical Gardens, Kew, Surrey; Decimus Burton and Richard Turner, designed 1844, executed 1845–8. Since those of the Jardin des Plantes by Rohault de Fleury in Paris, and the Great Store of Chatsworth, Derbyshire, have disappeared, this greenhouse is the most imposing surviving achievement in the genre from the first half of the nineteenth century.

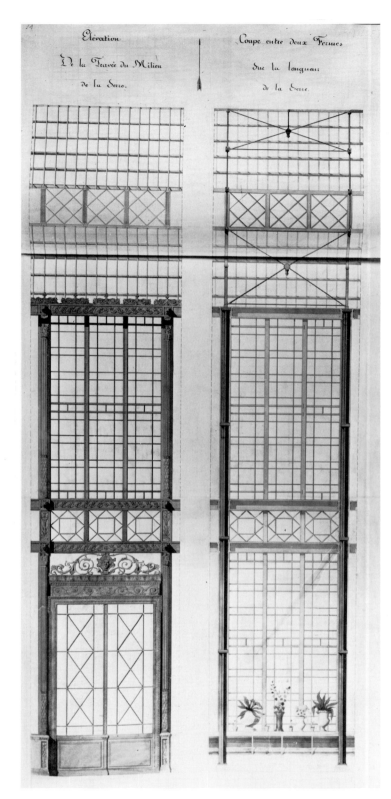

293 Greenhouse: design; Alfred Normand, 1843. Concours d'émulation de Serrurerie, École des Beaux-Arts, Paris.

tions and study tours. Captain Brown, who in 1817 had filed a patent application for a 'flat iron link', built the Union Bridge over the Tweed in 1820; it collapsed six months later. Cast iron was used first of all as a substitute for lineal frames, for stone voussoirs, or for cables; but progress was continuous.

In this respect the development of the chain suspension bridge is characteristic. In 1808 the American engineer James Finley patented a system for a chain suspension bridge on which he had been working since 1801. T. Pope expounded the system in his *Treatise on Bridge Architecture*, published in New York in 1811. The first modern cable-suspended bridge was built at Philadelphia in 1815. The great engineer Thomas Telford used this system for the Menai bridge (1820–6), since it lent itself particularly well to a marine site where the deck had to be high enough not to impede navigation. In 1821 the engineer Louis Marie Navier (1785–1836) was sent to England to study the suspension bridges there. Three years later Marc Seguin (1786–1875) published a study entitled *Ponts en fil de fer* (Paris, 1824), and tested his own system near Tournon on the Rhône (1823–4, destroyed 1965). With a span of 85 metres, this bridge was the first suspended from iron wire cables to be opened to wheeled traffic. During the following decades the firm of Seguin Brothers built more than eighty bridges of this type, and cables gradually replaced chains of bars or rings. Industry provided engineers with cables of ever increasing strength and the span between the pylons grew wider: 110 metres at Berwick on Tweed in 1820–6, 271 metres at Fribourg on the Sarine in 1834, and 198 metres over the Vilaine at Roche Bernard in 1836. The same was true in the United States, particularly of bridges built by John Roebling (1806–69) in 1854–7 across the Ohio (308 m) at Weeling, West Virginia, and Niagara Falls (1851–5, destroyed).

However, iron, stone or wood remained popular alternative materials. Cast iron was only *one* of the solutions put forward to solve the problem of fireproof construction, which continued to plague the whole of the nineteenth century. To quote one example, the Americans Latrobe, Mills or Strickland were more interested in 'fireproof' stonework than they were in metal frames. Sir Joseph Paxton, the English expert on greenhouses, continued to study conservatories constructed of timber and, as late as 1852, still had reservations concerning the use of wrought iron. He thought it too expensive, particularly as progress in the technique of laminating wood made it possible to produce large trusses (conservatory at Chatsworth, 1836–40; transept of Crystal Palace, 1850; King's

1779, the French took an interest in these structures from the beginning of the century (Pont des Arts, begun by Louis Alexandre de Cessart and Jacques Dillon in 1801, destroyed in 1981). Information was soon exchanged on an international scale and unending innovations were reflected in patents, publica-

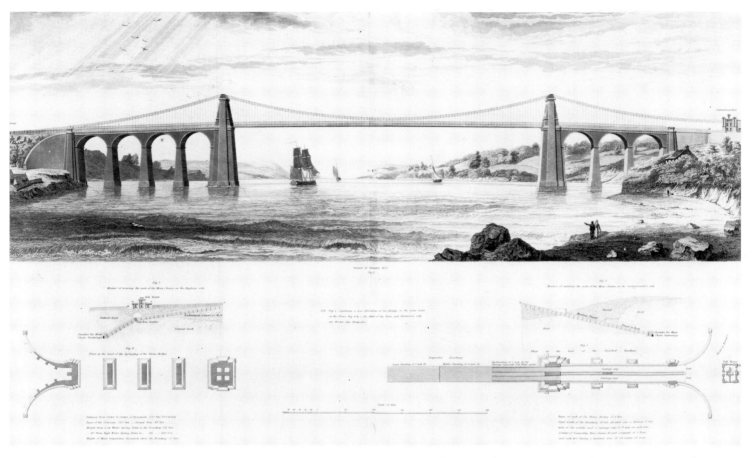

294 Bridge over the Menai Straits, between the island of Anglesey and Caernarvonshire, Wales, by Thomas Telford, 1820–6. The wooden deck of the bridge was replaced by one of steel in 1893 and the iron chains by steel chains in 1940.

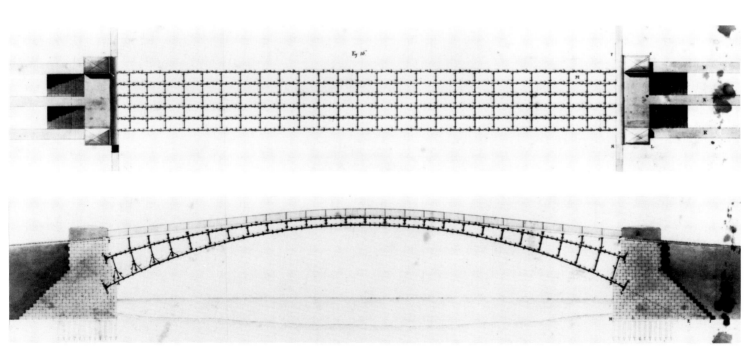

295 Cast-iron tubular bridge: design; Georg von Reichenbach, 1810.

296 Conway Bridge, Wales; Thomas Telford, 1826. This bridge, based on the same technical principles as the Menai suspension bridge, is still in its original condition. The crenellated piers were inspired by the castle built by Edward I to be seen in the background but they also reflect a more general symbolism of strength and solidity evoked by using in turn Egyptian, Roman and medieval forms. To the left, hardly visible in the photograph, is Robert Stephenson's tubular bridge, which is identical in design with the Britannia Bridge.

297 Suspension bridge over the Sarine, Fribourg, Switzerland; Joseph Chaley, 1832–4.

Cross station, 1851–2). Although stone for bridges was beginning to get more expensive, it seemed to last longer and look more dignified. The same engineers used either one or the other, depending on specific needs. Only five of the forty-two bridges built by Thomas Telford, famous for his metal bridge at Craigellachie (1815) and in particular for that over the Menai Strait (1820–6), are of cast iron. The French were interested in what the English were doing in metal: conversely, the latest advances in stereotomy by Perronet were adopted on a wide scale in England: modernity was also a feature (Grosvenor Bridge at Chester by Thomas Harrison with a span of 60 m).

The Aesthetic Quality of Metal

In the 1840s these new procedures began to spread all over Europe. The first iron bridges were built at Frederiksboro, Odense, Denmark, in 1844, and then at Seville, Spain, in 1845–52. These isolated experiments established new records for dimensions. The development of railways led to a considerable expansion of the iron industry. The price of cast and wrought iron began to compete seriously with that of timber. The perfected design of the Polonceau girder in 1837, and then of girders and trusses of riveted rolled iron sheets, enabled ever greater gaps to be spanned with confidence.

As long as cast and wrought iron were used in utilitarian structures (mills, docks, covered markets, bridges) and as ancillary elements in building construction (frames and floors), these technical innovations had no great impact on the taste and aesthetics of architecture. However, the glass industry was making parallel progress, and the conservatory began to assume monumental proportions. As a 'winter garden' it became a popular place for strolling and other leisure activities. Slim columns of cast iron, covered by large glass roofs, were used in new public spaces (shopping arcades and general stores) and became associated with the most innovative building designs (stations and exhibition halls). At this point the question of the aesthetic quality of metal structures became topical.

The aesthetics of iron revolve round two problems: the slenderness of columns made of metal and its unlimited plasticity. These problems were all the more acute in that they had an immediate bearing on what nineteenth-century architects felt to be their great weakness: the lack of any single reference system. Because of the outstanding compressive strength of iron pillars, their section-to-height ratio is quite different from that of stone columns. Their slenderness, which is one of their prime functional merits, puts them outside the modular systems of the ancient orders on which the aesthetic of architecture was still wholly based. Moreover, the fact that cast iron could be moulded into any shape did not help to solve the problem of defining a style suitable for the nineteenth century. As one architect put it, 'cast iron lends itself to all shapes, true, but once again do all these shapes lend themselves to architecture?'

During the first decades cast-iron architecture accorded well with the neo-classical aesthetics of the sublime and picturesque: in the Liverpool docks, the rough character of cast iron seemed to heighten the primitive massiveness of the columns; Canina suggested cast-iron columns reminiscent of Pompeian decors; Rickman, at St George's, sought an analogy with the ribs of flamboyant Gothic; and Nash, in the Royal Pavilion at Brighton, justified the bizarre proportions of his cast-iron columns by adopting an exotic vocabulary with Indian bases and palmiform capitals. But it was not very long before iron architecture was found to have a beauty of its own. As early as 1817 Loudon stated in his *Remarks on Hot-houses* that they could 'be beautiful without exhibiting any of the Greek orders or a Gothic design', and in 1837 the *Architectural Magazine and Journal* published an article with the significant title: 'Effects which should result to Architecture from the General Introduction of Iron Building'. The author, while suggesting picturesque and exotic associations (Gothic, Arabian, Indian and Chinese), stressed the 'great decorative possibilities' of iron roofs. 'Where circumstances warrant their being left visible inside the building, what beauty might be obtained by the combined effect of longitudinal and transverse members of cast iron above the level of the capitals.' In the Sainte-Geneviève Library Henri Labrouste was already at pains to work out a repertoire of motifs adapted in their styling to the nature of metal. The studied elegance of the design, its refinement and restraint, do

298   Jardin d'hiver (Winter Garden) on the Champs-Élysées, Paris; H. Meynadier and Rigolet, 1846–7 (destroyed in 1852).

299   Sainte-Geneviève Library, Paris: detail showing the metal girders of the reading room; Henri Labrouste, 1842–50.

not detract from its modernity. On entering stations, arcades, or huge glasshouses, contemporaries discovered enthralling light-filled spaces where unprecedented effects of transparency and reflection were to be seen. By covering a space so that it remained 'outdoors' in so far as lighting was concerned, the great roofs of glass and metal ushered in a radical novelty. The only parallel was the perfection of linear Gothic structures which transformed a wall into a stained-glass window.

When in mid-century stylistic certainties were tottering, a number of people thought that the rational approach of engineers who, through the exercise of their profession, assumed responsibility for the newest buildings of the industrial era, afforded a way out of the impasse. At the very same time when Europe's economic 'take-off' was, as it were, imparting a quicker rhythm to history, they thought they saw in the metal buildings the new style the century was waiting for. After Ambrose Poynter (*On the Effects which should Result . . . from the General Introduction of Iron in Construction Building*, 1842), William V. Pickett

published his *New System of Architecture* in 1845, in which he advocated the generalized use of metal. As early as 1846 César Daly, editor of the *Revue générale de l'architecture et des travaux publics*, asserted his hope that the station would be 'the principle that will renew our architecture' and that 'the great industrial creation will no doubt be partnered by an aesthetic one'.

Two years later, Jobard, director of the Belgian museum of industry, announced in the *Journal de l'architecture*, published in Brussels, the imminent disappearance of stone buildings:

. . . We are at last entering under full sail an iron-and-steel order which will display differences more clear-cut than those between Tuscan and Gothic architecture. For metals are amenable to all the shapes dreamt of by the most brilliant imagination of our artists, who are today so numerous, so excellent in their taste, and so pure in their talent. All the architectural masterpieces of the Thousand and One Nights, hitherto consigned to albums and keepsakes, can be executed in cast and wrought iron. There is nothing – not even the fearsome

biblical nightmare of the painter Martin, the mysterious brahmanic compositions of the scholar Coudère, or the elegant arabesques of the engineer Midolle – that cannot be transformed into cast-iron lacework illustrated by admirable windows. And remember that all these marvels will cost less than frost-riven stone, bloomed brick, and ephemeral wood, and will last a hundred times longer . . .

Elsewhere in this article he wrote:

What ease and economy is afforded by the power to cast hundreds of duplicated panels and identical angle pieces, ceiling roses, jamb linings and voussoirs; what a difference there is between shaping one wooden moulding pattern and carving a hundred models in stone, between casting from one mould a hundred hollow columns to serve as flues and cutting one hundred columns of solid marble!

This article with its somewhat prophetic tone was no doubt influenced by the messianic atmosphere that prevailed during 1848, the year of revolution, but it was not without an echo. Daly, although he thought Jobard was 'a little too ruthless about demolishing stone architecture', republished the article in his review in 1849, and it seemed to find striking confirmation when at the Great Exhibition in London the public discovered the magical space inside Paxton's Crystal Palace.

The idea of peaceful commercial and industrial confrontation on an international scale began to gather force in the 1840s. It culminated in January 1850 when it was decided to organize in London in 1851 an international exhibition. The Building Committee, comprising architects (Sir Charles Barry, Cockerell and Owen Jones) and engineers (Robert Stephenson (1803–59), William Cubitt (1785–1861), Isambard Kingdom Brunel (1806–59), launched an international competition on 13 March 1850. In April 245 projects were received; submissions from the Frenchman Hector Horeau (1801–72), who had built a winter garden at Lyons, and from the Irishman, Richard Turner, who was a specialist in greenhouses and had built the Palm House in Kew Gardens, received particular attention. However, the committee decided to entrust a small sub-committee elected from its own number with the finalization of a new project which was to be published in the *Illustrated London News* of 22 June 1850.

Meanwhile Joseph Paxton, who, like Turner, had made a name for himself as a specialist in the construction of large greenhouses, specifically those at Chatsworth (1845–50), having first been assured by a member of the committee on 7 June that a new project could still be considered, put his basic idea down on

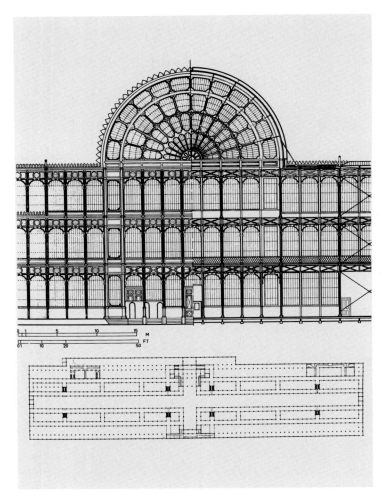

300 Crystal Palace, London: plan and section; Sir Joseph Paxton, 1850–1.

paper four days later: a giant greenhouse with a flat roof, made of cast iron and glass. He arranged to meet the committee the following week and spent the next few days perfecting the technical aspects. He returned to London, contacted the iron-masters Fox and Henderson, who worked for the railways, and the glazier Robert Chance, who had perfected the new cylinder process for making large sheets of glass for the Chatsworth greenhouse, and submitted his project to different members of the committee in the House; on 6 July he published it in the *Illustrated London News*. The simplicity of the architectural design shocked certain members of the committee. Sir Charles Barry threatened to resign unless the nave were covered by a barrel-vault. Finally a compromise was adopted according to which only one transept was to be vaulted; this had the advantage of saving some trees in the park by including them in the interior, the palace thus really serving as a greenhouse. With this modification the design was finally approved and adopted on 26 July. In seven weeks Charles Fox produced the detail drawings which were checked by Cubitt; on

301 Crystal Palace, London; Sir Joseph Paxton, 1850–1. The Great Exhibition in London, in the course of construction in Hyde Park. In the foreground can be seen the hollow columns and, behind, the great arches of laminated wood intended to cover the transept.

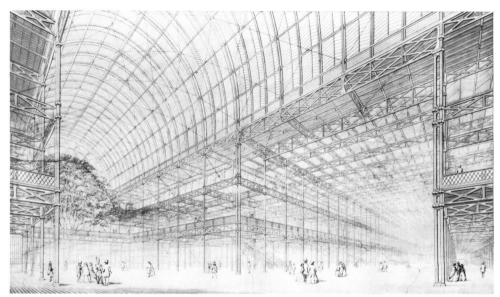

302 Crystal Palace, London: interior view before the exhibits were installed; Sir Joseph Paxton, 1850–1. The modular system and the new scale are brought out well by the draughtsman.

26 September the first column was erected in Hyde Park. The building was completed, ready to receive the exhibits, in January 1851. The exhibition opened on 1 May, the scheduled date; by 6 October, when it closed, six million people had visited it.

Joseph Paxton, the son of a farmer, began his career as an apprentice gardener; discovered by the Duke of Devonshire in 1826, he became his head gardener at Chatsworth and soon afterwards his agent. The construction of the Crystal Palace was for him the culmination of twenty years' experience in building greenhouses and also as a businessman. Adroit though Paxton may have been in exploiting his personal and political connections, the press and his relations with Midlands industrialists, his project was accepted only because time was running out: it was

'perhaps the only one which satisfies the essential condition of being capable of completion before the opening of the Exhibition planned for 1 May 1851' (*Revue générale de l'architecture*, 1855, p. 120).

In spite of its 3,800 tons of cast iron, 700 tons of wrought iron, 900,000 square feet of glass and 600,000 square feet of wood, the 'Crystal Palace' (the expression appeared in *Punch* on 2 November 1851) did not effect any revolutionary solution from the technical point of view. Paxton simply scaled up enormously the structural design with which he had experimented for the greenhouse built at Chatsworth in 1845–50 to protect the giant *Victoria regia* water-lilies; and his familiarity with industrial circles enabled him to obtain the assistance he needed to implement his plans. The building was constructed of a reduced

303 Crystal Palace, London; Sir Joseph Paxton, 1850–1. Photographed in Hyde Park before being taken down and transferred to Sydenham.

number of standard parts: cast-iron columns attached by a collar to horizontal lattice beams and covered by panes of glass arranged in a succession of ridges and troughs to guide the rain-water towards the hollow columns providing a runoff. All the dimensions of the edifice – 1,848 feet by 408 – were multiples or submultiples of a single module of 24 feet. The elements could be fabricated industrially and rapidly erected on a light foundation. As in the Chatsworth greenhouse, large semicircular trusses of laminated wood provided a roof for the transept, the dimensions of which (72 feet) were within two feet of those of the earlier project. This vault and the ceilings were glazed throughout. At the sides the gaps between the cast-iron columns were subdivided by intermediate wooden columns and closure was provided by planks and panes of glass.

The fantastic dimensions on the one hand and the simplicity of the design and the repetition of simple forms indispensable for rapid erection on the other, also had consequences for architecture. As Charles Downes remarked in the scientific description he gave in 1852 on the basis of the contractors' working drawings, 'it thus produces perfect symmetry and creates effects of great beauty through the distant views and the long perspectives opened up between the columns diagonally, as well as transversely and along the building.' The chronicle published in *The Ecclesiologist* expressed very well the astonishment tempered by reservations felt by contemporaries when faced with 'these unprecedented spatial effects'.

Such an extensive view that the atmospheric effect of extreme distance is truly new and distinctive, a general luminosity and fairy-like sparkle never dreamt of before, and above all – one of the most satisfying qualities, to our way of thinking – an evident and real structural straightforwardness which is beyond all praise. Thus form is lacking as well as the idea of stability and solidity. . . . We cannot help but think that the design would have been very different if it had been meant to be permanent. And finally the infinite repetition of the same elements – a necessity in such a building – seems to us to debar it from claiming great architectural merit.

304 Crystal Palace, London: design for the interior; Owen Jones, 1850.

305 The destruction by fire of the Crystal Palace, New York, 5 October 1858. Built in 1853, it was used as an exhibition hall for annual fairs and exhibitions.

These reservations are an echo of those of Horeau who called it 'this block of glass as monotonous as it is unsightly' and of Louis Auguste Boileau (1812–96) ('this large cubic cage of glass'), even though their acerbity owes something to the peevish disdain of unsuccessful competitors and ambitious rivals.

To offset the baldness of the architectural design, Owen Jones, who had been a student of polychromy for twenty years and had experience of winter gardens and greenhouses, was retained to decorate the structure. After a number of trials, which provoked great public debate, the exterior was painted white and blue and the interior in the three primary colours arranged in accordance with the latest chromatic theories. Five parts of red to three of yellow and eight of blue were the proportions recommended by G. Field for obtaining perfect balance (*Chromotography*, London, 1825); the coloured areas were separated by white to avoid the effect of simultaneous contrast, which had been studied by Eugène Chevreul (*De la loi du contraste des couleurs*, Paris, 1839). The curved surfaces were paint-ed yellow, the lattice girders blue, and the joists of the glass roof red; these colours were echoed by the large hangings suspended in every third bay, which created the effect of an arbour. The cast-iron columns and girders, which were naturally slim, were still further diminished by the floods of light coming down from the glass roof. Jones thought that the colour system 'by rendering each line of the building distinct would increase the height, length and mass'.

Contemporaries marvelled at the effects of light and colour. On 1 May 1851 the *Illustrated London News* columnist stressed

the extraordinary beauty of the view seen on enter-ing the south transept: the transept is all the more brilliantly illuminated in that the great vault is left open to the sky and not covered with hangings like the rest of the building. Away from this central point the light becomes softer in every direction, and while the eye travels along the perspectives, Sir D. Brewster's three primary colours strike the eye by their intensity in the foreground but, in the dis-

306 Glaspalast, Munich; August von Voit, 1854 (destroyed).

307 Glaspalast, Munich: section; August von Voit, 1854.

tance, blend together by the effect of parallax and the diminution of the visual angle and melt away in nature to a neutral grey. To appreciate Owen Jones' genius the visitor should stand at the end of the building and run his eyes along the nave with its endless lines of pillars to see the extreme brilliance of the spectacle melt into a misty softness which Turner alone could paint.

After the idea of keeping the building *in situ* as a huge winter garden had been turned down, the Crystal Palace was bought back by a company established by Paxton. It was disassembled and the elements reused for a new construction on a more ambitious plan at Sydenham in the south of London (1852–4), where it became the centrepiece of a large recreation park accessible from the capital by railway. It was destroyed by fire in 1936.

In the history of nineteenth-century European architecture, the Crystal Palace occupies a somewhat ambiguous position. It taught Europeans the remarkable architectural effects that could be achieved by combining iron and glass, and very soon crystal palaces were appearing all over the place. But their structural qualities were not always so evident, as is shown by the fires which destroyed nearly all of them, and their architectural quality invariably gave rise to reservations.

The decade 1841–51 was clearly marked by the discovery of the possibilities of iron in architecture. The jubilant utterances of contemporaries in the following decades when faced by these new spaces should not delude us; the proponents of stone did not retreat. Contrary to Jobard's hopes there was never more than a handful of somewhat cranky architects and ambitious engineers who thought that iron could oust stone.

Two French architects, Horeau and Boileau, appointed themselves the apostles of this new architecture. In order to 'put an end to the anomaly for which such fault is found with our century; namely that it is the only one not to have what is commonly called a style of architecture', as Boileau wrote, they tried to turn it into a universal system. With touching naïveté Horeau wrote innumerable pamphlets in which he rang the changes on this theme: 'samples of modern industry which enables us today to realize at little cost the dreams of the painters of Pompeii, an architecture which is light, rich, incombustible, durable, extensible, polychrome by nature, mobile and usefully dismountable'. In his works, *Nouvelle Forme architecturale* (Paris, 1853) and *Le Fer, principal élément constructif de la nouvelle architecture* (Paris, 1871), which present the history of architecture as that of the gradual victory of the void over matter, Boileau sees iron-and-steel architecture as the ultimate phase: 'where Gothic architects had to stop, the moderns can pass; they link up again with the tradition interrupted in the sixteenth century.' This theme is taken up again, word for word, in 1890 by the Belgian engineer Vierendeel in his book *L'Architecture métallique au XIXe siècle*, written under the powerful impression of the great achievements of the 1889 exhibition, the Eiffel Tower and the Galerie des Machines. 'These two monuments', he wrote, 'tell us of the power of metal and of modern industry. They symbolize in an imposing manner the power man has acquired over matter.'

The reference to Pompeian architecture and to Gothic architecture and the relegation of Horeau to the fringe after 1855 are very significant. So is the contrast between Boileau's success in the construction of the Bon Marché and the failure of the proposals of his father Louis-Auguste for 'cathédrales synthétiques' in metal. The determining factors continued to be historical and cultural points of reference and the particular nature of the specification. The idea of a universal iron-and-steel style – a myth kept alive until the end of the century by the engineers' phenomenal successes – became a dead letter.

On the other hand the practices of iron-and-steel construction were readily absorbed into architectural culture. Cast and wrought iron and steel were studied in the same spirit of constructive rationalism as stone and wood. Metallic architecture was, however, involved in the same disputes that were tearing apart stone architecture: archeological imitation versus invention of a new style; decorative eclecticism versus constructive rationalism. The picturesque Gothic of the church of St George at Everton near Liverpool designed by Rickmann in 1816–18 was followed by the archeological Gothic of Saint-Eugène in Paris in 1855. The architect, Louis-Auguste Boileau, stated openly that its cast-iron columns were inspired by those of the refectory of St Martin's-in-the-Fields. In St Jude's, built by George and Henry Godwin, in London, the polychromatic effect clearly points to modern Victorian Gothic.

New Materials

While refusing to make metal an exclusive material, architects as a whole knew how to use the new mode of construction, which had become economically attractive as an 'aid to masonry' and to the timber frame. One example may be quoted from among hun-

308 Infiorata: design; Hector Horeau, 1868. The winter garden (Infiorata) is the centre of a cultural, recreational and commercial complex (commercial galleries, assembly rooms, gymnasia, a theatre and even an observatory served by a lift). Although somewhat vague with regard to technicalities, the design has merit by virtue of what it sets out to do and because it embodies the dream of a universal iron architecture.

dreds: at the pumping station built in Copenhagen in 1857–9, the pump is covered by a timber framework whereas the steam-engine driving it has a metal one to reduce the risk of explosion.

Between 1850 and 1855 wooden floors were replaced everywhere by floors on girders of metal, which in 1851 had become cheaper than those of the traditional material. Metal frameworks continued to be used for new churches and in the restoration of historic monuments (Trinité Church, dome of Val-de-Grâce in Paris). For the dome of the Capitol in Washington (1855–65) Thomas Ustick Walter (1804–87) made use of cast-iron trusses, just as Auguste Ricard, called de Montferrand, had done for

Saint Isaac's Cathedral in St Petersburg (Leningrad), completed in 1841; in the Paris Opéra, Garnier used large metal girders to limit the fire risk and also to leave an unprecedentedly large space over the staircase. No architect refused the resources provided by the most modern technologies. Their lightness and strength made cast-iron columns and metal frames routine features in certain well-defined types of structure: greenhouses, markets, workshops, passengers' concourses at railway stations, shops, temporary pavilions for exhibitions, and libraries. On this point there was a general consensus. In the eclectic practice of associating certain styles and types of building, metal had reserved to it, as it were, those specifications to whose needs it seemed perfectly adapted, and no objection was raised to it being exposed.

Greenhouses – 'of all constructions those where iron is most appropriately used' (Blouet) – were built in increasing numbers all over Europe, from Rennes (Thabor greenhouses, 1862–3) to Barcelona (Umbraculo and El Invernaculo in the park of the Citadel,

309 Saint-Eugène, Paris: view of the interior; Louis Auguste Boileau, 1854. The constructional layout has close affinities with that of the Sainte-Geneviève Library, cast-iron piers carrying plaster vaults on iron lathing, but the piers are inspired by those of the refectory of Saint-Martin-des-Champs.

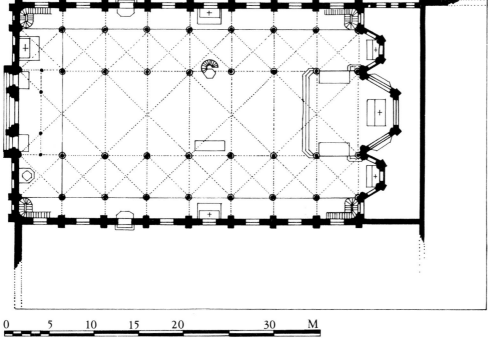

0   5   10   15   20   30   M

310   Saint-Eugène, Paris: plan; Louis-Auguste Boileau, 1854.

311 Refectory of Saint-Martin-des-Champs, Paris. A project for restoring the refectory had been put forward by Jean-Baptiste-Antoine Lassus in the Salon of 1837. Execution of the work may have finally been entrusted to Félix Louis Jacques Duban.

312 St Jude's, South Kensington, London; George and Henry Godwin. Victorian polychromy, exposed roof beams and cast-iron piers. After *The Builder*, 13 May 1871.

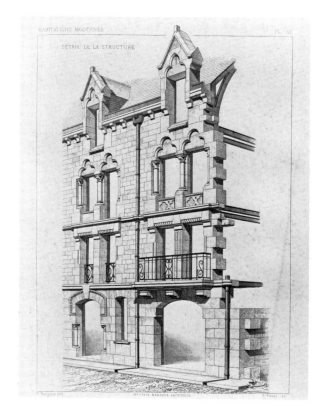

313 Apartment-house, Chalon, Saône-et-Loire: design; Félix Narjoux, 1875. 'The floors and the roof-frames are of iron, as indicated in the detail drawing of the construction... The façades recall the attractive houses of Cluny, as if the architect had wanted to adapt that architecture to our modern needs.'

1883–7). They ranged from small greenhouses for middle-class houses and winter gardens attached to the façades of apartment blocks to monumental greenhouses which are the pride of royal and public parks. The finest example today, without doubt, is the winter garden of the Royal Park of Laeken near Brussels, built in 1875–6 by Alphonse Balat (1819–95).

Similarly, after modest trials at the beginning of the century (Marché de la Madeleine, 1824, by Marie Gabriel Vignon, in Paris; Hungerford Market, 1830–3, by Charles Fowler in London), Victor Baltard (1805–74) adopted, after some hesitation, a system of metal umbrellas for the Halles in Paris (1853–8), as did James Bunston Bunning for the New Metropolitan Castle Market in London (1854–6). An editor of the *Revue générale de l'architecture* noted in 1857:

> Under these circumstances unreserved praise is due to the use of cast iron. The columns are slim, delicate, light, and the eye is satisfied, for what it seeks is the most economical and beneficial use of space ... each pavilion as a whole has a sufficiently monumental appearance without forfeiting the character of a light construction such as is appropriate to a market hall which, when all is said and done, brings to mind an open-air sale.

Les Halles ensured the success of this kind of design in Paris, in the provinces, and abroad – as the *Gazette des bâtiments* emphasized in 1864 in connection with the inauguration of the Marché Saint-Honoré (p. 265). In Paris alone well over thirty market halls were built between 1857 and 1900, more than half between 1865 and 1870; only six have survived, among them the Marché du Temple (1863–5) and the Marché Saint-Quentin (1866). Among dozens in the provinces we may mention the Marché Saint-Nicolas in Lille (1867), the Marché des Lices in Rennes (1868–71) and the market at La Roche-sur-Yon (1890). At Auxerre, on the other hand, the project for a new market hall built of metal, designed in 1867–8, was not completed until 1900–3. Among market halls in Spain one may mention those of La Cebada and Los Mostenses (1870–5) in Madrid, El Borne (1875–6) in Barcelona, and those at San Antonio (1876–82), Valladolid (1878–82) and Salamanca (1898–1909). In Brussels the covered Marché de la Madeleine, roofed with Polonceau trusses, designed by Pierre Cluysenaar (1811–80) in 1847–8, was followed by the Halles Centrales, built to the design of Léon Suys in 1872–4, the street markets at Etterbeek in 1873, at Saint-Géry in 1881 by Adolphe Vanderheggen, and the abattoirs at Anderlecht, designed by Émile Tirou

314 Notre-Dame de la Croix, Paris; Louis J. A. Héret, 1863–80. The use of cast-iron vaulting ribs hardly detracts from the impression of coherence.

315 St Pancras Station, London; W. H. Barlow and R. M. Ordish, 1865–7. Detail showing the springing of the metal girders.

316 Royal greenhouses at Laeken, near Brussels; Alphonse Balat; winter garden, 1875–6; palm house, 1885–7.

317 Royal greenhouses at Laeken: interior view of the winter garden, Alphonse Balat, 1875–6. Thirty-six Tuscan columns from which spring the same number of metal arches surround a central rotunda, 40 metres in diameter, while an annular gallery almost 8 metres in width runs under the supporting flying buttresses.

318 Winter garden for a country mansion: design; Edward William Godwin. After *Artistic Conservatories*, 1880, Pl. 12.

319 Palm House, winter palace, Pau, Pyrénées-Atlantiques, late nineteenth century (destroyed).

320 Les Halles Centrales, Paris: Fish market; Victor Baltard, 1855–7, 1860–6 (destroyed in 1973).

321 Les Halles Centrales, Paris: section; Victor Baltard, 1855–7, 1860–6. After *Gazette des architectes et du bâtiment*, vol. VII, 1869–71.

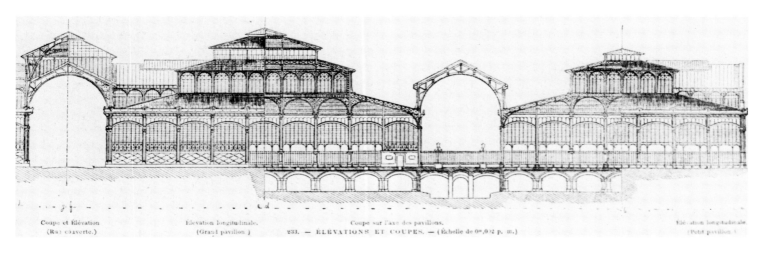

Coupe et Élévation
(Rue couverte.)
Élévation longitudinale.
(Grand pavillon.)
Coupe sur l'axe des pavillons.
233. — ÉLÉVATIONS ET COUPES. — (Échelle de 0m,0½ p. m.)
Élévation longitudinale
(Petit pavillon.)

322 An Athenaeum for a Capital City; Paul Henri Nénot, 1877. First grand prix, École Nationale Supérieure des Beaux-Arts, Paris. It was intended to have meeting rooms, a library, and a conservatory.

in 1889–90; these are of impressive size, forming a square measuring 100 by 100 metres.

Iron-and-steel architecture is the natural choice for specifications as different as swimming baths, where it is desired to create an outdoor atmosphere (Diana-bad in Vienna by Karl Etzel in 1841–3; Brill's Baths in Brighton by Sir George Gilbert Scott in 1866), stations, where wide-span trusses allow subsequent rearrangement of the lines and slim cast-iron columns do not block the platforms, theatres, race-courses, arenas and circuses where it is essential to span wide spaces without interrupting the view (Pernambuco theatre, race-course of the Pont d'Alma in Paris, 1878, and of Roubaix, 1880, arenas at Valencia, 1860–70, Madrid, 1874, and Bilbao, 1882).

It was the concern with the fire hazard and its elimination that determined the use of metal structures for libraries. The example set by Labrouste was followed in the British Museum (1854–7) by Sidney Smirke

(1798–1877) and at the University of Copenhagen (1856–61) by Johan David Herholdt (1808–1902), a design which Labrouste echoed in the great reading room and bookstacks of the Bibliothèque nationale (1857–67).

Around 1845 progress was made in the technique of building iron bridges. Engineers discarded 'analogical' designs and invented specific systems: tubular bridges of riveted plates (Britannia Bridge over the Menai Strait, 1845–50); plate lattice decks (Crumlin Viaduct near Newport, 1853–7). With the invention of the Bessemer converter, steel could be produced on an industrial scale. This made possible feats of an ever more spectacular nature (e.g. Forth Bridge, 1882–90; Viaur Viaduct, France, 1896–1902).

It is quite logical for pavilions used in world exhibitions to be metal constructions. The modernity of these buildings, breaking away as they did from the showiness of late classicism, delights us today perhaps even more than stations or big department stores do. However, in the context of the nineteenth century, this modernity, we must remember, was a necessity that was accepted as a precise solution to specific pro-

blems and needs. Intended as temporary buildings and designed to be erected rapidly, these pavilions could make do with a sober architecture which did not overshadow the exhibits. They utilized a spectacular form of engineering that reflected the successes of modern industry. An iron-and-steel style was held to be most appropriate to this type of building, according to the eclectic conception of architecture. But once they were conceived as permanent 'exhibition palaces', it is hardly surprising that they should have been endowed with all the features of palatial architecture.

The most prestigious of these buildings are inconceivable without the experience gained in other types of construction – greenhouses for Paxton's Crystal Palace, railway bridges for the Galerie des Machines or the Eiffel Tower. More generally, they are unthinkable without the support of the railway industry, whose expansion ensured that research was carried out in every field of metal technology. Conversely, they also provided an opportunity to pull off technical 'firsts', which were something more than publicity stunts. The most prestigious of these buildings had such novel spatial qualities that they changed architectural sensibility in a quite drastic manner.

Not only did the area covered grow markedly from one exhibition to the next – that of the London exhibition of 1851 was doubled in Vienna in 1873 and tripled in Philadelphia in 1876 – but the number of external pavilions round the main pavilions also

326 Reading Room, Bibliothèque nationale, Paris; Henri Labrouste, 1857–67.

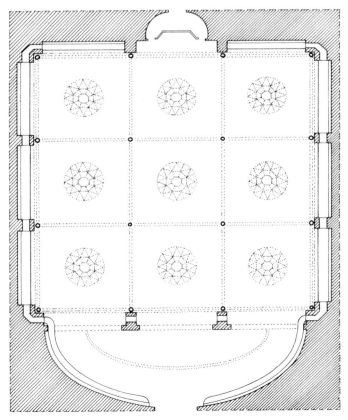

327 Reading Room, Bibliothèque nationale, Paris: plan; Henri Labrouste, 1857–67. After *Nouvelles Annales de la construction*, vol. 15, 1869, Pl. 21.

328 Crumlin Railway Viaduct, near Newport, Monmouthshire, Wales; Charles Liddell, engineer, and Thomas W. Kennard, entrepreneur, 1853–7. One of the first bridges with metal piers and a lattice deck.

329 Bridge over the Elbe, Hamburg, 1877. The horizontal deck is hung from two parabolic suspension booms. This is a monumental version of an idea which Isambard Kingdom Brunel used twice (Chepstow Bridge over the Wye, 1852, and King Albert Bridge over the Tamar, 1854–9).

330 Müngsten Bridge over the Wupper; A. Rieppel. With a span of 160 metres and a height of 69 metres, this railway bridge is still one of the highest in Germany.

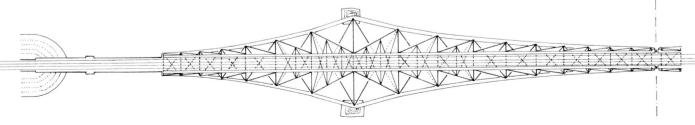

333a Bridge over the Rhône between Tournon and Tain,
France; Marc Seguin, 1824–5. Two equal spans of 85 m are
suspended from two abutments and a central tower by twelve
cables (six on each side), each consisting of 112 strands of iron
wire with a diameter of 3 mm, the strength of which had been
proved by Seguin to be two to five times greater than a bar of
equal section.

331 Forth Bridge over the Firth of Forth, near Edinburgh,
Scotland; Sir Benjamin Baker, Sir John Fowler and Sir William
Arrow, 1882–90.

332 Viaur Railway Viaduct, Tarn, on the Rodez-Albi line;
Paul Bodin and the Société des Batignolles, designed 1887, executed 1896–1902. The span of the central arch is 220 metres, that
of Gustave Eiffel's Garabit viaduct only 165 metres. A metal
design was adopted instead of the masonry bridge originally
envisaged in order to reduce the slope.

333 Viaur Railway Viaduct, Tarn, on the Rodez-Albi line;
Paul Bodin and the Société des Batignolles, designed 1887, executed 1896–1902.

multiplied. Efforts were redoubled to achieve the
spectacular, culminating at the 1889 Paris exhibition
with the Galerie des Machines (destroyed in 1910) by
Charles Dutert (1845–1906). This had arches spanning 115 metres, whereas those of the 1867 exhibition
had a length of only 35 metres. Gustave Eiffel's 300-
metre tower had what looked like a triumphal arch at
the entrance; it was the first wonder of the world in
the industrial epoch. This rather futile predilection
for breaking records of scale was glaringly apparent
at the Chicago Universal Exhibition in 1899, when it
was decided to make the arches of the Manufactures
and Liberal Arts Building a few feet longer in order
to beat the world record set by the Galerie des Machines.

The austerity of the Crystal Palace, due not to aesthetic preferences but to lack of time, was never seen
again. Greater care and attention were naturally paid
to the architecture of the envelope when designing a
permanent exhibition hall, and as the number of exhibitions multiplied the idea of a permanent building
came to be accepted. This explains the contrast between the 'Palais d'industrie' built in 1855 by Jean-
Marie Viel (1796–1863) and Alexis Barrault
(1812–67), which was meant to last (it was not demolished until 1900, in order to make way for the
Grand Palais), and the temporary pavilion designed
by Léopold Hardy (1829–94) for the 1878 exhibition,

334 World Exhibition, Vienna: general view; 1873.

335 World Exhibition, Paris: main entrance from the Champ-de-Mars; Léopold Hardy, 1878. Note the pilasters of riveted sheet metal decorated with polychrome tiles.

and between the latter and the Palais du Trocadéro of Davioud (1823–81), which stood until 1937. It is significant that the Great Hall, built by Francis Fowkes for the London exhibition in 1862, revived the external walls of brick and the large central glazed dome from the Building Committee's design of 1850, which had to be dropped for lack of time. From one exhibition to the next the dimensions of these domes went on growing, like those of the arches spanning the naves: 102 metres in Vienna in 1873 and 110 metres in Lyons in 1894.

Up to the end of the century the universal exhibitions retained the ambiguous quality which contemporaries had experienced when visiting the Crystal Palace. The sparkling and tinsel magic of these spaces went well with exhibition palaces but a renewal of architecture could never come from such a source. Universal exhibitions were nevertheless an opportunity for striking technological feats and effected permanent changes in urban layouts.

For the sake of convenience, we have considered these various buildings according to the category of specification they fulfilled. However, there were obviously also a number of composite structures. The design with double cylindrical vaults buttressed by stone walls is to be found in very different types of building; so is that of a dome with metal bracing. Polonceau trusses spanned indoor markets as well as stations, and the same architects built closed arcades and halls. These designs were not the prerogative of engineers. A classical architect like Viollet-le-Duc or a neo-Gothic architect like Scott adopted them whenever the work in hand made their use expedient (the former's Archives Hall for the law-courts in Paris; the latter's Brill's Bath at Brighton in 1866).

A number of people were also greatly taken with the aesthetic qualities of the new materials. Throughout the century the glazed interior courtyard featured with growing frequency in the most varied types of building and steadily increased in size. As early as 1815 Étienne Éloy de Labarre covered the courtyard of the Bourse, built to a design by Brogniart and Louis Hippolyte Lebas (1782–1867) with an iron framework, the central part of which was glazed. This design was copied for the Hôtel des Monnaies in Nantes in 1825. It was not long before glazed roofs, the development of which was clearly bound up with

336, 337 The Eiffel Tower in the course of construction, June and September, 1888. The designs for this tower, which Gustave Eiffel planned as a monumental entrance to the World Exhibition in Paris in 1889, were prepared in 1884–6; erection began in 1887.

338, 339 The Galerie des Machines at the World Exhibition of 1889, Paris; architect: Charles Dutert; engineer: V. Contamin, 1887–9 (destroyed in 1910). The gallery had white glass with some blue patterning. It was 420 metres in length and 115 metres in width (compared with the 73 metres of St Pancras Station in London, the previous record, established in 1868). 'In spite of the development of some fine side galleries, it is somewhat difficult for the eye to accustom itself to these previously unimaginable dimensions,' wrote a visitor.

that of shopping arcades, increased in size and covered the whole courtyard.

This design, which introduced into the heart of the building a light-filled space of an almost outdoor character, held such appeal for contemporaries that it was soon found everywhere: in private houses, where it merged with the winter garden, to which it was akin, and also in public and semi-public buildings. Among the latter we may mention commercial exchanges (Coal Exchange, 1846–9, in London by Bunning, Berlin Bourse, 1859–63, by Hitzig, Corn Exchange, 1861–3, in Leeds by Cuthbert Brodrick, Brussels Bourse, 1868, etc.); aristocratic clubs (Reform Club, 1837–41, by Sir Charles Barry); group residences (Sailors' Home, 1846–9, in Liverpool, by John Cunningham; Cité Napoléon, 1849–53, by Veugny; Guise Workers' Co-operative, etc.); hotels (Hôtel du Louvre, 1853–5 and Hôtel Terminus, 1889, in Paris, Hôtel Thiriez, 1874, Lille, Palace Hotel, 1874–5, San Francisco); educational buildings (University Museum, 1855–7, at Oxford by Woodward; University of Brussels, 1892, by E. Hendrickx); commercial complexes (Bon Marché, 1868–72, Paris; Palais du Midi, 1875, Brussels); banks (Comptoir d'Escompte, 1880–9, Paris, by Corroyer); and office buildings (Guaranty Loan Building, 1888–90, Minneapolis, by E. Towsend Mix). This feature may either be incorporated from the outset or else introduced later as at the École des Beaux-Arts in Paris, where, in 1871, Ernest Georges Coquard (1831–1902) glazed over Duban's court in the Palais des Études built in 1833. Similarly, at the Royal Exchange in London, William Tite's courtyard of 1841 was given a glazed roof in 1880. Just as the open loggias of the Renaissance had been closed with glass in the eighteenth century, certain courtyards of sixteenth-century Florentine villas were covered with glazed roofs carried by cast-iron pillars (Villa della Petraia near Florence).

Similarly, and on a more modest scale, cast iron was used for the verandas and glazed awnings which became popular as additions to façades (façade for the Marquess of Salisbury, 20 Arlington Street, London, c. 1869; Hermes Villa, Lainz Tiergarten), and enabled large surfaces to be left free for glass in commercial and office blocks (Oriel Chambers, 1864, Liverpool, by Peter Ellis).

Being prefabricated and transportable, iron-and-steel architecture also seemed well suited to the needs of the colonies, where qualified architects and skilled workmen were in short supply. When in the 1840s the catalogues of architectural components published by the design offices of British foundries began to grow thicker, it was but a short step to façades and houses

340 World Exhibition of 1889, Paris: the axial rotunda; Jules Bouvard. It was designed to form a temporary matching piece to the permanent exhibition hall of the Trocadéro, built in 1878 by Gabriel Davioud.

made entirely of metal. The Britannia Iron Works, which had been producing the famous 'Derby castings' since 1818, embarked about 1848 under Andrew Handyside on the manufacture of exportable metal houses. So did its competitors Edwin May in Liverpool, Henning in Bristol, E. T. Bellhouse & Co. in Manchester, Charles D. Young & Co. in Edinburgh, and others. Similar research was carried out in France and Belgium but not in such depth.

The architectural journals followed these experiments with interest. These metal houses proved to be less suitable for colonial needs than had been hoped. Nevertheless, the exportation of ornamental castings went on to the end of the century, when prefabricated cast-iron verandas had become features of the townscapes in Johannesburg and at the Cape, in New Orleans and in San Francisco.

In the United States cast-iron façades composed of prefabricated elements were a great success from 1848 onwards and did not fall out of favour until the 1870s. Structures built on these lines were by no means immune to the risks of fire, as was claimed by one of their main propagandists, James Bogardus (1800–74), who

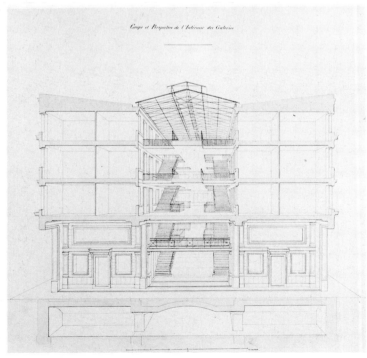

341 Cité Napoléon, a workers' town, Paris: general view; Marie Gabriel Veugny, 1849–53.

342 Cité Napoléon, a workers' town, Paris: section and perspective of the interior of the galleries; Marie Gabriel Veugny, 1849–53.

343 Pouhon, Spa, Belgium: view of the interior. The metal framework and the vegetation combine harmoniously.

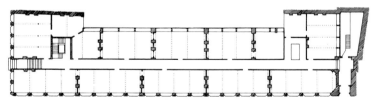

344 Oriel Chambers, Water Street, Liverpool; Peter Ellis, 1864. The oriel windows lighting the offices can be generously dimensioned thanks to the metal framework between the slender stone columns in highly stylized Gothic style.

345 Oriel Chambers, Water Street, Liverpool: plan; Peter Ellis, 1864.

346 A factory; James Bogardus, Center and Duane Streets, New York, 1848 (destroyed).

347 Haughwout Building, Broadway and Broome Street, New York; John P. Gaynor, 1857. The cast-iron elements were supplied by the Daniel Badger Corporation.

designed his New York factory on these lines in 1848 as an advertising stunt. It was not so much a question of creating apertures for glazing as in European shops but rather of producing rapidly façades of an elegance that evoked all the prestige of stone architecture. The foundries supplied not only columns and frames but even motifs in the style of Florentine ceiling bosses. Harper's Building (1854) and Haughwout Building (1857) by John P. Gaynor convey a better idea of this most popular style than do the buildings that have been destroyed. The early examples were destroyed or disfigured (Bogardus factory, New York, and John Milhau drugstore, 1848; Laing stores, 1849). In 1858, Bogardus reported, there were some fifteen of these designs in New York and the same number in other American cities (Baltimore, Chicago, Philadelphia, San Francisco). The firm of Daniel Badger seems to have operated on a still larger scale, since, in a catalogue published in 1865, it quoted more than six hundred projects it had carried out (including 55 façades of between two and six floors in height) all over the United States. There were still other foundries (Cincinnati Iron Foundry, Eagle Foundry) with a similar scope of business. In a new country, where economic expansion was proceeding very rapidly, this form of design made it possible to give façades the prestigious appearance of stone architecture at a time when qualified sculptors and architects were unable to meet all needs.

In France, in 1852, Bruyère also submitted a design for a metal house in the 'General Construction' competition of the École des Beaux-Arts, but in the 1860s research concentrated rather on lineal metal structures intended to reinforce stone or brick buildings. The substitution of iron for wood is noticeable in the design published by Viollet-le-Duc in his *Entretiens sur l'architecture* (1863–72), but as early as 1867 François Liger devised systems with girders of riveted plate. These found their way into many utilitarian

348 Iron cottage with a fine cast-iron front: design No. 14; Charles D. Young & Company. A house of this type, the Villa Corie, built about 1885, still exists at Geelong, Australia.

349 Iron dwelling house with shop on ground-floor and fine cast-iron front: design No. 15; Charles D. Young & Company.

buildings (factories, barracks, schools, hospitals). At the same time, however, more elaborate research was in hand to characterize an aesthetic appropriate to iron. Some architects and engineers, with a robust frankness, continued simply to take advantage of the potentialities of iron constructions – rivets, butt straps, joints and lattices – 'four elements capable of producing very original decorative effects and unfortunately too much neglected up till now', as the engineer Arthur Jules Vierendeel observed in 1890.

To overcome the slimness of the metal members, use was first made of paint, as we have seen. This seemed all the more rational in that iron must be painted in any case in order to protect it from rust. The studies of colour begun by Owen Jones in the Crystal Palace continued until the end of the century, but then, in the 1870s, it was thought that more body could be given to iron architecture by combining it with panels of coloured ceramics. Experiments were made along these lines in several exhibition pavilions, particularly in Paris in 1878, and in a number of medium-sized stations, especially in France and Spain. Commenting on Jean Camille Formigé's (1845–1926) station design exhibited at the Salon in 1876, Paul Sédille (1836–1900) called attention to the slim columns of iron, picked out in strong colours, which subdivided the large area of glazed gable, and noted that the use of 'enamelled earthenware in association with iron . . . mitigates its chilliness.' For the outside of his pavilion at the Exposition Universelle in Paris in 1878, Hardy also made extensive use of slabs of enamelled earthenware. At the 1889 exhibition these polychrome effects were still further enriched by contrapuntal ironwork in the Grand Palais, built to a design by Formigé, which foreshadowed, if not the design, at least the syntactical role of ironwork in Art Nouveau.

350 House with cast-iron front, 5 rue de l'Aqueduc, Paris 10: elevation; A. Lefèvre, 1878. After *Revue générale de l'architecture*, series 4, vol. 6, 1879, Pl. 26.

351 House with cast-iron front, 5 rue de l'Aqueduc, Paris 10: detail of wall pier; A. Lefèvre, 1878. After *Revue générale de l'architecture*, series 4, vol. 6, 1879, Pl. 27.

352 Barracks of the Garde Républicaine, rue de Schomberg, Paris 4; Jules Bouvard, 1883. After J. Lacroux, *La Brique ordinaire*, Paris, 1878, vol. 2, Pl. 70.

353 Palais des Beaux-Arts et des Arts Libéraux, World Exhibition, 1889, Paris; Jean Formigé. After P. Chabat, *La Brique et la terre cuite*, Paris, vol. 2, Pl. 79.

354 Collège municipal Chaptal (Lycée Chaptal), boulevard des Batignolles, Paris 8; Eugène Train. After *Revue générale de l'architecture*, 1880, Pl. 17.

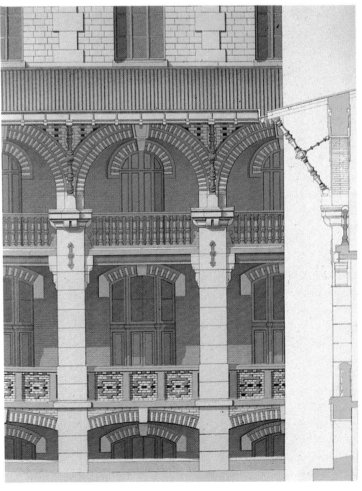

355 Menier chocolate factory, Noisiel, Seine-et-Marne; Jules Saulnier, 1871-2. The substitution of iron for wood is still palpable in this case.

356 Offices of the Compagnie des chemins de fer de l'Est, 144 rue du Faubourg-Saint-Denis, Paris 10: Adrien Gouny, 1887. Note the frank statement of the materials used: coloured brickwork, lintels of riveted sheet metal, small cast-iron columns and glazed tiles.

357 Pavilion of the Ministry of Public Works, World Exhibition, Paris; de Dartein, 1878. A typical example of the modern 'brick and iron' style in utilitarian constructions.

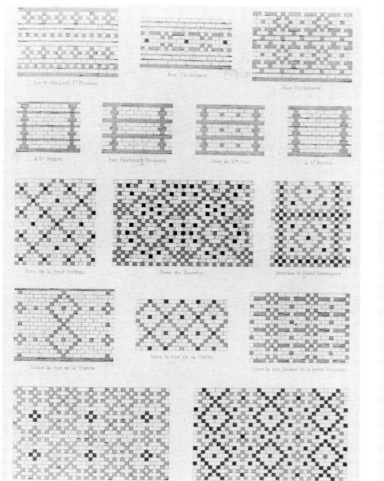

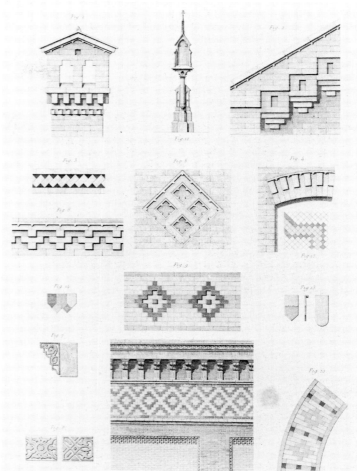

358, 359   Brickwork constructions in Munich and at Troyes.
These two plates clearly show the interest in abstract patterns
formed by playing with colour and arrangement of the tiles.
They were modelled on modern German compositions and old
French ones from Troyes.

Transcending these decorative answers to the
problem, Boileau, with reference to his work in the
Bon Marché department stores, emphasized that in an
iron building 'all the architectural clichés' become
useless 'once there is no surface available to receive
them'. 'Since such a monument cannot sustain serious
comparison with stone buildings,' he went on:

It should once and for all avoid imitating them and
be considered from another point of view (. . .): it
is no longer the solids of the building that should
be envisaged but rather the void it envelops; that
is to say, instead of seeking to make light play on
three-dimensional forms, it must be opposed to

itself in the ambient air circulating through the
construction and, by its plenitude or its exiguity,
create highlights, half-lights, or reflections which
make the brightness of space scintillate as fires are
called forth from the crystals of chandeliers when
they are cut into a diversity of prisms. In this concert of light the solid architecture will play the part
of a setting for a fine jewel: it must figure just sufficiently to lend the greatest possible vibrancy to
this interior daylight, which the translucent glazed
surfaces and the surrounding half-lit depths will
have made more gay, more sonorous, more enriched, as it were, than the pure and simple daylight
outside.

This acute insight into an aesthetic appropriate to
iron remains an exception. For the majority of architects iron was just one of many sculptural and conf-
structive tools and its use was a matter either of constructive rationalism or of decorative eclecticism.

Building for a Purpose: Prisons and Hospitals

'The plan of a mental hospital is an essential matter which ought to be left solely to the architect. A mental hospital is a means of healing.'
(Docteur Esquirol, *Des établissements d'aliénés en France*, Paris, 1819)

Purpose Prevails over Style

The splintering of architectural language and the imitation, whether naïve or academic, of the styles of the past are the most conspicuous and at the same time the most superficial characteristics of nineteenth-century architecture; for they mask the inwrought features of a less obvious but more essential modernity composed of structural techniques and layouts. 'For a long time the battles still sometimes waged between the different styles of architecture have ceased to flutter the dovecotes', the architect Adolphe Étienne Lance (1813–74) noted in 1858. In 1859 and 1860 these sentiments were echoed by César Daly in an editorial in the *Revue générale de l'architecture et des Travaux publics*: 'in France questions of style have not been in the forefront of architects' concerns since 1852; activities serving national production, the need to manufacture rapidly and on a large scale have caused the practical questions of our profession to outweigh all others.' Towards mid-century some more perspicacious observers began to see quite clearly what it was that, beyond and in spite of the diversity of styles, constituted the unity and modernity of their epoch: the solution of novel and ever more complex problems concerning technology and layout which originated in the new characteristics and the needs of bourgeois industrial civilization.

The use of industrially produced materials – floors and frameworks of iron, enamelled ceramics and terracotta; the introduction of modern amenities – central heating and ventilation, gas and electricity, shower rooms and flush toilets: all these practical questions, which figured prominently in every architectural journal, had an unobtrusive effect on the most traditional of designs. 'The Reform Club shows some essentially modern features,' wrote César Daly in 1857:

We are not referring either to the architectural style of the façade, which is of the Italian school, nor to the layout of the plans, intelligent though it is, but to something more intimate which does not strike the eye, and at first does not even attract one's attention, but which nevertheless makes itself felt everywhere and in everything and which has for its purpose the achievement of *comfort* in its broad sense.

It is in the buildings devoted to the needs of large associations of individuals, like hotels, societies, clubs etc., that the development of these characteristics of the architecture of the future can best be seen. It is here that one can see how private needs are catered to by the multifold resources of steam power and electricity, by the various processes of heating, ventilation and lighting, by the means of transporting, silently and without fuss, luggage, fuel and food to every storey and to every room.

The problems of layout, which were growing continuously more complex, also claimed greater attention by architects. They had to design buildings to meet entirely novel requirements. As the American Henry van Brunt noted in 1886, the nineteenth-century architect

in the course of his career, is called upon to erect buildings for every conceivable purpose, most of them adapted to requirements which have never

before arisen in history . . . Railway buildings of all sorts; churches with parlors, kitchens and society rooms; hotels on a scale never before dreamt of; public libraries the service of which is fundamentally different from any of their predecessors; office and mercantile structures, such as no pre-existing conditions of professional and commercial life have ever required; school houses and college buildings, whose necessary equipment removes them far from the venerable examples of Oxford and Cambridge; skating-rinks, theatres, exhibition buildings of vast extent, casinos, jails, prisons, municipal buildings, music halls, apartment houses, and all the other structures which must be accommodated to the complicated conditions of modern society . . .
Out of [the] . . . eminently practical considerations of planning must grow elevations, of which the essential character, if they are honestly composed, can have no precedent in architectural history.

In the eighteenth century buildings serving the needs of the community were few and far between and there was little to distinguish them in their typology. With the Enlightenment, the idea of joint civic action began to dawn in towns and their environments. As liberal ideas spread, an ever denser network of public buildings came to be established: schools and town halls, museums, hospitals, prisons, etc. The specifications for them became increasingly complex but also repetitive and standardized. Side by side with architects, specialists began to play an ever more crucial role. Experts in other domains of public health, penology, education and museology had an influence on the design of hospitals and prisons, schools and museums. The publication of the first models of American schools was linked with the meeting of the two first national conventions of the Friends of Public Education, who were alarmed at the lack of national standards. And this set the international pattern. At the beginning of the century all these projects were still experiments and it was the best architects who were invited to study them; then about 1830–40 their typology became fixed. Very soon precise administrative regulations limited the architect's scope of manoeuvre and laid down the area, the cubic air space, and the cost per pupil, patient or prisoner. As Paul Planat wrote in his architectural encyclopaedia at the end of the century: 'The architect's work in designing a school is quite naturally laid down by the regulations in force. . . We can therefore restrict ourselves here to reproducing the ministerial rules and regulations of 1880.'

These unobtrusive and progressive shifts and changes affecting architectural practice, although less spectacular than the battle of styles, were no less characteristic of nineteenth-century architecture. We will select here two particularly illuminating examples – the hospital and the prison – in which the thought devoted to form was especially closely associated with that given to function.

The Nineteenth-Century Prison

Prison architecture, like that of hospitals, which had a very similar history, was a favoured field of rational layout in the nineteenth century. This is a fascinating development since the spatial arrangement of prisons may be explained by an analysis of the programmes which it, so to say, translated into space.

At the end of the eighteenth century incarceration became the main penalty imposed by the courts, with the objective of bringing about the reform of the prisoners. The filth, promiscuity and disorder of the existing prisons, described in the admirable inquiries conducted by John Howard (1726–90), *The State of the Prisons in England and Wales*, 1777–84; *Appendix to the State of the Prisons*, 1788, appeared to be the main obstacle to achievement of this goal. The study of the penitentiary system by penologists throughout the nineteenth century who published their findings at international congresses (the first held in Frankfurt in 1846) led to the formulation of contrasting systems. To meet these requirements architects engaged in a variety of formal experiments while seeking to remain within the budgetary limits fixed by the authorities.

'To introduce a complete reform in prisons, to ensure the present good conduct of the prisoners and the correction of their faults, to establish health, cleanliness, order and industry in these places, hitherto infected by moral and physical corruption . . . *by a simple architectural idea*' – this was the express aim of Jeremy Bentham's *Panopticon*, published in 1791. It was one of the first manifestations of a quest for close agreement between architectural form and function that gave the nineteenth-century mind no rest. In this work Bentham put forward a design for six storeys of cells arranged circumferentially round a circular or polygonal building. In the middle was a three-storey tower, separated by an annular glazed wall, containing the chapel and the warders' quarters. This central structure was encircled by curtained galleries, so that a discreet watch could be kept on the simple barred cells. To eliminate the risk of fire, Bentham proposed to employ 'iron wherever it could be used' in place of wood. A modern construction in regard to materials,

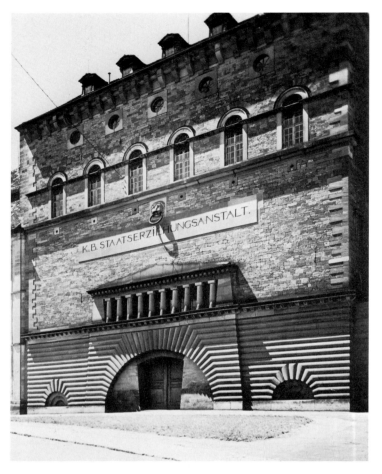

360 Women's prison, Würzburg; Peter Speeth, 1809–10. In a style close to that of Ledoux, an attempt has been made to produce an expressive and intimidating façade.

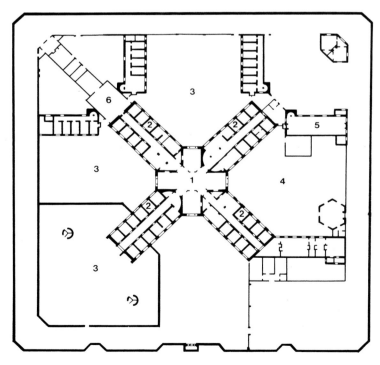

361 Suffolk County jail, Ipswich, England: plan; William Blackburn, 1784–90. 1 governor's house; 2 cells; 3 courtyards; 4 women's courtyard; 5 hospital; 6 study.

Bentham's prison is of particular interest because of its layout. It was Bentham's hope that 'this new type of inspection which appeals to the imagination rather than the senses' would procure the reform of prisoners 'associated in small selected groups' of three or four per cell: 'being continually under a warder's eye is tantamount to losing the power of doing wrong and even the wish to do it'.

Detached from the utopian moral ideas underlying Bentham's project, panoptic layouts enabling dozens of cells to be kept under surveillance from a central point never failed to fascinate nineteenth-century architects. A semi-circular panoptic plan was adopted in 1791–5 for the Bridewell in Edinburgh, but in general the circular (or semi-circular) plan gave way to one in which the detention quarters radiated from a centre with surveillance concentrated on the inter-connecting corridors or galleries rather than on the cells themselves. Ipswich prison (1784–90), built by William Blackburn (1750–90), a friend of Howard, was the prototype of this design: a tower containing the warders' quarters was the central point from which radiated the detention quarters with corridors arranged along the same axes as those of the dwelling.

In the following decades a score of prisons of this type were built in Great Britain and on the Continent, but a balance between the needs of domesticity and surveillance was rarely achieved with such success as at Ipswich. At Bury St Edmunds in Suffolk (1803–5) the central tower was isolated by a ditch and connected to the detention quarters by two gangways, no doubt with the intention of avoiding a dangerous proximity: security had taken precedence over the panoptic ideal. In the prison of Geneva (1822–4), where two detention quarters radiating from a tower were contained in a semi-circular enclosure, the architect discarded a focal point of surveillance in favour of a convenient arrangement of the communal services, visiting rooms, chapel and infirmary round the staircase of the central tower. Here the panoptic ideal was sacrificed to uninterrupted traffic flow and convenience of layout. Lebas took the same design on a bigger scale for the house in which young prisoners were quartered at the Petite Roquette in Paris (1826–36). In 1829 appeared Louis Pierre Baltard's (1764–1846) *Architectonographie des prisons ou parallèle des divers systèmes de distribution dont les prisons sont susceptibles*, which summed up the experience acquired in Europe.

The quality of the Geneva prison, like the Petite Roquette, is due to the clarity of layout and also to the penitentiary system itself. This was based on a method already practised in the eighteenth century in the

214

362 House of Correction, Bury St Ed-
monds, Suffolk, England: plan; 1803–5.

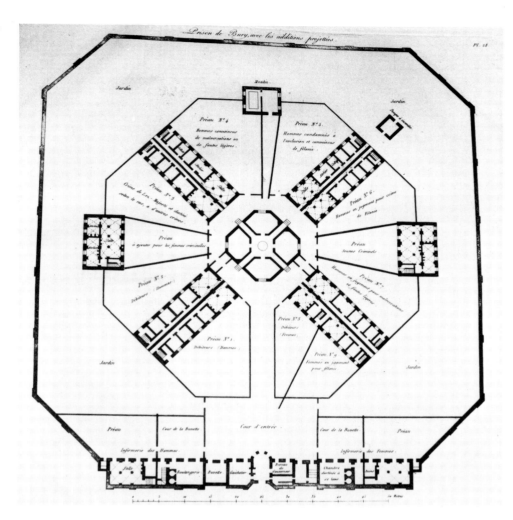

363 Prison, Geneva: plan of second
floor; M. Osterrieth, 1822–5. 1 infirmary;
2 chapel; 3 warders' room; 4 cells; the
workshops are on the first storey below
the cells.

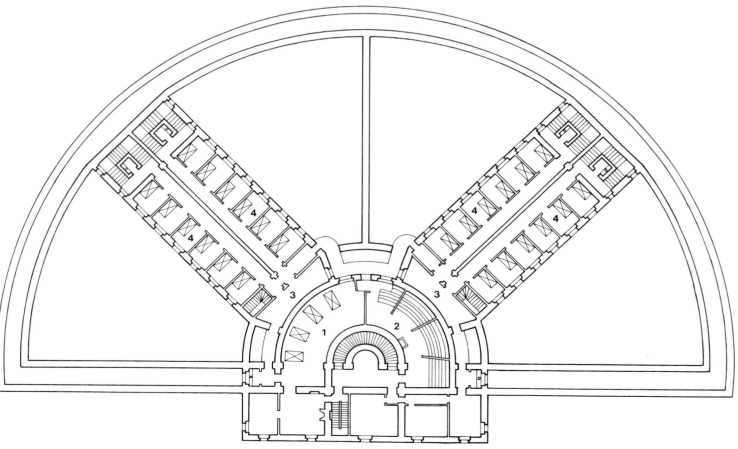

364   La Petite Roquette, prison for young delinquents, Paris: general view; Louis Hippolyte Lebas, 1826–36 (destroyed 1974).

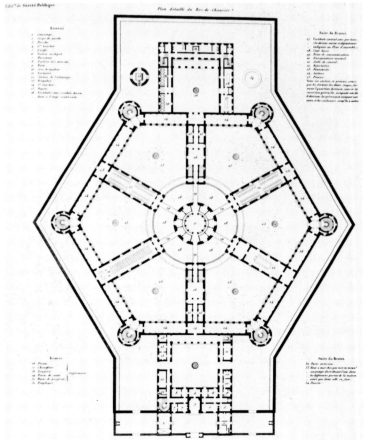

365   La Petite Roquette, prison for young delinquents, Paris: ground-floor plan; Louis Hippolyte Lebas, 1826–36 (destroyed 1974).

San Michele prison in Rome (1702–4) and at Ackerghem near Ghent (1772–4). It combined daytime labour in workshops with confinement to individual cells at night, the penologists fearing that criminal behaviour was contagious. In the 1820s a penitentiary system was devised in Pennsylvania which was based on even stricter segregation of the prisoners. They were shut up day and night in fairly spacious cells where they were able to sleep, work and stretch their legs. 'In Philadelphia the walls are the punishment of crime; the cell puts the prisoner in his own presence; he is forced to listen to his conscience, he seeks to banish his persecutor; the work which his hands have perhaps never known before appears to him to be less forbidding.'

The layout of prisons built on this pattern is more complex in its details since each cell must be, in a way, a private prison. The prison is merely a juxtaposition of identical cells which the prisoners do not leave. The simplicity of this design allows a return to the panoptic ideal. The prototype was built by John Haviland at the Cherry Hill penitentiary (Eastern penitentiary) in Philadelphia (1823–9). Administrative offices and outbuildings occupied the entrance to the complex, and one had to go through them in order to reach the central rotunda. From this radiated seven one-storey blocks through which ran long corridors, on either side of which were the cells, each with its own small exercise yard. From the central room on which all the corridors converged it was possible to keep the whole of the penitentiary under surveillance. Haviland combined the cellular design, first seen in the San Michele prison in Rome, the radial plan of Blackburn's prisons, and Bentham's panoptic ideal.

The flexibility of this design is not the least of its virtues, since the number of wings can be reduced or increased at will, extended in length or even heightened by the addition of extra storeys (but in this case individual yards must be provided where the prisoners can be taken in turn). Haviland demonstrated this flexibility in Trenton prison (1833–6), where he designed five wings arranged like the radii of a semicircle, but at first built only two of them.

Cruel as it was, the Pennsylvanian system became nothing short of inhuman if the cells were not sufficiently large. After a revolt by convicts held in cells that were too small, the director of Auburn prison in New York state, where at that time the Pennsylvanian system was in operation, had canteens and workshops built in which the prisoners ate and worked in association, going back to their individual cells only at night – a return to the system followed at Ackerghem – but in addition he imposed the rule of silence. This was

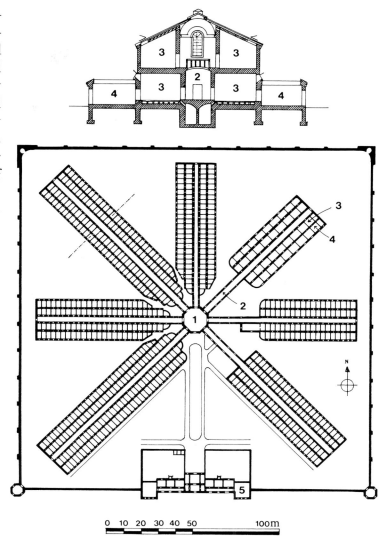

366 Cherry Hill prison (Eastern Penitentiary), Philadelphia, Pa.: section and plan; John Haviland, 1823–9. 1 warders' room; 2 corridor; 3 cells; 4 small courtyard; 5 heating ducts; 6 administration.

the novel feature in the Auburn system (1823). Being built on empirical lines, this prison naturally had a less uniform plan, and in this respect was less attractive than Philadelphia and Trenton, whose formal perfection at the hands of John Haviland goes some way to explain their extraordinary subsequent history.

When, about 1830, with the advance of liberal thought, people began to ponder the penitentiary system more deeply, Europeans took a keen interest in the Americans' achievements, which at the time were among the most modern, along with the Swiss. The two systems of Auburn and Pennsylvania henceforth became standard and criminologists took their bearing from these two poles. Around 1840, after lively controversy, most European countries were won over to the Pennsylvanian system. Architects rang the changes on Haviland's radial panoptic model. Par-

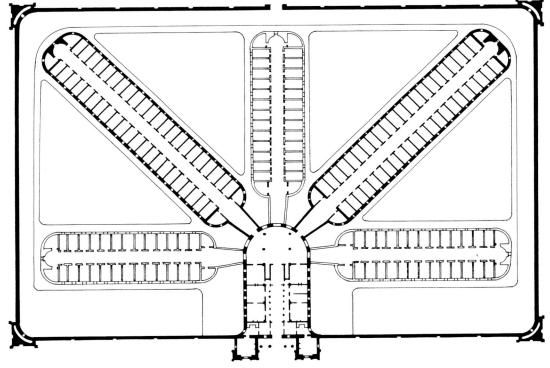

367 New Jersey State Penitentiary, Trenton, N. J.: entrance; John Haviland, 1833–6. Because of its massive proportions and its symbolic values, the Egyptian style is particularly appropriate for prisons.

368 New Jersey State Penitentiary, Trenton, N. J.: plan; John Haviland, 1833–6.

adoxically enough, it found little favour in the United States, where most prisons were erected on the Auburn pattern with a very loosely-knit plan (Sing-Sing, New York, 1825; Columbus, Ohio, 1834; Waupun, Wisconsin, 1851; Joliet, Illinois, 1856–8; Western Penitentiary, Pittsburgh, 1882; Nashville, Tennessee, 1895, etc.).

The first structure on the Pennsylvanian pattern to be erected in Europe was Pentonville prison in London, built in 1840–2 by Sir Joshua Webb and Sir Charles Barry (it is much altered today). With its four cell blocks radiating in a semicircle from a central watch-tower, in front of which the common utilities are grouped, the plan is borrowed directly from Trenton. The only new idea, which was to be widely copied, was that of circular walks, divided into individual sections by walls radiating from a central watch-tower. It was to provide inspiration for later English prisons: Berkshire County Gaol, Reading (1842–4), by Sir George Gilbert Scott and W. B. Moffat; Holloway prison, London (1849–52, destroyed), by James Bunston Bunning. It also served as a halfway house between the American prototypes and the first continental buildings.

After inspecting it with his architect Busse, Frederick William IV of Prussia decided to adopt the Pennsylvanian system for the first Moabit prison in Berlin (1844). The system was also adopted at Münster (1845) and Breslau, now Wrocław (1844–52). But at Bruchsal (1848) we again find the radial layout of

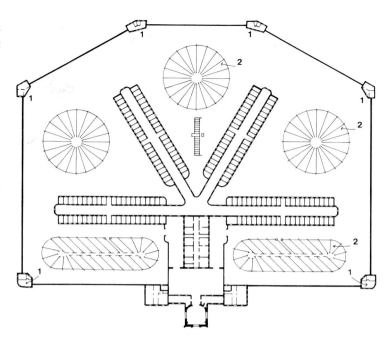

369 Pentonville prison, London: plan; Sir Joshua Webb and Sir Charles Barry, 1840–2. 1 warders' room; 2 exercise yard.

370 Holloway prison, London: façade; James Bunston Bunning, 1849–52 (destroyed).

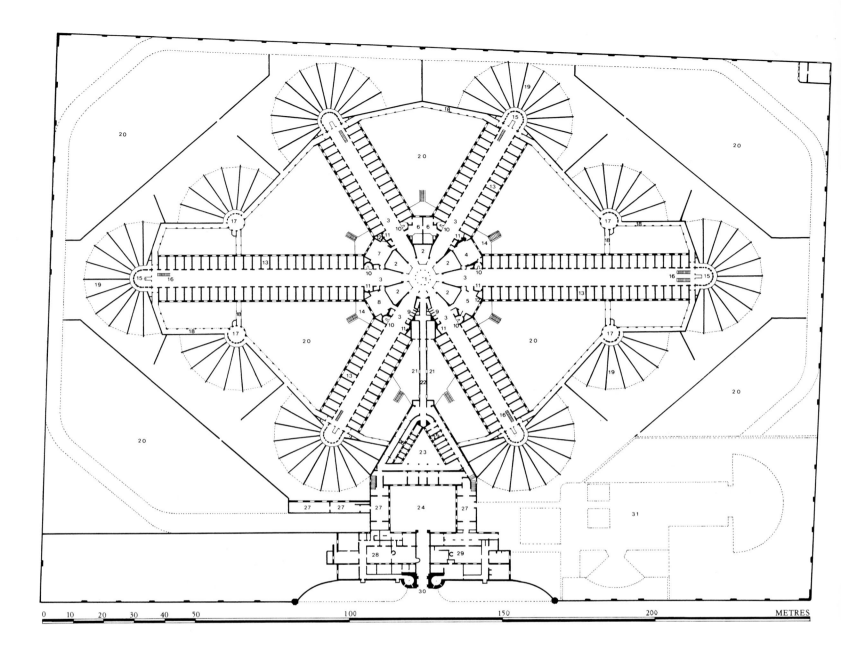

the cells but not the central surveillance point, the central tower being occupied, as in Geneva, by the common utilities.

After a tour of England undertaken at the instance of the Belgian minister of justice, during which he visited Pentonville and Reading, Joseph Dumont (1811–59) built an important series of prisons of the Pennsylvanian type in Belgium: Louvain (1846–58); Brussels (1847–8, destroyed); Liège (1850–1); Verviers (about 1850) and others.

In France, Duchatel, minister of the interior, authorized publication in 1841 of *Instruction et programme pour les constructions des maisons d'arrêt et de justice*. This marked the official acceptance of the Pennsylvanian system by the government. The atlas accompanying

371 Prison, Louvain, Belgium; Joseph Dumont, 1846–58. The prison was built below a boulevard, the ground-floor of the cells (Nos. 1-20) is at the level of the basement of the administration building (Nos. 21-30). It contains 600 cells on three floors: 1 central watch-tower; 2 divisions of the chapel intended for prisoners on the ground-floor; 3 corridors of the cell wings; 4 kitchen; 5 dispensary; 6 bakery; 7 warders' dormitory; 8 warders' refectory; 9 rooms for firemen; 10 staircases of cell wings; 11 ablutions and hoists for distributing rations; 12 main ventilation shafts; 13 cells; 14 circular connecting passages in basement for supplies; 15 bedrooms for warders on duty and observation points for inspecting courtyards; 16 service staircases to courtyards; 17 observation point; 18 passage for observation and communication between courtyards; 19 courtyards; 20 land for cultivation; 21 steam wash-house and outbuildings; 22 main entrance for prisoners; 23 courtyard; 24 entrance yard; 25 cells, baths and fumigation for arriving prisoners; 26 baths, showers, etc.; 27 cellars for stores; 28 governor's flat; 29 deputy governor's flat; 30 entrance porch.

220

372, 373   Cell area of the Maison centrale de Beaulieu, Caen, Calvados: view looking from the watchtower over a cell wing; Romain Harou, after 1844.

it is a most astonishing compilation of variations on this pattern. Abel Blouet, Romain Harou (1796–1866) and Hector Horeau (1801–72) proposed numerous variants on the panoptic model with its radial cell blocks as well as on Bentham's panoptic circular layout and its semicircular variant, which they believed they had rediscovered.

Beaulieu prison, near Caen, where the new cell block, built by Jean-Baptiste-Philippe Harou and rebuilt by his son Romain, is a perfect example of the spatial qualities achieved in radial panoptic prisons. The model building in Paris was the house of deten-

tion of Mazas, built by Jean François Joseph Lecointe (1783–1858) and Émile Jacques Gilbert; it has, however, few new ideas to show and it is rather the quality of its technical features that attracts. The work was authorized in 1840 and a contract placed in 1842, but it was not completed until 1850.

The circular design could not fail to fascinate people in a century when the pattern of Soufflot's Panthéon was constantly present in their minds. André Berthier adopted it in the prison at Autun (1847–56; closed down and placed on the List of Historical Monuments), where access to the fifty individual cells arranged in three tiers was by way of metal galleries round a circular room covered by a dome lit by an oculus. Its higher costs of construction explain the gap between the number of buildings de-

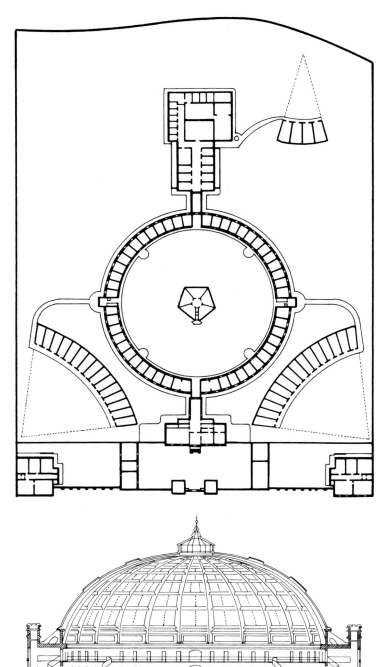

374, 375   Prison, Arnhem, Netherlands: plan and section;
1884. The prison resembles the circular prison of Autun, France
(1847).

signed and that actually built and the general preference shown by the administration for radial plans.

In the following decades prisons on the circular plan were unusual. We may mention those at Dinant, Belgium and Arnhem, Netherlands (1884, undergoing alteration), the most spectacular embodiment of

this design. It has two hundred cells in four tiers round a large circular room, 45 metres in diameter with a dome borne on visible metal trusses. The pattern of cell blocks radiating from a central vantage-point won the day everywhere. In Belgium, seventeen of the twenty prisons built in the nineteenth century were of this type. In Germany there are forty, and there are others in Scandinavia (Langholm near Stockholm), the Iberian countries (Vitoria, 1859; Madrid, 1877; Lisbon, 1880; Valencia, 1887, etc.), Argentina (Buenos Aires, 1872) and Japan, where the opening up of the country to the West also led to adoption of its penitentiary system (Miyagi prison, Tokyo, built by an English engineer in 1879). However, if the typology remained that of prisons in the style of John Haviland, who was known humorously as the 'jailer of the world', the layout continued to grow more varied and complex: in the Saint-Gilles prison in Brussels (1847) the surveillance room and the chapel were superimposed dramatically, a happy compromise between the Genevan and Pennsylvanian models; in Le Nuove prison in Turin (1860-9/70) the cell blocks were organized on a plan shaped like a double cross; and comparison of the plans of the prisons at Philadelphia (1823) and Louvain (1846–58) shows the progress achieved in twenty-five years – progress which was seen to justify the optimism of the nineteenth century.

A more extended analysis would necessitate study of the development of legislation from one country to another. This alone would allow one to give a detailed account of the different buildings. In the second half of the century the opposition between the Auburn and the Pennsylvanian systems tended to become less marked. Certain penologists proposed mixed or progressive systems and the pattern of cell blocks radiating from a central vantage-point, a departure from the Pennsylvanian system, was a feature of all designs.

Pennsylvanian prisons were two to four times more expensive than those of the Auburn type. This, and the suicide rate among prisoners, explain why officials looked on them with increasing reserve. Belgium, the Netherlands and most Scandinavian countries remained faithful to the principle of individual confinement, with the inmates' isolation relieved by authorized visits along the lines advocated by the Belgian penologist Edouard Dupectiaux. In Great Britain, and later in Germany, Spain and elsewhere, it was the 'progressive' or Irish system, proposed by Walter Crofton in 1853, that was adopted. After a period of total isolation the prisoners were put on to an Auburn-type regime. Other penologists, particularly in France, were favourably inclined to the

376 Alt-Moabit prison, Berlin; Herrmann, 1869–71 (state about 1920).

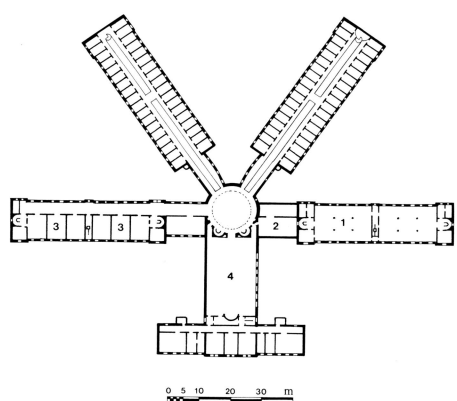

377 House of Correction, Rendsburg,
W. Germany: plan; 1870–2. 1 workshops; 2 school; 3 dormitories; 4 chapel.

0 5 10   20   30   m

adoption of regimes which were diversified to meet the character of the prisoners: solitary confinement for prisoners awaiting trial, the Auburn system for convicts, and collective confinement for political offenders and debtors. Thus, after 1850, many prisons were mixed in layout, being designed half for cellular confinement and half for collective confinement, or half Pennsylvanian and half Auburn, or diversified in character depending on their nature (remand prison or penitentiary: Holloway (1849–52) in London, La Santé (1862) in Paris, Rendsburg (1870–5) in Germany).

The abandonment of a more or less uniform concept concerning the execution of a sentence by no means involved abandonment of the panoptic radial plan, as could be seen in the new remand prison in Lyons, called the Saint-Paul prison, designed by Antoine-George Louvier (1818–92); it comprised a cell block and five blocks for collective detention with heated rooms, canteens and dormitories radiating from a central watchtower with a chapel on the first floor. However, this development no doubt explains why, at the end of the century, the radial plan was abandoned for a 'comb' layout in which the cell blocks were arranged at right angles to a narrow traffic corridor (Wormwood Scrubs, London, 1874–91; Fresnes prison near Paris, 1898), a system which recalls that of English hospitals. Prison and hospital architecture naturally interacted with each other, as they had in the past.

However, if practical considerations and problems of layout remained dominant, prison architecture was also one of the favourite fields for expressive architecture: the elevations had to be a metaphor of the moral universe of the prison, a sign of its function.

> The architectural style of a prison is a matter of no slight importance. It offers an effectual method of exciting the imagination to a most desirable point of abhorrence (. . .). The exterior of a prison should therefore be formed in the heavy and sombre style which most forcibly impresses the spectator with gloom and terror. Massive cornices, the absence of windows or other ornaments, small low doors and the whole structure comparatively low, seem to include nearly all the points necessary to produce the desired effect ('Prisons', *Encyclopaedia londoniensis*, vol. 21, London, 1826, p. 421).

This effect, which Peter Speeth (1772-1831) succeeded perfectly in attaining in the women's prison (1809–10) at Würzburg, as Romain Harou did at Beaulieu near Caen (after 1844), remained a constant preoccupation for nineteenth-century architects.

The Mazas prison is not merely a building in its own right and an administrative agency, it is a work of art; the general style of the monument requires it to be simple, noble, severe to the point of austerity. Its nature is, as is right and proper, imprinted in its form and, on approaching it, one feels it is something forbidding (*Encyclopédie de l'architecture*, 1853, col. 181).

The image of the fortress often underlay the design; and with the medieval revival, prisons readily assumed the appearance of castles and medieval keeps, from Cherry Hill prison to Holloway, and from Brussels prison to that at Auxerre. 'Towers, bartizans, narrow windows, bars, crenellations – all these evoke force, the surrender of liberty. The prison must be severe in style. It is even a good thing for it to be an intimidating deterrent to crime. Such is the wish of the law that has decreed the punishment of incarceration,' wrote the *Journal de l'architecture* with regard to the prisons of Dumont: 'on viewing one of these prisons, it is impossible to imagine that it could serve any other purpose.' Only a few prisons can be regarded as a success in this respect. The effects were often nothing but ornamentation; the coloured crenellations and the rustic gate of Auxerre prison were the product of the picturesque in prison design rather than of the sublime, which is attained only by one or two rare masterpieces such as the prison of Trenton or The Tombs in New York, where Haviland discarded the Gothic attempted at Cherry Hill in favour of the Egyptian style.

The Nineteenth-Century Hospital

When in the mid-eighteenth century disease ceased to be a stroke of fate and became a pathological fact, hospital architecture allowed greater scope to notions of hygiene and medical practice. Between 1760 and 1790 comparative studies conducted by the Englishman Howard, the Frenchman Tenon, and the Austrian Hunczovsky demonstrated statistically the link between the rate of mortality, certain medical practices and spatial arrangements. They condemned the traditional system of the multi-purpose hospital, where those with infectious diseases, the wounded, and women in childbirth lay cheek by jowl, and called for the creation of specialized hospitals. They underlined the importance of ventilation and the orientation of rooms, criticized the traditional plan of a square or cross with interconnecting wards, and advocated adoption of the pavilion hospital. The prototype of this was Stonehouse Hospital, Plymouth, designed by Rovehead in 1760.

In France these ponderings over health questions were accompanied by a vast output of graphic work – several dozen projects – inspired by the problem of reconstructing the Hôtel-Dieu (1772–88) in Paris. The plan drafted by the architect Bernard Poyet in 1788 to illustrate Tenon's *Mémoire sur les hôpitaux de Paris* became accepted as a model. In 1809 Jean Nicolas Louis Durand published a variant in his *Précis d'architecture*. The pavilions, which were to contain no more than sixty beds on two floors, were distributed in two parallel rows (for men and women), separated by a distance equal to two and a half times their height. The pavilions were connected by porticos on either side of a square courtyard, the far end of which was occupied by the chapel. In 1786 the Académie des Sciences advocated adoption of this layout for new hospital constructions, but the subsequent nationalization of the property of the clergy made it pointless to erect new hospitals. Instead the sick were housed in former monasteries and convents.

These principles were applied half-heartedly at Bordeaux (1810) and disregarded in the hospital at Saint-Mandé (1828) near Paris. They were never implemented properly until after 1830, when they were embodied in the Hospice de la Reconnaissance (or Hospice Brezin) at Garches; the first design (1835) for this was drafted by Marie-Antoine Dellanoy (1800–60) but it was built between 1836 and 1846 by Martin Pierre Gauthier (1790–1855), the architect of the Paris municipal hospital administration. Another example was the hospital of Saint-Jean de Bruxelles (1837–43, destroyed), built by Henri Partoes (1790–1873) after a detailed study of the most up-to-date hospitals in Europe. The most modern hospital, which was epoch-making until Casimir Tollet perfected an improved system in 1872, was that named for Louis-Philippe, later called Lariboisière, in Paris. It was designed by Martin Pierre Gauthier in 1839 and built between 1846 and 1854. The military hospital at Vincennes, the Bégin Hospital (1856–8), has a more closely-knit layout; so, too, does the Hôtel-Dieu (1864–76) by Émile Jacques Gilbert and the chief architect of Paris Arthur Nicolas Diet (1824–90).

In Great Britain the implementation of the new principles was delayed longer. In 1853 a hospital commission was set up. It recommended that the pavilion layout should be adopted. In 1858 *The Builder* devoted articles to the subject and in 1859, in her *Notes on Hospitals*, Florence Nightingale (1820–1910) waged a campaign for the pavilion system. She specified architectural features which were the most advantageous from the point of view of hygiene. The first large hospital to be erected in accordance with the latest

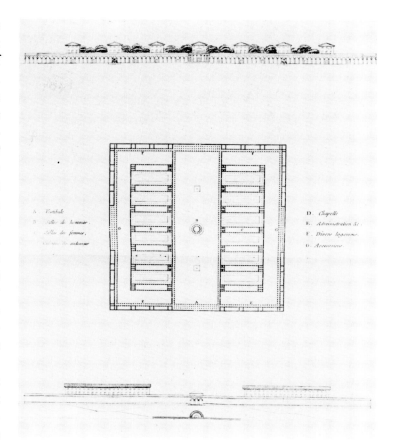

378   Model of a hospital based on the hospitals designed by Bernard Poyet. After Jean Nicolas Louis Durand, III, Pl. 18.

principles was the Royal Herbert Military Hospital, Woolwich, which was built in 1860–4 by Sir Douglas Galton. Similar constructions followed: St Thomas's Hospital, London (1865–71) by Henry Currey, the Royal Infirmary, Edinburgh (1870–9) by David Bryce, and the Sick Children's Hospital, Pendlebury near Manchester (1872–8) by Pennington and Bridges. In these the pavilions, isolated from one another as in France, were arranged not round a courtyard but at right angles to a circulation corridor at the centre of which stood the administration building. This comb-type layout was also found in the United States (Free Boston Hospital; Moser Taylor Hospital, Scranton, Pa.; Roosevelt Hospital, New York); in Sweden (Sabbatsberg, Stockholm, 1879); Australia (Prince Alfred Hospital, Sydney, 1882); Spain (Huelva Hospital, by Green, 1883); Persia (Teheran Hospital, by the Englishman Ernest Turner, 1890–1).

Germany remained faithful to traditional layouts for a greater length of time (Stadtkrankenhaus, Hanover-Linden, 1829–31; Bethany Diakonissenkrankenhaus, Berlin, 1845–7; Militärkrankenhaus, Hanover, 1846–56). The modern pavilion layout did not appear until about 1870: Augusta Hospital, Berlin

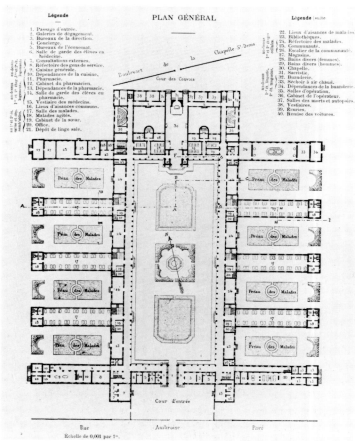

379   Hospital of the Order of Deaconesses, Bethany, Berlin; Stone, 1845–7. After designs by Ludwig Persius, Friedrich August Stüler and, for the towers, King Frederick William IV.

380   Hôpital Louis-Philippe (later Lariboisière), Paris: plan; Martin Pierre Gauthier, designed 1839, executed 1846–54. After Tollet, 1894, Pl. 3.

381   Hôpital Lariboisière, Paris: view of the courtyard; Martin Pierre Gauthier, designed 1839, executed 1846–54. To the left and right are the pavilions, communicating on the ground-floor by a portico and above by a terrace; in the background is the chapel.

382   New Royal Infirmary, Edinburgh, Scotland: main façade; David Bryce, 1870-9. A corridor connects the four pavilions with the main building. After *The Builder*, 17 December 1870.

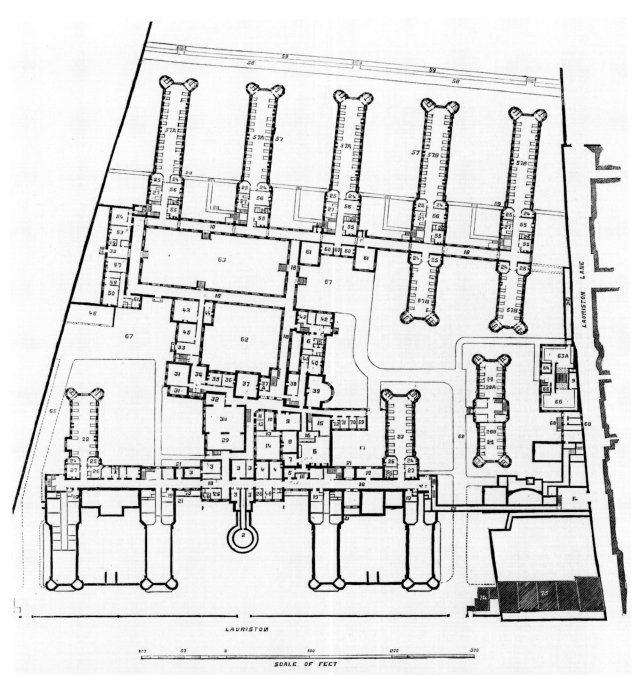

NEW ROYAL INFIRMARY, EDINBURGH.

Plan of Principal Ward Floor, Medical Hospital; and Basement Floor, Surgical Hospital.

REFERENCES.

1. Surgical Hospital.
2. Ice House.
3. Beer and Wine Cellars.
4. Porters' Rooms.
5. Housemaid's Closet.
6. Kitchen.
7. Cook's Store and Office.
8. Probationer Nurses' Dining Hall.
9. Servants' Hall.
10. Shoe Place.
11. Weighing Place.
12. Brushing Place.
13. Covered Passage.
14. Court.
15. Scullery.
16. Service Place.
17. Kitchen Court.
18. Corridor 12 ft. wide.
19. Coals.
20. Tunnel for conveying Dead Bodies from Surgical Hospital to Mortuary.
21. Space for Cross Ventilation.
22. Ward for Foul Discharges.
23. Erysipelas Ward.
24. Doctor.
25. Sisters, Nurses.
26. Bath.
27. Private Ward.

28. Fever Hospital :—
    A. Female Ward.
    B. Male Ward.
29. Nurses' Linen Store.
30. Patients' Linen Store.
31. Store Room.
32. Linen Store for Officers.
33. Entrance.
34. Hall.
35. Mending Room.
36. Work Room.
37. Matron's Office.
37a. Grocery.
38. Bread Store.
39. Nurses' Dining Room.
40. Matron's Dining Room.
41. Pantry.
42. Sick Students' Rooms.
43. Museum.
44. Curator's Room.
45. Preparing Room.
46. Covered Standing or Carriages.
47. Male Reception Room.
48. Lavatory.
49. Examination Room.
50. Female Reception Room.
51. Infectious Room.
52. Drive.

53. Out-door Patients' Waiting Room.
54. Dispensary.
55. Ward Kitchen.
56. Convalescent Room.
57. Medical Hospital :—
    A. Male Ward.
    B. Female Ward.
58. Walk.
59. Sloping Bank.
60. Wards. Special Cases.
61. Class Room.
62. Watson's Hospital Dress Ground.
62a. Underground Passage from Mortuary to Medical Hospital.
63. Garden or Dress Ground.
63a. Washing House.
64. Dirty Clothes.
65. Clean Linen.
66. Laundry House.
67. Gravel Space.
68. Upholsterer's Department.
69. Larder.
70. Milk Store.
71. Butter and Eggs.
72. Vegetables.
73. Area for Light.
74. Lodge.
75. Wharton-place.

383   New Royal Infirmary, Edinburgh, Scotland: plan; David Bryce, 1870–9. After *The Builder*, 17 December 1870.

384   New Royal Infirmary, Edinburgh, Scotland: rear view; David Bryce, 1870–9.

(1869), municipal hospital, Dresden (1870–6). Preference was often given to a design which was stricter from the hygienic point of view but more loosely knit architecturally, with pavilions spaced out in a park so as to be totally isolated. This plan was derived from the hutments of military hospitals, a layout evolved during the Crimean War and American Civil War. It was featured in the Friedrichshain Hospital, Berlin (1870–4), by Gropius and Schmieden, the Carola Hospital, Dresden (1876–8), the municipal hospital, Wiesbaden (1876–8), the general hospital, Hamburg (1884–9), and also in Kiel, Leipzig, Tübingen and elsewhere.

A more detailed history of nineteenth-century hospitals should also take note of two opposed phenomena:

— the relinquishment for financial reasons of official ideal standards (at the Hôtel-Dieu in Paris, for example, the density of beds was four times greater than it ought to have been);

— the methodical improvement of details in the basic design and the ever increasing stringency of the standards adopted.

The circulation of vitiated air, which was thought to be responsible for phenomena of contagion, attracted particular attention. In 1872 the engineer Casimir Tollet proposed an arched section for the wards, which would make for better evacuation of polluted air. This was a significant echo by a health engineer of the rationalist interpretation of Gothic architecture. At the Universal Exhibition of 1878 his system drew the attention of Austrian and English physicians. The

Tollet company built a dozen hospitals of this type in France: Hôpital Bichat (Paris), Saint-Denis, Le Havre, Epernay, Bourges, Le Mans, Montpellier (1884), and others at Broni to the south of Pavia in Italy (1893) and Madrid in Spain (1894). In Antwerp hospital (1878–80) the Belgian Baeckelmans tried out the system of covered circular pavilions which was used elsewhere together with one of rectangular pavilions. Discussion turned to the role of corridors, which seemed to be essential for the convenience of the staff but were said to promote the transmission of disease. The Free Hospital, Boston, took steps to remedy this. At the end of the century two major publications, Henry C. Burdette's *Hospitals and Asylums of the World* (London, 1891–3) and Casimir Tollet's *Les hôpitaux modernes au XIXe siècle* (Paris, 1894) took stock of the experience garnered. The spacing of beds, the isolation of wards, ventilation, heating installations, circulation of air, cost per patient, and mortality rates were studied systematically and compared to international criteria.

At the time when the pavilion system typical of the nineteenth century was entering upon its final form in Europe, it was beginning to be discarded in the United States. A better understanding of infection made lavish use of space pointless once passive hygiene had become outdated. It was again possible to regroup departments and wards, perhaps even in a more tightly knit form than before, because vertical traffic could now be handled by lifts large enough to transport a bed. New York Hospital, built in 1877 by George Brown Post, was the prototype of the new block de-

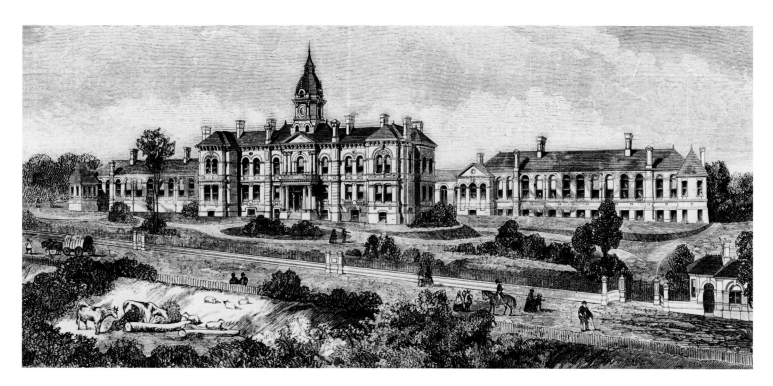

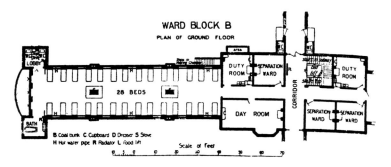

WARD BLOCK B

PLAN OF GROUND FLOOR

28 BEDS

LOBBY

BATH

DUTY ROOM

SEPARATION WARD

DUTY ROOM

DAY ROOM

CORRIDOR

SEPARATION WARD

SEPARATION WARD

B Coal bunk C Cupboard D Dresser S Stove
H Hot water pipe R Radiator L Food lift

Scale of Feet

386   St Saviour's Union Infirmary, Champion Hill, London;
Henry Jarvis & Son. Elizabethan picturesque style and clarity of
layout. After *The Builder*, 30 April 1887.

387   St Saviour's Union Infirmary, Champion Hill, London:
plan of a pavilion; Henry Jarvis & Son. After *The Builder*,
26 February 1887.

230

◁385 Hospital for Sick Children, Pendlebury, near Manchester; Pennington & Bridgen, 1872–8. This time the style is Italian but the layout is like that of the hospitals in Edinburgh and Paris. After *The Builder*, 26 October 1872.

sign for hospitals which was to dominate the twentieth century.

The appearance of specialized hospitals for surgery, maternity and convalescence resulted in all sorts of variant designs which exhibited the architect's resourcefulness in handling layout. An example is Barnes convalescent hospital, Cheadle near Manchester (1875), where the architect, Lawrence Booth, provided large public rooms and a monumental winter garden.

Designs for lunatic asylums naturally required still more specific study. As early as 1785 Colombier recommended a pleasant site, airy and shady. He classified patients into four categories – raving, quiet, imbecile and convalescent – and allocated them to four square blocks, built on one floor around a courtyard with galleries. In a report published in 1819, Jean Étienne Dominique Esquirol (1772–1840), who had inspected several Danish buildings, revived the question. With the aid of the architect Louis Hippolyte Lebas he defined the plan of an ideal asylum. Round a central axis occupied by common service departments and the administration two rows of blocks were arranged in a U-shape at a single level, allowing the patients to be classified. This design was implemented at the Saint-Yvon asylum near Rouen (1821–5) by Jouannin and Grégoire, at Marseilles (1838) by Penchaud and at Charenton (1838–45) by Gilbert, where, however, the principle of independent blocks was not rigorously observed. This overtheoretical ideal design, which reflects psychiatric nosography in the floor plan, was shared neither in England nor Germany. In 1851 Maximilien Parchappe, whose study *Des principes à suivre dans la fondation et la construction des salles d'asile* remained the authoritative work until the end of the century, stated that 'the subdivision of a lunatic asylum must not and cannot correspond to scientific classifications.' Very naturally, psychiatric hospitals were also interested in panoptic layouts (Glasgow asylum, 1810; Erlangen asylum, Germany, 1834–46), but they were generally used only for blocks for disturbed patients. Their plan

388 Hospital ward on the Tollet system; 1872. A, B, C: air intakes and vents for used air. After Tollet, 1894, Pl. 83 i.

389 Hospital, Antwerp: plan of a ward; Baeckelmans, 1878–80. After Tollet, 1894, Pl. 76.

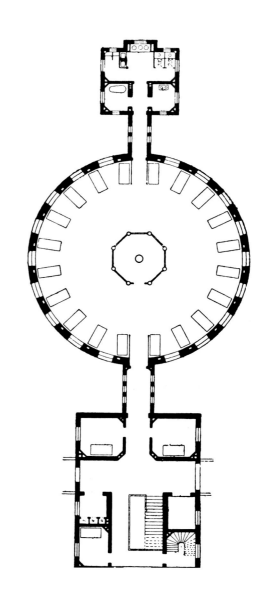

390 Johns Hopkins Hospital, Baltimore, Maryland; 1873–92. After *Encyclopédie de l'architecture et de la construction*, vol. IV, p. 428, Pl. 66.

stands out strongly in contrast to that of others where cells are arranged in a radial fashion round the nurses' central observation post, each extended by its own little garden, as in the Sainte-Anne Hospital in Paris (1861–7).

In France, Germany and England hospital architecture remained extremely sober during the first half of the nineteenth century. Government committees, like architects, with the approval of the journals, took pride in the fact. 'We are far from proposing a sumptuous monument, a model of architectural beauty, a masterpiece of art,' wrote the committee set up to examine the projects for Lariboisière Hospital. 'In-deed, we feel that the patients' interests have too often been sacrificed to purely exterior perfection. What we want is a model hospital designed in the interests of the patients and with a view to improving the services.' Gilbert's Charenton, with its sublime por-ticoed terracing culminating in a chapel designed as a Greek temple, remains an exception in Europe. How-ever, if practical considerations and problems of lay-out were dominant, hospital architecture felt the cur-rents and tensions of architectural culture as much as any other type of building. The Charenton hospital was matched by the small picturesque hospitals of the English countryside. The latter were in Tudor Gothic,

391 New York Hospital: main façade;
George Brown Post, 1877. After Tollet,
1894, Pl. 41.

392 New York Hospital: plan of
ground-floor and upper storey; George
Brown Post, 1877. After Tollet, 1894,
Pls. 42-3.

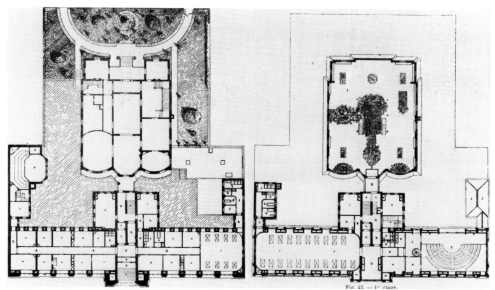

393 Hôpital Sainte-Anne, Paris;
Charles Auguste Questel, 1861–7. In the
centre of the esplanade are the administration, service and auxiliary buildings; to left and right, the men's and
women's quarters; on the periphery the
three blocks for disturbed patients with
their individual courtyards.

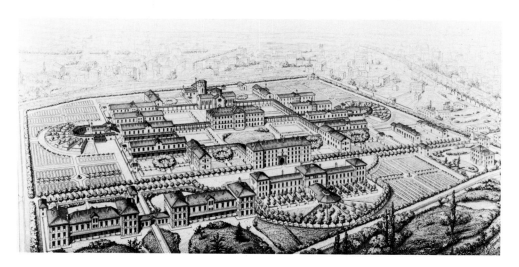

394, 395   Mental Hospital (Hôpital Esquirol), Charenton, Saint-Maurice, Val-de-Marne; Émile Jacques Gilbert, 1838–45. The porticoed courtyards centred on the chapel are terraced along the hill-side above the Marne.

396   École nationale professionnelle (now Lycée technique), Armentières, Nord: detail of design for façade; Chipiez, 1883–7. After *Revue générale de l'architecture*, 1886, Pl. 48.

397 Cottage Hospital, Savernake, Wiltshire, England: view and plan; Sir George Gilbert Scott. During the mid-century a picturesque style, half Gothic and half Old English, became accepted for small country hospitals. After *The Builder*, 8 March 1873.

Elizabethan or Italian style but this did not affect the quality of the layout. Casimir Tollet's indignation was misplaced when he wrote of the Royal Infirmary of Edinburgh that 'the most serious criticism one can level at it is the extravagance of its construction – its corner turrets are a luxury out of all keeping with their utility.' In point of fact these turrets contained toilets and urinals and their overhang allowed them to be isolated better from the wards – an amusing echo of the picturesque rationalism of Pugin and the Ecclesiologists.

After 1850 the French and Germans sought a style which was still economical but was also given an unobtrusive picturesque note by recourse to coloured or glazed bricks and ceramics (Asile Impérial, Vincennes, 1855–7, by Eugène Laval (1818–69), Friedrichshain Hospital, Berlin, 1870–4). This style with multicoloured bricks is also found in contemporary school architecture. The most striking expression is no doubt the École nationale professionnelle (1883–7) at Armentières in the north of France, by Charles Chipiez (1835–1901).

Temples of the Modern Era

'Railway termini and hotels are to the nineteenth century what monasteries and cathedrals were to the thirteenth century. They are truly the only representative buildings we possess.'
(*Building News*, 1875)

Shopping Arcades and Department Stores

The shop window for the display of goods, the arcade and the general store were invented between 1800 and 1830. They were followed by department stores in 1850–70. In the nineteenth century commerce became a public show, the shop a subject for architects, and the store a monument.

At the beginning of the nineteenth century most shops differed very little from those of medieval times. They usually still had a counter fronting on the street; or at best, following a style introduced during the seventeenth century, had a display window of small wooden-framed panes.

Between 1800 and 1830 the fall in the price of glass, a boom in the fashion trade, and the imagination of certain shopkeepers brought into being a new type of shop which was very similar to that of today. The contrast is evident from two descriptions by Balzac. In the *Maison du Chat-qui-pelote*, he writes, 'through the heavy bars of iron which protected the shop outside, one could just descry packets wrapped up in brown canvas, as numberless as herrings'. In *César Birotteau*, the 'Petit Matelot' is full of 'painted signs, coloured streamers, displays of shawls draped like swings, ties arranged like castles of cards, and a thousand other commercial inducements: fixed prices, bands, posters, illusions and optical tricks of such perfection that shop windows have become commercial poems'.

Architectural studies were devoted to the shop window, as may be seen from the number of books on the subject published in the 1830s both in London (Thomas King, *Shop Fronts*, 1830; Nathaniel Whittock, *On the Construction and Decoration of Shop Fronts of London*, 1840) and in Paris (Thiollet, *Serrurerie et fonte de fer récemment exécutées*, 4ᵉ cahier, *Boutiques et galeries vitrées*, 1832). Cast-iron pillars came into general use after the 1820s. These, along with copper rods and panes of glass that grew steadily in size as the glass industry developed, soon made it possible to replace the elegant but minutely partitioned shop windows of wood (Woburn Walk, London, 1822) by a wall of glass divided at regular intervals by the slenderest columns.

The first shops with display windows of cast iron and glass appeared simultaneously in London, Paris and New York at the end of the 1820s and rapidly grew in number during the following decades.

It is significant that in 1843 *La Revue générale de l'architecture* published an article with a plate showing how the whole weight of a façade could be borne by iron pillars so as to allow the installation of two shops. The shops in the Vero-Dodat covered arcade in Paris (1826), Asprey's in Old Bond Street in London (*c.* 1860) and Benson's in London (1866) still convey a good idea of this kind of front.

While these improvements were in progress, efforts were being made to build co-ordinated rows of shops. In 1784 Philippe d'Orléans, Duke of Chartres, had already had timber arcades constructed between the courtyard and the garden of the Palais Royal. Modest though their architectural design may have been, they played a part in the life of Paris which we today find difficult to conceive. There were three rows of stalls, bookshops and fashion shops, which formed two arcades covered by a timber frame. Two

398 Shop in the Galerie Vero-Dodat, Paris 1, 1826 (present state).

399 Galerie Vero-Dodat, Paris 1, 1826 (present state). Built in 1826 for the butchers Vero and Dodat, it is 4.5 metres wide and 80 metres long, and connects the rue du Bouloi to the rue Jean-Jacques Rousseau. The twin pillars which project slightly form a discreet demarcation between the different shops. Note the regular alternation of painted ceilings and areas through which light can penetrate, and also the classical friezes decorated with palmettes.

400 Burlington Arcade, London; Samuel Ware, 1818–19.

fruitful ideas were born here: Parisians discovered the pleasure of a covered walk with shop window displays on either side; shopkeepers saw the advantage of having a concentration of shops which brought together crowds and created an atmosphere that was good for business.

As early as 1770 a glazed roof with a metal frame had been used to cover the avenues lined with shops of the Foire Saint-Germain. The toplighting produced such a complete change in the appearance of these spaces that it could be said that a new form of architecture was born: the modern passage or arcade. This type of structure became extremely popular all over the world, assuming monumental proportions between 1825 and 1840. By the end of the century it had undergone a variety of developments and extensions.

The late eighteenth-century idea that led to the reshaping of the Grand Gallery of the Louvre as a museum, which was to be treated as a modern crypto-porticus covered by a glazed barrel-vault, punctuated at intervals by arcades and columns, undoubtedly played a crucial part in the creation of this type. The poetic and functional qualities of this toplighting caused it to be used for traditional-type shopping alleys through blocks of buildings (Passage du Caire, 1799; Passage des Panoramas, 1800) in Paris and also for the peripheral galleries of theatres (Royal Opera arcade, London, 1816).

401 Passage Pommeraye, Nantes, Loire-Atlantique; Hippolyte Durand-Gosselin, 1840–3. Sixteen columns are topped by allegorical statues (Agriculture, Industry, Fine Arts, Navigation, etc.). The passage with a gallery links two roads; the difference in height is 9.4 metres.

402 Galerie Saint-Hubert, Brussels; Jean Pierre Cluysenaar, 1846–7. This arcade is notable for its Italian style; the two upper storeys point the way for subsequent developments.

The care which architects bestowed upon such galleries soon became more lavish. (In Paris at this time the term *galerie* replaced *passage*.) Examples of this include Burlington Arcade, London, 1818–19, by Samuel Ware; Galerie Vivienne, 1825, and Galerie Vero-Dodat, 1826, in Paris. According to Thiollet in 1832, the latter 'takes pride of place for the richness and unity of its decoration'; the public admired 'the fine effect produced by the double row of uniform shops with transparent glass fronts joined by strips of burnished yellow copper in imitation of gold, with their doors, likewise of glass, surmounted with a splendid arrangement of gilded rosettes and palm-leaf mouldings', 'the picturesque and brilliant effect created by the gas-lighting globes placed between the capitals of the two coupled pilasters dividing one shop from the next with reflecting glass in the space

in between', 'the chequered marble floor' and the ceilings 'painted with landscapes and other subjects'.

One can readily imagine the success enjoyed by these paved and covered spaces, light-filled by day and illuminated in the evening by gas lamps, which appeared in the Passage des Panoramas in 1817 (the iron roof structures reduced the risk of fire), with on either side attractive shop windows co-ordinated and glazed. Patterned round rotundas (Galerie Vivienne, Paris) or arranged on several levels (Passage Pommeraye, Nantes, 1840–3, by Hippolyte Durand-Gosselin) displayed an enormous variety of detail. Lighting effects played no small part: simple glazed saddle roof (Passage de l'Opéra, Paris, 1822); glazed barrel-vault (Galerie d'Orléans, Paris, 1829); a structure enlarged to admit a small central saddle roof (Galerie Saint-Hubert, Brussels, 1846–7, by Jean

Pierre Cluysenaar) or punctuated instead by stone arches (Burlington Arcade, London; Galerie Vivienne, Paris; Lower Arcade, Bristol, 1824–5) and later by slender metal arches richly decorated (Galleria Mazzini, Genoa, 1875; Thornston's Arcade, 1878, and County Arcade, Leeds, 1898).

At the end of the 1820s galleries had begun to increase in size. This change of scale was noticeable in the Galerie d'Orléans, which replaced the eighteenth-century timber arcades at the Palais Royal. A large barrel-vault of glazed ironwork, double the span of all previous arcades, gave unity to the entire space. The model was then extended vertically with the addition of first one and later two storeys: Sillem's Bazaar, Hamburg, 1845; Galerie Saint-Hubert, Brussels, 1847; Kaisergalerie, Berlin, 1871–3, etc. These arcades really became covered streets. In 1855 William Moseley and Paxton had the notion of creating in London a 'Crystal Way', accommodating an underground train and a covered arcade more than 30 metres in height. In 1866 Hector Horeau even suggested covering the Parisian boulevards! In Italy the confidence inspired by the newly unified kingdom and also, no doubt, a traditional taste for urban life were conducive to developments of this kind. The Vittorio Emanuele Arcade in Milan was built in 1865–75 by Giuseppe Mengoni (1829–77). Its creation was associated with a redesigning of the square in front of the cathedral. It took the form of a veritable covered boulevard, arranged in a cruciform pattern round a central dome. Its grandiose scale was still further inflated in the Umberto I Arcade, Naples (1887–90), built by E. Rocco.

France remained aloof from this movement. Under the July monarchy the last Parisian projects of this kind to be carried out, as their names intimate (Passages Jouffroy, Verdeau and de la Madeleine in 1845), like the Passage des Princes in 1860 and the London Royal Arcade in 1879, reveal an architectural quality which is definitely inferior to that of contemporary arcades in Belgium and Germany.

This loss of popularity was perhaps due to the new and carefully laid-out boulevards; it was above all caused by the early development in France of the big department store. This sprang from the success of the fancy goods store combined with a particular type of arcade, known by the oriental term bazaar.

In function and typology they were, of course, very similar to *galeries*. The terms *passage* and *galerie* emphasize the communicative function, whereas *bazar* stresses the commercial function. Since these two functions always co-existed, contemporaries inevitably confused them.

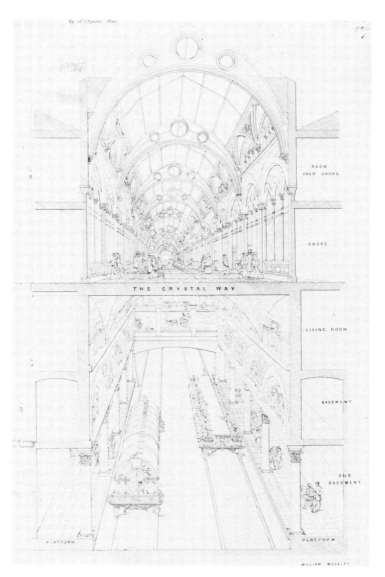

403 'Crystal Way' with a railway below: design; William Moseley, 1855.

We shall use the term 'bazaar' for that particular form of gallery where shops are not lined up along a thoroughfare but are organized on several floors around an open courtyard. The relationship between certain 'shopping courts', such as the Cour Batave in Paris, and these covered bazaars may have resembled that between the open passages of the eighteenth century and the passages and galleries of the nineteenth.

In the years from 1820 these bazaars grew in number both in London and in Paris. In 1816 the Soho Bazaar in Regent Street was the first of some fifteen similar projects in London which ranged from the Queen's Bazaar (1820–5) to the Pantheon (1835), both in Oxford Street. In Paris, following the Grand Bazar opened in 1825, which does not seem to have been a commercial success, we have the Bazar de l'Industrie (1827–30) by Paul Lelong, Boulevard

241

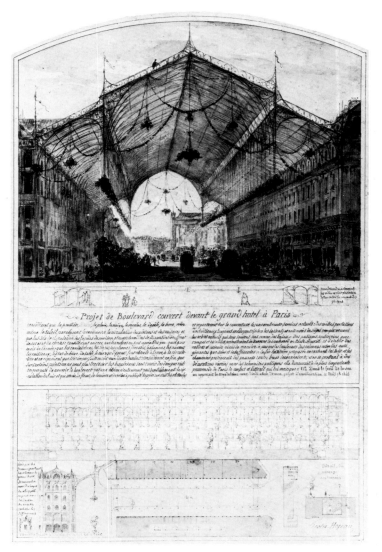

Projet de Boulevard couvert devant le grand hotel à Paris

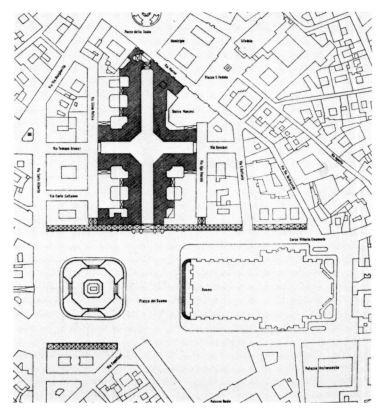

404 Roofed boulevard: design; Hector Horeau, 1866.

405 Galleria Vittorio Emanuele, Milan: general view; Giuseppe Mengoni, 1865–75. The arcade, which is nearly 200 metres long, connects the Piazza del Duomo and the Piazza della Scala, which were rebuilt on this occasion.

406 Piazza del Duomo with Galleria Vittorio Emanuele, Milan. After Geist, 1969.

407 Galleria Vittorio Emanuele, Milan: section through central octagonal dome; Giuseppe Mengoni, 1865–75.

408 Kaisergalerie, Berlin; Kyllmann & Heyden, 1871–3 (destroyed). The use of brick is part of the Berlin tradition.

409 Galleria Umberto I, Naples: entrance next to the Teatro San Carlo; Emanuele Rocco, 1887–90. The soberly neo-classical style is in contrast to the polychrome marble, rich stucco work and graceful wrought-iron work.

410 Galleria Umberto I, Naples; Emanuele Rocco, designed 1855, built 1887–90, opened 1892. Even more than the Galleria Principe d'Italia (1876–83), this second Neapolitan gallery is modelled on its Milanese predecessor; it is more than 10 metres higher.

411 Department store, Zurich: design; Heinrich Ernst, 1890. This project was never executed.

412 GUM Stores (state stores), Moscow; Alexander Nikanorovich Pomerantsev, 1888–93. The building is neither a gallery in the true sense nor a real department store but rather a modern version of the oriental bazaar with small shops fronting on covered streets.

413 Comparative sections of nineteenth-century galleries and passages (after Geist, *Passagen*): 1 Passage des Panoramas, Paris, 1800; 2 Burlington Arcade, London, 1818–19; 3 Galerie Vivienne, Paris, 1825; 4 Galerie d'Orléans, Paris, 1829; 5 Sillems Basar, Hamburg, 1845; 6 Galerie Saint-Hubert, Brussels, 1846–7; 7 Galleria Vittorio Emanuele, Milan, 1867; 8 Kaisergalerie, Berlin, 1871–3; 9 Cleveland Arcade, Cleveland, 1890; 10 Galleria Umberto I, Naples, 1887–90.

414 County Arcade, Leeds, Yorkshire, ▷ England; Frank Matcham (?), 1898–1900 (state in 1904).

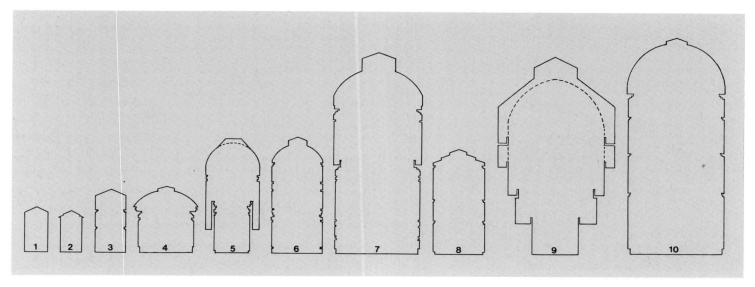

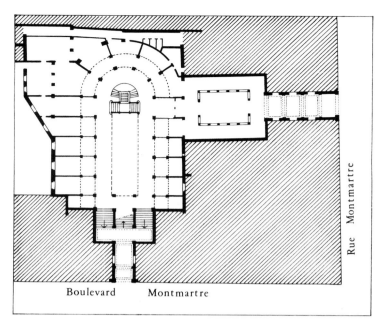

415 Bazar de l'Industrie Française, boulevard Montmartre, Paris: section; Paul Lelong, 1827–30 (destroyed). After Louis Marie Normand, *Paris Moderne*, Paris, 1834–57, vol. II, Pl. 139.

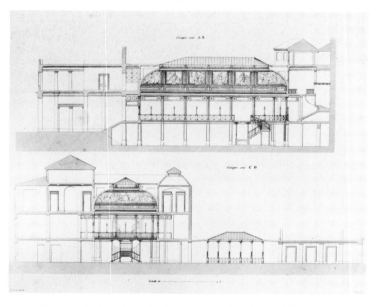

416 Bazar de l'Industrie Française, boulevard Montmartre, Paris: plan. After Louis Marie Normand, *Paris Moderne*, 1834–57, vol. II, Pl. 140.

Poissonnière, la Galerie de Fer or Bazar Bouffers, Boulevard des Italiens (1829), the Bazar Montesquieu or Bazar de Fer (1830), and the Galeries du Commerce et de l'Industrie (1838). Although we are best informed on the bazaars in London and Paris, similar emporia must have been established elsewhere.

These covered shopping 'courts' also grew in size in the second half of the century. Examples are Barton Arcade, Manchester (1871), Cleveland Arcade, Ohio (1890). The commercial complex in Moscow (now

GUM), built in 1888–93 by Alexander Nikanorovich Pomerantsev, combines several galleries like an oriental bazaar. Access is given by balconies and gangways, as in French bazaars, but on a scale that recalls the arcades of Italy.

These bazaars, which were a combination of a number of shops, were similar in function to the arcades of our shopping centres, but their architectural design already foreshadowed that of the big department stores. A comparison between the plans for the Bazar de l'Industrie of 1827, the first multi-level shopping area with toplighting, and those of Bon Marché or Printemps will make the kinship plain. There is a monumental entrance from the street and a courtyard or large central hall covered by a large glass roof, surrounded by galleries carried on slim pillars of cast-iron on one or two floors; access is by way of a monumental staircase opposite the entrance.

In the 1820s such shops were patronized by local clients, but with the development of urban transport and then of railways, together with new business techniques such as fixed prices, catalogues and publicity, they were able to attract a larger clientèle drawn from the whole of Paris and then also from the provinces. Shop-owners with a very original turn of mind had an opportunity to do a fantastic amount of business. Boutiques on the ground floor soon spread to the mezzanine, and then to the upper floors, at first by a process of trial and error; cast-iron columns made façades and dividing walls disappear. 'The fancy goods store "Aux Statues de Saint-Jacques" has just added to its shop a huge gallery in which the lighting and amenities leave nothing to be desired,' we read in one advertisement. The big modern department store made its appearance at a time when large fancy goods shops, then undergoing a process of wholesale reorganization and restructuring, were able to make the typical bazaar pattern their special perquisite by increasing the number of counters and the amount of goods on offer.

These modern stores came into being more or less at the same time but independently. In New York Haughwout and Co. appeared in 1857, and Steward & Steward in 1859. In Cincinnati, Ohio, the second John Shillito store, with a glass-covered inner court, was built in 1878. In Paris the first store to organize its counters on three floors round a large glass-roofed hall, 'Au Coin de Rue', was opened in 1864. It was followed by 'La Belle Jardinière' in 1866–7 and 'A la Ville Saint-Denis' in 1869. The 'Bon Marché', the most famous, was in fact the last of this first generation of large stores. The new premises, built by Boileau, were begun in 1869 and opened in 1872.

417 'Au Bon Marché' stores, rue de Sèvres, Paris 7: staircase; Louis Charles Boileau, 1872–4 (former state). A plan and section of this staircase were published in the *Encyclopédie de l'architecture et des travaux publics*, 1876.

418 Roosevelt Stores (afterwards James Wilde Jr & Co), Broadway, between Grand and Broome Streets, New York. In this building the cast-iron framework allows generously dimensioned windows to be used for commercial purposes.

In 1873 and 1876 several architectural journals published plans of the 'Belle Jardinière' and 'Au Bon Marché', thus helping to fix this typology, which attained its full flowering in the 'Grands Magasins du Printemps'. Established in 1865 and reconstructed in 1874, this store burned down in 1881. The new store, which was run up quickly in 1881–3 by Paul Sédille, gave ultimate expression to the formula. The premises occupied a complete block and were devoted to selling; gas lighting was replaced by electricity.

'Le Printemps' served as a model for all subsequent projects in Paris ('Magasins Dufayel', with a more broadly-based clientèle, Boulevard Barbès, 1890; 'Nouvelles Galeries de la Ménagère', 1898) as well as in the provinces ('Nouvelles Galeries de Bordeaux', 1893). After 1890 similar stores made their appearance all over Europe. By way of example we may quote: in Copenhagen, Kongens Nytorv, the 'Magasin du Nord', by Albert Christian Jensen

(1847–1913) and Henri Glaesel, 1893; in Rome, on the Corso, the 'Magazzini Boccioni' (today 'La Rinascente') by Giulio de Angelis, *c.* 1895; in Berlin, in the Leipziger Strasse, the 'Tietz stores', by Sehring and Lachman, 1898; in Zurich in the same year, 'Jelmoli', by Stadler and Usteri; in Brussels, 'Old England', by Paul Saintenoy, 1899, and 'L'Innovation', by Victor Horta, in 1900–1. In England events moved more slowly. The first of the big stores in the continental manner, Selfridge's, was not begun until 1908.

All of them took the Printemps design as their basis: a steel framework, light and transparent enough to enable the counters to be detached while at the same time minimizing the fire risk; a central space, consisting of a glass-roofed hall and forming a large well of light, quite indispensable at a time when artificial lighting was an avant-garde luxury. The *Lichthof*, as it was called in Germany, was co-ordinated with a monumental staircase.

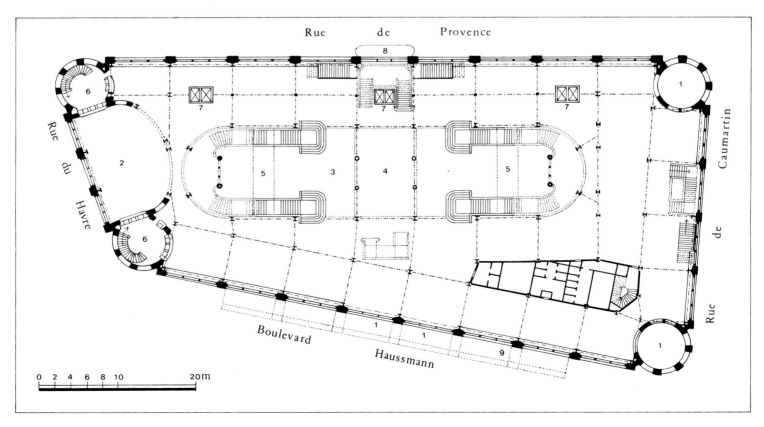

The first lifts came into use in 'A la Ville Saint-Denis' in 1869, but the staircase nevertheless remained the indispensable showpiece of every store: a bravura masterpiece which flaunted its ironwork curlicues at the end of a large glass-roofed hall opposite the entrance. Cast-iron pillars and steel frames were accepted because they were fireproof and light. Cast iron enabled the display windows and the sales areas to be uninterrupted by supporting structures. It created fluid and transparent spaces in which the principal decoration was the goods displayed for the women shoppers to feast their eyes on.

In the design of the fronts, even though the big all-glass windows went on increasing in size, there were two somewhat contrary tendencies. Some shops left the steel structure visible and glass took possession of the whole front. Others treated the store as a palace: an imposing façade was constructed over the framework and majestic columns and pediments crowned the ground-floor windows.

In Paris the big department stores were modelled on the great apartment blocks favoured by Haussmann. Like them, they went back to the grand classical style. The ground-floor and the mezzanine formed a base for a fine array of pilasters extending up two floors, between which the wall disappeared completely to make way for large steel-framed windows.

Façades of moulded cast iron as used in New York conduced to the more regularly and simply organized designs in which superimposed orders of columns were uniformly repeated. But Richardson, at the 'Marshall Field Wholesale Store' in Chicago (1885–7), designed a façade entirely in stone, making for a monumental sobriety.

In Europe stone-faced façades are also found in the Northern Stores in Copenhagen. The massive structure is punctuated by domed pavilions embodying a resurgent late classicism. Elsewhere stores were built entirely of iron and glass combined in a diversity of patterns. In Berlin the 'Tietz stores', where all the metal pillars were set back, have a huge surface of glass 26 metres long and 17 metres high. There are three entrances in stonework, sculptured with caryatids and atlantes, the genii of commerce. In Zurich the 'Jelmoli' façade is entirely in steel but partitioned, like the contemporary 'Schlesinger & Mayer' store (now 'Carson, Pirie & Scott') in Chicago (1899–1904) by Louis Henry Sullivan (1856–1924). In Brussels Horta wove flamboyant Art Nouveau wrought-iron work to create a counterpoint to a huge smooth wall of glass.

The great department store of the nineteenth century is to be found, we need hardly say, in Émile Zola's *Au Bonheur des Dames* (1888). With the archi-

419 'Les grands magasins du Printemps', boulevard Haussmann, Paris 9; Paul Sédille, 1882–9 (former state before the building was heightened). Note the way the walls have been dissolved between the pilasters, the picturesque belvederes and the quality of the details (ironwork, mosaics, imbricated roof).

420 'Les grands magasins du Printemps', boulevard Haussmann, Paris 9: the central hall (no longer extant); Paul Sédille, 1882–9. The coloured glass of the dome, the wrought iron of the balustrades, and the cut-outs in the riveted girders mitigate the severity of the exposed structure.

421 'Les grands magasins du Printemps', boulevard Haussmann, Paris 9: ground-floor plan; Paul Sédille, 1882–9. 1 entrances; 2 main vestibule; 3 central court; 4 connecting passage at mezzanine level; 5 ditto at first-floor level; 6 main cash desks; 7 lifts; 8 goods entrance; 9 large glass roof. After *Encyclopédie d'architecture*, 1885.

422 'Jelmoli' department store, Zurich; Hermann August Stadler and Jakob Emil Usteri, 1898 (state in May 1903). Apart from the Art Nouveau vocabulary, which is lacking, the design foreshadows that of Frantz Jourdain's 'La Samaritaine' in Paris (1905–7).

423 'Hermann Tietz' department stores, Leipzigerstrasse, Berlin; Sehring & Lachmann, 1898. All supports, all pillars, are removed from the façade and placed in the interior. One only notices the glazed surfaces (26 metres long and 17 metres high).

424, 425, 426 'Schlesinger & Mayer' stores (now 'Carson, Pirie, Scott & Co'), Chicago; Louis H. Sullivan, 1899–1904.

tect Frantz Jourdain (1847–1935), who was to rebuild the 'Samaritaine' in 1905, as his adviser, he was able to conjure up an all-round picture: it takes due note of the effect of the 'cut-off corner', the 'mirrors', the 'somewhat vulgar' décor 'of two allegorical figures, two bare-bosomed women leaning back and unfurling the shop sign "Au Bonheur des Dames"': 'the air and light entered freely, the public walked round at its ease below the bold span of long girders; it was the cathedral of modern commerce, solid and light, made for a nation of women customers.'

Railway Stations: the Modern Cathedrals

No doubt there will come a day when railway stations will be among the most important buildings; for them architecture will be called upon to mobilize all its resources and the construction will have to be monumental. These stations will then be put on a par with those huge and magnificent monuments in which public baths were housed by the Romans.

These lines were written by César Daly in 1846, at a time when, after the first pioneering efforts of the English (1830–45), French engineers took the initiative (1845–60). It was they who thought out in detail how these new buildings should be planned and what architectural expression would be appropriate to them. Daly describes the trend of the century, as it were, and, in prophetic tones, foreshadows later developments in Germany and America, where railway stations did indeed become the modern equivalent of the thermal baths of antiquity (Pennsylvania Station, New York, 1906–10).

Thirty years elapsed between the first locomotive experiments – Richard Trevithick's steam carriage (1801) – and the inauguration of the first modern railway lines between Liverpool and Manchester (1830) and Baltimore and Ohio (1831). In the following decade the first experimental lines, modelled on those in England, were opened in all European countries: Lyons-Saint-Étienne, 1832; Brussels-Malines, 1835; Nuremberg-Fürth, 1835; Vienna-Brünn, 1837 and so on. Within twenty years the first modest experiments had become a worldwide industrial phenomenon.

From then to the end of the century the construction of the thousands of bridges, viaducts and tunnels needed as the network expanded provided an incentive for feverish experiments in the art of engineering which had repercussions on every kind of construction. Of all railway installations, stations were the only ones that gave scope for proper architectural expression. Although they accounted for only a small part of the money invested by the companies concerned, the latter soon wanted to make them a symbol of their success. The Birmingham-London line, which cost more than £5.5 million to build, arrived triumphantly in London under Euston Arch, built in 1835–9 by Philip Hardwick (1792–1870) for £35,000, which stood like a true propylaeum of travel.

In 1830 Crown Street Station, Liverpool, the first railway station in the modern sense of the term, together with that of Liverpool Road in Manchester, was a simple rectangular building with a ticket office and a waiting room on the ground-floor and station-master's quarters upstairs, installed along the tracks which were covered at the same height as the station building by a wooden roof. This elementary original arrangement was the most common during the first decade and was adopted everywhere: at Malines in 1835; at St Petersburg in 1837; at Potsdam in 1838; and for the Nordbahnhof in Vienna in 1839. In 1840, in an article 'Sur la Disposition et le Service des Gares', undoubtedly the first of its kind (*Revue générale de l'architecture*, vol. I, col. 523), it is still described as 'the best' by Camille Polonceau and Victor Bois. Until the end of the century it remained the most natural solution for intermediate and through stations but it ceased to be used for termini and railheads. Newcastle, by John Dobson (1787–1865), was the last big station of this type (1846–55).

As the travelling public expanded and the number of tracks increased, more sophisticated designs had to be evolved. In 1837 three new arrangements were tried out at the same time: at Reading Brunel strung out the arrival and departure buildings on one side only, a design repeated by Francis Thomson at Derby (1839–41) and Chester (1847–8); in the London station of Nine Elms, Tite grouped the services in an arrangement enclosing the lines at the head, a layout copied at Brighton in 1840; and at Euston Robert Stephenson arranged departure and arrival tracks on both sides.

This latter layout suited English practice perfectly: there was no baggage control and passengers had free access to the platforms. The monumental propylaeum, designed by Philip Hardwick, gave access to the departure concourse intended to serve the termini, while a small courtyard at the head of the tracks enabled carriages to be loaded direct on to waggons (freight cars) by a method which recalls modern car-ferry trains. Under the protection of porticoes the passengers had free access to the platforms and, on their return, could transfer directly from the railway

427 Crown Street Station, Liverpool; George Stephenson (?), 1829–30 (demolished). The first modern station, prototype of the through station, in its original state.

coaches to the cabs awaiting them in the arrival courtyard. The noteworthy clarity of this design made it a certain success. It was imitated with only minor modifications in all the big London stations: King's Cross (1851–2), Paddington II (1852–4), Cannon Street (1854), Charing Cross (1854) and St Pancras (1863–5).

The English designs were carefully scrutinized by continental engineers but for technical and aesthetic reasons their stations developed on rather different lines. The practice of keeping passengers in different classes of waiting room until the time of departure and the systematic examination of baggage by *octroi* (city toll) officials demanded a much more complex arrangement.

At first Frenchmen and Germans were attracted by a more architectural design, with the services organized at the head of the tracks round a large entrance hall with waiting rooms. This layout was adopted by Eduard Pötsch (1803–89) at the Thüringer Bahnhof, Leipzig (1840–4), by Friedrich Bürklein (1813–72) in Munich (1849) and by François Léonce Reynaud (1803–80) in the first Gare du Nord, Paris (1845–6).

But the bilateral arrangements used in Paris for the Gare de Montparnasse (1848–52) and the Gare d'Orléans-Austerlitz finally struck Pierre Chabat about 1860 as 'the best layout for a station'. They were adopted fairly generally throughout Europe: for example in France (Gare de Lyon-Perrache, 1855, by François Alexis Cendrier, 1803–92; Gare de Metz).

Whereas the bilateral system might have become the stock design in medium-sized stations like Metz or Lyons, larger stations, where there had been a considerable expansion of services, required intermediate solutions. In 1847 François Duquesney borrowed the layout of the Gare du Nord I for the Gare de l'Est, expanding it with broad lateral developments. In 1861–5 Hittorff adopted the bilateral layout for the Gare du Nord II but arranged the suburban services at the head. The growth of traffic continually outstripped forecasts and explains the construction of

427a Paddington Station, London; Isambard Kingdom Brunel and Matthew Digby Wyatt, 1852–4. The train shed, 238 feet wide, is covered by three arched roofs; the central nave is wider than the others, the space being unified by two transepts. Every third iron rib rests on a metal column and the intermediate ones on longitudinal girders. Wyatt designed the decorative treatment of the ironwork and notably the iron arabesques in the glazed arches.

428 Euston Station, London: entrance portico; Philip Hardwick, 1835–9 (demolished 1961).

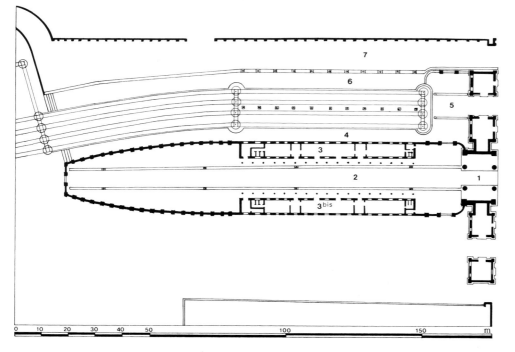

429 Euston Station, London: plan; designed Robert Stephenson, executed Philip Hardwick, 1835–9 (original state): 1 entrance portico; 2 departure courtyard; 3 booking-office and 1st- and 2nd-class waiting rooms; 3bis departure building intended for the Great Western Railway (Bristol-London), which preferred to have its own station at Paddington; 4 departure platform; 5 driveway for private carriages; 6 arrival platform; 7 arrival courtyard.

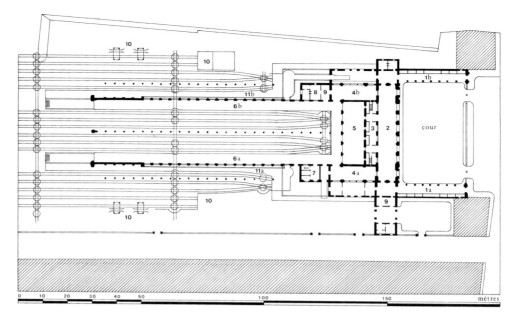

430 The First Gare du Nord in Paris: plan; François Léonce Reynaud, 1845–9 (demolished). 1a departures portico; 1b arrivals; 2 vestibule; 3 booking-office; 4a baggage departures; 4b baggage arrivals; 5 waiting room; 6a departure platform; 6b arrival platform; 7 saloon; 8 stationmaster's office; 9 toilets; 10 entrance for mail-coaches, etc.; 11a suburban departures; 11b suburban arrivals.

two or three successive stations on the same site. It also led to expansions and arrangements to the importance of which we would simply call attention here.

The misgivings of the French engineers, Auguste Perdonnet and Pierre Chabat, which led to the first systematic inquiry into typology, were also due in part to a clash between considerations of arrangement and aesthetics.

The lateral arrangement, which is very convenient for the passenger service and railway operation, is less satisfactory as an architectural expression. It does not mark out clearly enough the entrance to the railway and, for its main aspect, often presents merely the gable end of the main hall. The other system affords a more monumental façade and greater ease of access (*Revue générale de l'architecture*, 1859).

In England the bilateral layout was in fairly general use. The gable end of the arrival and departure hall was decorated with picturesque battlements and triumphal arcades (Temple Meads, Bristol, by Brunel, 1839–40), with a railway hotel backing up against it in pragmatic fashion. The development of this design, eminently suitable for large metropolitan stations, can be followed by comparing York Station (1840–1) and St Pancras (1868–74). This arrangement came late to France and was never widely adopted. Examples are Gare Saint-Lazare (1887), by Juste Lisch (1828–1910), where the hotel is located in front of the station and communicates with it, and Gare d'Orsay (1898–1900) by Victor Laloux (1850–1937).

Dissatisfied by the over-sublime style (Euston) or the over-picturesque (Austin, Connecticut), by pala-

431 Central Station, Munich; Friedrich Bürklein, 1849. The façade is an elegant variation in Pisan Romanesque on the composition of the Gare de l'Est, Paris.

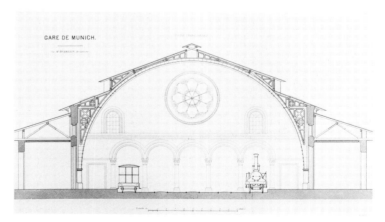

432 Central Station, Munich: cross-section; Friedrich Bürklein, 1849. Note the timber framework of the station hall.

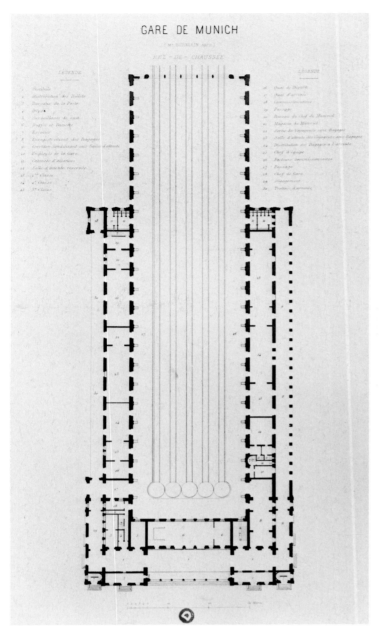

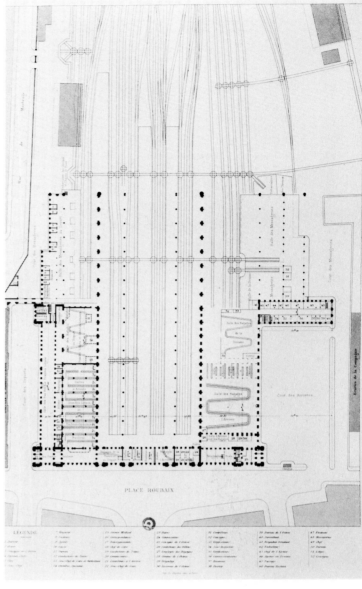

433 Central Station, Munich: plan; Friedrich Bürklein, 1849.

434 The Second Gare du Nord, Paris: plan; Jacques Ignace Hittorff, 1859–65 (original state).

tial or religious analogues (Leipzig and Munich), French engineers and architects set themselves to formulate an architecture appropriate to the functioning of a railway station.

In his *Traité élémentaire des chemins de fer*, 1856, Auguste Perdonnet tackled the problem of 'the architectural decoration of stations' in these terms:

The architecture of a monument must disclose its intended purpose. Railway stations, particularly termini, have their special architecture. Apart from the peristyle, the most typical feature of the main façade is a monumental clock, and, if this façade encloses the station, a large arch or a huge orna-

mental front accentuates the shape of the roof covering the arrival and departure hall.

Two examples in particular engage one's attention. In the Gare Montparnasse (1848–52) Victor Lenoir's façade is a clear and sober statement of the two arrival and departure bays which enclose the clock featured there. This design was echoed by Lewis Cubitt in his design for King's Cross (1851–2), but with a little more breadth for the clock-tower.

In the Gare de l'Est (1847–52) Duquesney endowed this design with more elegance. A neo-Florentine peristyle links two pavilions, and a large semi-rosette pierced in the gable end marks the arrival and depar-

435   The Second Gare du Nord, Paris: façade; Jacques Ignace Hittorff, 1861–5. A peculiarly felicitous adaptation of the classical vocabulary to a new type of building.

ture hall in the façade. This arrangement continued to be admired until the end of the century. It remained a permanent model for the whole of Europe, even though other architectural versions differed in their interpretation of details: a restrained classicism in the Gare du Nord, Paris, or in the East Station, Budapest, by Rochlitz (1881–4); Baroque and medieval eclecticism at Antwerp (1899) by Louis Delacenserie; Anhalter Station, Berlin (1872–80), by Franz Schwechten, the finest since the Gare de l'Est in Paris; Gare du Sud, Nice (1892) – a version of the Gare du Nord, Paris, on a reduced scale; Porta Nuova Station, Turin (1866), by Alessandro Mazzuchetti.

The boldness of the arrival and departure hall very soon acquired a symbolic value. 'When they are covered by roof frames combining vigour and elegance, very big stations, like those of the Gare du Nord or of the Gare de l'Est, assume an imposing character which is in harmony with the importance of the railways of which they form the head', wrote Perdonnet in 1846 (*Portefeuille de l'ingénieur des chemins de fer*, vol. I, pp. 500–86). The way in which these halls evolved between 1830 and 1880 can be seen very well from the successive reconstructions of Lime Street Station in Liverpool: the first station, built in 1836, was still open and covered by a wooden trussed roof; in Lime Street II, in 1851, Richard Turner spanned a distance of 46 metres with iron; and finally, between 1876 and 1896, the width of the vault was increased to 60 metres.

436 Former Station, Karlsruhe; Friedrich Eisenlohr, 1841–2. One of the first railway campaniles to be built.

437 Great Joint Station (London Bridge Station), Southwark, London; Henry Roberts, 1844. Since enlarged and altered. The model of the Italian *palazzo* has been adapted to the railway station.

438 Gare de l'Est, Paris; François Duquesney, 1847–52 (original state before being enlarged). By framing the passenger hall by two pavilions connected by a portico, Duquesney invented a formula which was to have a great future.

439 King's Cross Station, London; Lewis Cubitt, 1851–2. Queen Victoria is shown arriving for the train to the York races.

440 King's Cross Station, London: plan; Lewis Cubitt, 1851–2. 1 booking-office; 2 platform; 3 baggage; 4 cab drive.

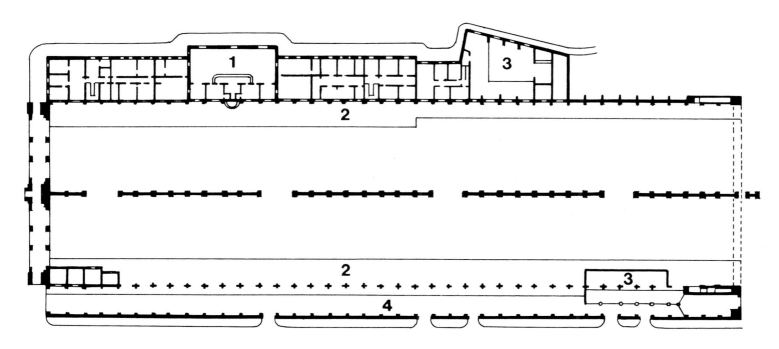

441 St Pancras Station, London: passenger hall; William Henry Barlow and Roland M. Ordish, 1863–5. The metal framework covered a single span of 210 metres for a length of 73 metres and a height of 30 metres, a world record until the construction of the Galerie des Machines in 1889.

It will be noted that cast iron, which in almost every case was used for the pillars from the outset, was often first combined with a timber framework. This system was still in use at the Central Station in Munich in 1849 and at King's Cross in 1851–2, where the train-shed roofs had originally been of a laminated structure, a technique perhaps inspired by the Czar's riding school in Moscow and used also by Paxton for the Crystal Palace. The present iron-ribbed roofs date back to 1869–70 in the eastern shed and to 1886–7 only in the western shed.

With its plain stock-brick screen of semicircular openings following the twin train sheds, King's Cross appears in retrospect to be the most surprisingly modern of the Victorian stations. In fact this rigidly astylar simplicity recalls the smooth surfaces of Sir John Soane's stables in Chelsea Royal Hospital (1814–17) and the primitivist and utilitarian aspects of Durand's projects.

On the Continent, in France particularly, the effect was completed by an allegorical or decorative sculptured décor. In the Gare de l'Est, Paris, the capitals of the peristyle are decorated with symbols of the agri-

cultural products grown along the route; the Seine and Rhine wind round the clock; and the pediment is crowned by a statue of the city of Strasbourg. This somewhat ingenuous railway iconography, which hardly took in its contemporaries (cf. P. Planat, 'Les Chemins de fer', *Revue générale de l'architecture*, 1873, pp. 209–10), nevertheless continued to enjoy an unbroken success for want of an alternative.

As the railway network continued to ramify and intermediate, medium and small stations grew in number, research was instituted to standardize and categorize types. In the early 1860s the types were finally 'fixed', as may be seen from the publication of Pierre Chabat, for whom 'the only problem that is not completely solved is that of properly utilizing local resources and deriving from their use an interesting and sound architectural expression.'

In large stations engineers were happy to use neo-Greek, neo-Renaissance and classical styles, but they deliberately opted for the picturesque in small country ones. Francis Thomson's stations on the North Midland Line or David Mocatta's on the Brighton line drew their inspiration from the architecture of

442 Midland Grand Hotel and St Pancras Station, London; Sir George Gilbert Scott, 1868–74. The hall is hidden by the hotel which was designed by Scott as a manifesto to show the ability of Gothic style to adapt itself to all requirements.

443 Station, Chathill, Northumberland, England; Benjamin Green. An example of how the model of the Gothic-Tudor villa could be adapted to the needs of a small provincial station.

444 Station, Stoke-on-Trent, Staffordshire, England; H. A. Hunt, 1850. The North Staffordshire Railway Company had its stations built in a uniform style but its architect, Hunt, knew how to bring out the contrast between medium-sized and small stations.

445 Station, Stone, Staffordshire, England; H. A. Hunt, 1848.

446 Station, Huelva, Spain; Font, 1880. 'If the town is Gothic, let the station be Gothic; if the town is Moorish, let the station be Moorish.'

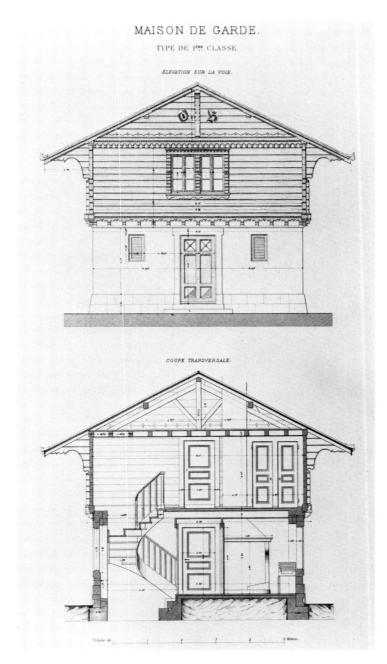

MAISON DE GARDE.

TYPE DE 1RE CLASSE.

ÉLÉVATION SUR LA VOIE.

COUPE TRANSVERSALE.

447   Signalman's box of Western Swiss Railway: elevation and section. After Chabat, vol. II, Pl. 38.

cottages in Gothic; those by H. A. Hunt in Staffordshire are in Jacobean style. Elsewhere the quaintness of vernacular buildings was the mode chosen. 'Along some lines, in picturesque valleys, they have borrowed the architecture of chalets', Perdonnet noted in regard to Etzel's Swiss stations. He was also an admirer of the small railway stations of Baden, which 'are simply elegant peasant houses, gracious chalets'.

In France it was common practice to seek symbolic analogies of style, as was recommended by Perdonnet. 'The architecture of intermediate stations located in large cities must be related to that of the principal buildings of the city. Thus at Nancy, an eminently monumental city, the architecture of the station is reminiscent of one of the fine creations of Stanislas.' Following this rule Vitré (1857) would be neo-medieval, reflecting the city it served, Montpellier neo-classical and Valençay neo-Renaissance.

Abroad French engineers were sometimes freer to develop this slightly naive symbolism with more poetical inventiveness. On the Seville-Huelva line an engineer named Font, working between 1870 and 1880, favoured for small and medium-sized through stations a 'Moorish' style reduced to the exaggerated horseshoe arch motif, which appears in a still more opulent version on the façade of the terminus of Huelva.

There were also small stations designed on quite rationalistic lines, like that of Caudos on the Bordeaux-Bayonne line, which Chabat recommends as a model. 'The external ornamentation looks for its elements solely to the expression of the standard design, to the form of construction and to such fixtures as the clock and the name-boards of the station.'

Even more than Auguste Perdonnet's *Nouveau Portefeuille* (1857–60), Pierre Chabat's publication of 1860, which is an account and summary of this experimentation, concludes this second phase in which French engineers played a leading role.

About 1870–5 there were striking new developments in different directions. When the volume of traffic increased and the arrival and departure of several trains took place at such close intervals that they could not be handled on the single external tracks, the bilateral arrangement showed its shortcomings; as tracks became increasingly interconnected, rail-head stations became an obstacle.

German architects then seized the initiative and rethought the typology of the station. They returned to frontal or unilateral layouts but created huge concourses, introduced multi-level arrangements, and increased the number of subways and footbridges over the tracks. The most striking examples are without doubt the stations at Frankfurt am Main, Hanover, Magdeburg and Strasbourg.

448   Anhalter Bahnhof, Berlin: façade; Franz Schwechten, designed 1871, executed 1872–80. Schwechten took over the composition with twin towers of the Thüringer Bahnhof from Eduard Pötsch, 1840–4, but proposed to show the exposed metal gable above his arcades. The polychrome brick reflects the heritage of Schinkel.

449   Anhalter Bahnhof, Berlin; Franz Schwechten, designed 1871, executed 1872–80. In quest of a more artistic solution, the architect finally decided to embody his metal gable in large arcades, thus reverting to a solution closer to that of the Gare de l'Est, Paris.

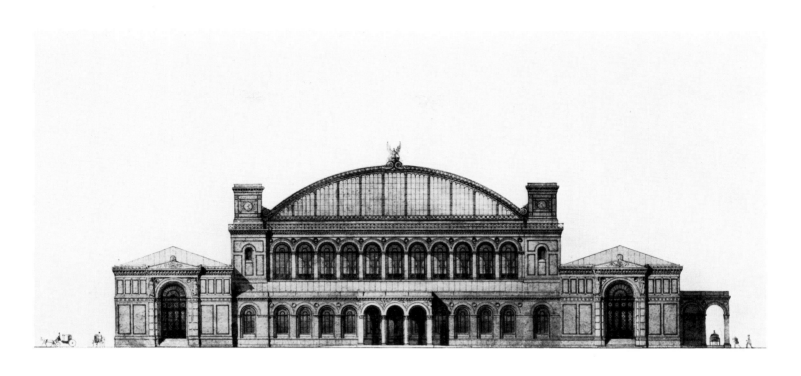

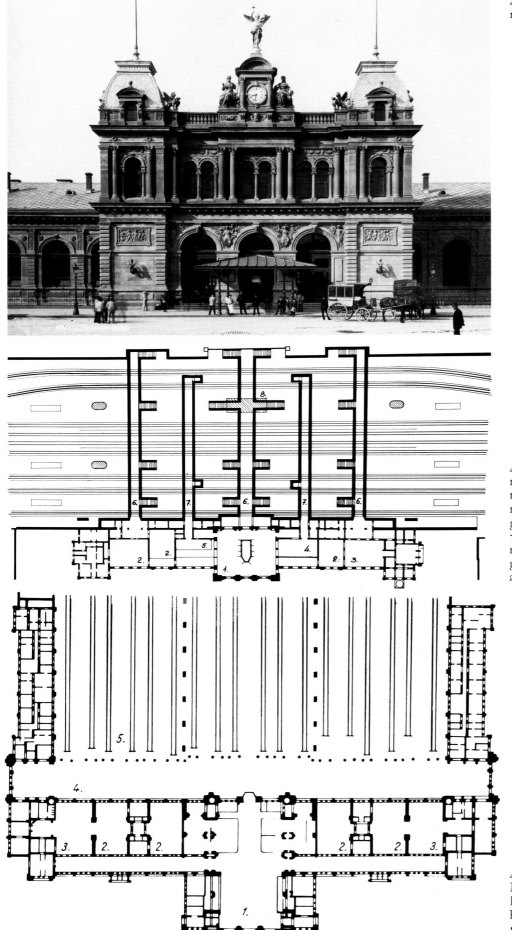

450 Central Station, Mainz, W. Germany; Philipp Berdellé, 1880–4.

451 Central Station, Hanover, W. Germany: plan; Hubert Stier, 1877–9. 1 entrance hall; 2 waiting rooms; 3 refreshment room; 4 baggage arrivals; 5 baggage departures; 6 tunnel for passengers; 7 tunnel for baggage transport; 8 refreshment room at platform level for passengers travelling in the direction of Berlin and Cologne.

452 Central Station, Frankfurt-am-Main, W. Germany: plan of arrival hall; Hermann Eggert, 1881–8. 1 entrance hall; 2 waiting rooms; 3 refreshment rooms; 4 cross platform; 5 platforms.

453 Central Station, Frankfurt-am-Main, W. Germany: principal façade; Hermann Eggert, 1881–8.

454 Central Station, Frankfurt-am-Main, W. Germany: elevation and view of the passenger hall; Hermann Eggert, 1881–8.

455 West Station, Budapest: Gustave Eiffel, 1874–7. Undoubtedly the first example of a monumental station in which the gable of the passenger hall is boldly exposed in the façade without a rose window or arcades.

456 East Station, Budapest; Gyula Rochlitz, 1881–4. Return to the formula of the Gare de l'Est. The monumental architecture expresses little despite its massiveness.

457 Station, Le Havre: façade; Juste Lisch, 1888. After Chabat, *La Brique et la terre cuite*, vol. II, Pl. 48.

458 First Termini Station, Rome; Salvatore Bianchi, 1874 (destroyed). Modelled on the Gare de l'Est in Paris, the contrast between the classic pavilions and the metal gable is stated with greater boldness. This design was reflected in that of Atocha Station in Madrid, 1888.

459 A terminus station: design, Jean Camille Formigé. Exhibited at the 1876 salon, Prix Duc. 'The two pavilions for departures and arrivals give balance to the overall design...; iron pillars picked out in bright colours divide up the large glazed gable' (Paul Sédille, 1876).

460 Central Station, Antwerp, Belgium: main façade; Louis Delacenserie, 1899.

Similar developments occurred in the United States, where entrance halls also assumed giant proportions: St Louis, 1891–6, by Theodore Link; Chicago, 1892–3, by Bradford Lee Gilbert. At the same time the balance achieved around 1850 between the classical tradition and those features peculiar to the railway station was upset in different ways. In some cases no attempt was made to characterize stations as such and in others their special character was emphasized to excess.

As entrance halls grew in number and circulation areas expanded in front of steel-built halls, bringing the classical type of station closer to the monumental, architects drew the logical conclusion. They began to treat stations like any other public building, ornamenting the façade with the same showy array of columns and pilasters of late classicism as were used for the fronts of ministries and law-courts. It was the natural consequence of the unexpected success of such designs that the station, whose architectural typology had sometimes been dominated by the picturesque, should become indeed, as César Daly had prophesied as long ago as 1846, the modern equivalent of the ancient thermal baths.

Taking the contrary line, certain French engineers made no bones about featuring the steel gable end of the station building plainly in the façade, without attempting to frame it elegantly in a rose window or a window befitting a spa. This was Eiffel's approach at Budapest (1874–6) and Salvatore Bianchi's in Rome (1874); but Franz Schwechten shrank from such a solution in Berlin.

A better way was to use iron stanchions picked out brightly in colour to subdivide the huge glazed gable end, together with glazed tiles or polychrome bricks, such as had appeared in 1857 on the side of the Gare de Perrache in Lyons. Combining with the iron and relieving its austerity, those bricks transformed the chilly functional gables into a brilliant display piece. Preferably with an arrival and a departure wing at either end for balance, they became the colourful centrepiece of the composition. A design of this kind, exhibited at the salon of 1876, is undoubtedly the prototype of a highly original series of provincial sta-tions (*Encyclopédie d'architecture*, 1876, p. 54, Pls. 267, 400).

French stations in this 'flamboyant steel style' fell victim to both the modernism and post-classicism of the 1920s. Almost all of them have now disappeared. Among them were the Gare du Nord, Amiens, 1878; Calais, Le Havre, 1888; Tourcoing, 1888; Roubaix, 1905 – the last of the series to be built and the only one to survive apart from Tourcoing.

Sheltered by its economic backwardness, Spain still has today the best examples in Europe: the Estación de Delicias (1878) in Madrid, by the French engineer E. Cachelièvre; Estación de Atocha (1888) by the Spaniard A. de Palacio; and the Estación de Abando (1900), Bilbao, by S. Achucarro.

As early as 1840 some architects had toyed with the motif of the clock tower, treating it either as a Chinese pagoda or, more often, as an Italian belvedere in keeping with the neo-Florentine style of the main buildings: London Bridge Station (1844), by Henry Turner.

After 1870, no doubt under the influence of the massive compact Romanesque Revival style made popular by Richardson, there appeared more monumental versions of this feature which, when located asymmetrically, gave balance to the low building of the station: at Park Square Station (1872), Boston, by Peabody and Stearns; Union Station (1875–7), Worcester, Mass., by Ware and van Brunt; Michigan Central Station (1882–3), Detroit and Dearborne Station (1883–5), by Eidlitz (1853–1921). After 1890 there were echoes of this American design in Europe.

When, at the end of the century, the American J. R. Coolidge stated that stations were the characteristic buildings of the age, he repeated a notion which had been current everywhere since 1846. He did not mention the contrasting layouts and the diversity of the architectural designs with which we have been concerned here.

The station was a building on which progressive architects had set great hopes for the renewal of their art, but it proved to be riddled with the same contradictions, the same divergences and to have hidden unity as the most conservative specifications.

Private Houses

'If there is any one thing in which English architects of the latter half of the nineteenth century excelled, it is in their domestic work.'
(J. M. Brydon, 'The Nineteenth Century', *Architectural Association Notes*, 1901)

From the end of the century onwards there was no doubt in the minds of English, German and French critics that one of the greatest, indeed 'the one great achievement of the nineteenth century', was the 'artistic regeneration of the home', a field in which English-speaking architects were uncontested leaders. Even though there were new and spectacular revivals of the castle and the aristocratic town mansion in the nineteenth century, a new type of dwelling – the private house – crystallized with the growth of a large middle class and there was also a marked development of the apartment block. These were new departures in architecture which, from the 1860s onwards, were to constitute its modernity for contemporaries.

Opulent blocks of flats lined new roads, which were laid out on a scale contrasting sharply with the traditional streets and made Paris, Vienna and Berlin the first modern capitals. Private houses set the scene in middle-class residential suburbs and seaside and winter resorts, the development of which was to leave its distinctive imprint on urban geography in the second half of the century.

The opening of omnibus services around the major European cities about 1820, followed by the development of suburban railways in the 1840s, gave an impetus to the development of suburbs where private houses, answering the needs of an increasingly prosperous middle class, rapidly mushroomed. Although the most felicitous designs were undoubtedly to be found in England, the phenomenon was an international one: Neuilly, Auteuil and Passy, Le Vésinet, Le Raincy, Enghien and Croissy around Paris; Richmond and Bedford Park to the south-west of London; the Tiergarten district round the Nollendorf-Platz and the Lichterfelde quarter in Berlin.

English cottages, Swiss and German chalets, Italian villas, French maisonettes and Indian bungalows – the very variety of the names used for this 'new class of private buildings' underlines the international dimension of the trend: it also suggests links with the picturesque architecture of the first half of the century and with academic architecture. Whether more classical in appearance in the residential areas of towns or more picturesque in resorts, whether a *cottage orné* or a 'small' country seat, the private house seemed to spring from a successful hybridization in which classical pleasure houses (summer-houses of Italian villas, small classical *maisons plates*, Rococo follies), picturesque buildings (rustic houses, cottages, chalets, retreats) and modern amenities were united.

It was from the picturesque buildings that the private house derived its irregular plan and silhouette and its predilection for structures in vernacular style (half-timbering, bonded brickwork, rough stonework), and from the classical country seat that it inherited the convenience and spaciousness of its layout; but as a result of cross-cutting and cross-fertilization certain elements from the vocabulary of classical architecture (Scandinavian Mannerist gables, rusticated stonework in Louis XIII style, Queen Anne

461 Avenue de l'Opéra with view of the Place de l'Opéra. An example of the boulevards characteristic of the 'Nouveau Paris'.

462 Wittenbergplatz with Tauentzienstrasse, Berlin. A new urban scale was attained here, as in Paris and Vienna.

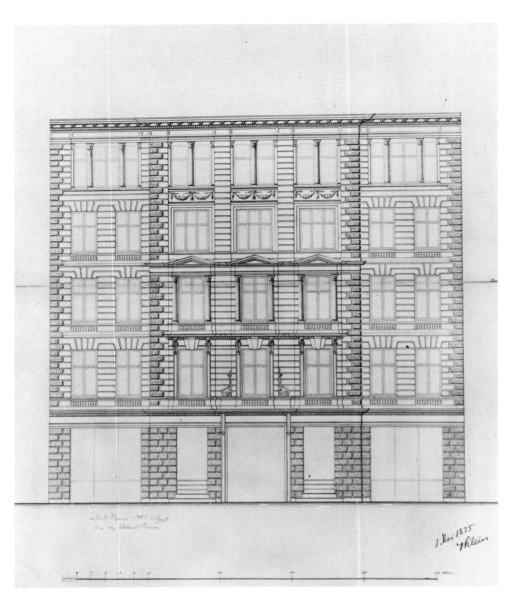

463 Apartment block on Store Kongensgade, Copenhagen: design; Vilhelm Klein, 1875. The persistence of the Italianate style is evident.

464 Leon House, Vienna: façade facing the Schottenring; Heinrich von Ferstel, 1870–3. The trend towards more marked sculptural effects, parallel to that observable in public buildings, is noticeable here.

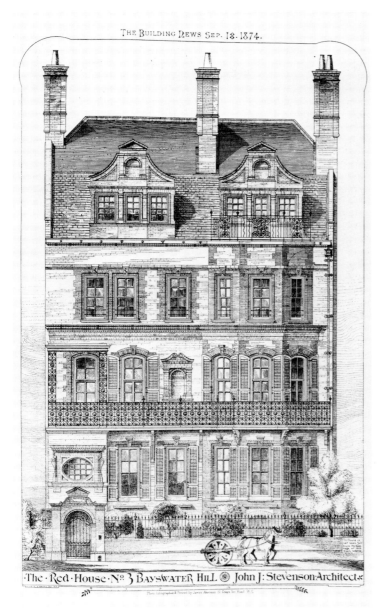

465 The Red House, 3 Bayswater Hill, London; John James Stevenson, 1871–3 (demolished). In this house, which stands in the line of traditional 'terrace' houses in London, Stevenson succeeded in showing the qualities of the 'free classic' style, also called Queen Anne, for urban apartment blocks. Like its French equivalent, Louis XIII style, it represents a compromise between classical and picturesque elements.

466 Apartment block in François I style, place Jussieu, Paris 5, about 1855.

467 Apartment block, place du Prince-Eugène (today place Léon-Blum), Paris 11; Brouilhony, about 1860. A fine example showing the resemblance to the Henri IV style.

468 Old Swan House, 17 Chelsea Embankment, London;
Richard Norman Shaw, 1875–7, for Wicklam Flower, a solicitor
close to the Morris circle. Here the symmetry is perfect but Shaw
seems to have sought an imaginative variety in the design of the
windows: large oriels, inspired by those of Sparrowe's House at
Ipswich, one of his leitmotifs, on the first storey; very slender
windows on the second with alternation between flat and bay
windows.

mouldings) gave extra piquancy to the range of picturesque styles (rustic, exotic, Gothic), just as the irregularity of the picturesque plans modified the
symmetrical designs of academic architecture.

Two ways of reading the pattern are necessary: the
diachronic method enables us to follow throughout
the century the persistence of the different picturesque modes and their metamorphoses. The other
method, the synchronic, enables us to see more clearly
the effort to differentiate between the houses of the
working, lower-middle and middle class, between the
dwellings of artists, men of letters and businessmen,
between suburban and seaside villas.

Riots and epidemics, particularly of cholera in
1832, underlined the importance of the problem of

working-class housing, but in social, economic and
hygienic rather than artistic terms. In England, from
the eighteenth century onwards, landlords provided
lodges and cottages for the workers on their estate,
such lodgings sometimes taking the form of a village.
Manufacturers naturally adopted this concept of the
estate village. After an initial experiment in 1849, Co-
lonel Akroyd developed the idea at Haley Hill near
Halifax, soon known as Akroydon (1855), just as
Sir Titus Salt built Saltaire near Bradford (1854–72),
or Lever, the soap manufacturer, Port Sunlight from
1888 onwards. Krupp in Germany, Menier in France
and many other paternalistic employers proceeded
along similar lines.

Numerous philanthropic societies tried to improve
the standard of working-class housing. The Society
for Improving the Conditions of the Labouring
Classes, founded in 1844 and supported by Lord Ash-
ley and Prince Albert, seized the opportunity of the
Great Exhibition in 1851 to promote a prototype by
his architect, Henry Roberts (1803–76), who was
much taken up with the problem.

The modern element was the concept of a basic unit
which could be repeated horizontally and vertically.
From this time onwards, similar experiments with
standardized and basic workers' cottages of cheap
materials (brick, brick and iron, wood), can be observed, but not until Tony Garnier's Cité Industrielle
was this theme approached from an artistic angle.

From 1790 to 1850 there appeared in England, and
also in France, Germany and the United States,
several dozen books testifying to the popularity of the
picturesque country retreat. As examples we may
quote those by John Papworth, *Rural Residences*,
1817, John Claudius Loudon, *Encyclopaedia of Cottage,
Farm and Villa Architecture*, 1833, Francis Goodwin,
Rural Architecture, 1836, P. F. Robinson, *A New Series
of Designs for Ornamental Cottages and Villas*, 1838, all
published in London; Urbain Vitry, *Le Propriétaire
Architecte*, published in Toulouse in 1827; and Andrew Jackson Downing, *Cottage Residences*, 1842, and
The Architecture of Country Houses, 1850, published in
New York. These books, usually compiled on the
double principle of stylistic variety and typological
progression from the garden pavilion and peasant
cottage to the country seat, enable us to observe the
birth, as it were, of the middle-class private house.

The true prototypes of the modern middle-class
house seem to be the pavilions and gardener's and
porter's lodges of country parks, and especially country vicarages and the modest villas that were the rural
retreats of artists and men of letters, all of which were
featured in many of these books.

468a Model worker's cottage; Henry Roberts, 1851. Built in connection with the Great Exhibition of 1851 in Hyde Park and subsequently rebuilt in Kensington Park. Planned with a central staircase, it was conceived for four families, but the idea was that this module might be extended lineally or vertically.

469 Cronkhill, Shropshire, England: entrance and garden façade; John Nash, about 1802.

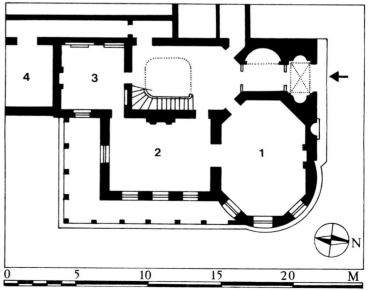

470 Cronkhill, Shropshire, England: plan; John Nash, about 1802. 1 dining-room; 2 drawing-room; 3 study; 4 services.

471, 472 Cottages, Blaise Hamlet, near Bristol, Gloucestershire, England; John Nash, 1811. Two variants of picturesque rustic style: tall chimneys, bow-windows, porticoes, contrasting roofs of tile and thatch.

473 Boileau hamlet, Auteuil, Paris 16: publicity brochure, about 1845. The villa on the right, designed by Jean Charles Léon Danjoy, is still extant. The octagonal staircase turret, the timber-framed avant-corps, and the L-shaped plan were to become recurrent features in the middle-class French villa of the late nineteenth century.

474 Redleaf Cottage; 1826.

Whether in rustic style (from Marie-Antoinette's *hameau* of 1780 at Versailles through Boileau's *hameau*, 1845, to Sauvestre's neo-Norman villa, 1880, or to that of Lavezzari at Cabourg, from the cottages of Blaise Hamlet, 1811, to Redleaf Cottage, 1826, and to Roundwick House at Kirdford, 1868) or in the Italian style (from the gardener's lodge in the park of Sans Souci in Potsdam, 1828–9, to the Garbald Villa at Castasegna in Bergell, Grisons, 1862, designed by Gottfried Semper) the formal genealogy is evident, just as it is from the exotic follies of the early century (Nash's Royal Pavilion at Brighton) to Frederick Church's oriental villa on the Hudson by Calvert Vaux in 1870, or the Chinese villa at St Adresse, Le Havre, by Poulpert, about 1880.

Similarly, in his book *Rural Architecture or a Series of Designs for Ornamental Cottages* (1st ed., 1822, 4th ed., 1836) P. F. Robinson is early on the scene with a design for a Swiss cottage, sketched in 1816 on his return from Italy (Pl. 8). He gives an example of the application of the Old English style of architecture to residences.

As early as 1800 John Plaw had provided a design for a cottage 'with a virando in the manner of an Indian bungalow', and in 1802 John Nash organized Cronkhill in Shropshire round a belvedere tower in the manner of Italianate rural villas. Verandas, bay windows, projecting chimneys – these picturesque motifs, which struck Andrew Jackson Downing in mid-century as 'the most general truths in domestic architecture', betrayed this typological genealogy.

However, after 1850, a wilfully eclectic architectural culture favoured an intermingling of styles: the Henschel Villa at Kassel (1868) by Richard Lucae (1829–77) has an Italian belvedere but neo-Grecian proportions and outline. Conversely, the development of national archeologies was conducive to differentiation. The picturesque rustic style which had

475 Villa, near Cabourg, Calvados; Lavezzari. Neo-Norman half-timbering and picturesque handling of the roofs, an example of the way in which the rustic picturesque style was resuscitated for the middle-class holiday house. After *Revue générale de l'architecture*, 1881.

476 Villa Garbald, Castasegna, Grisons, Switzerland: preliminary design; Gottfried Semper, 1862.

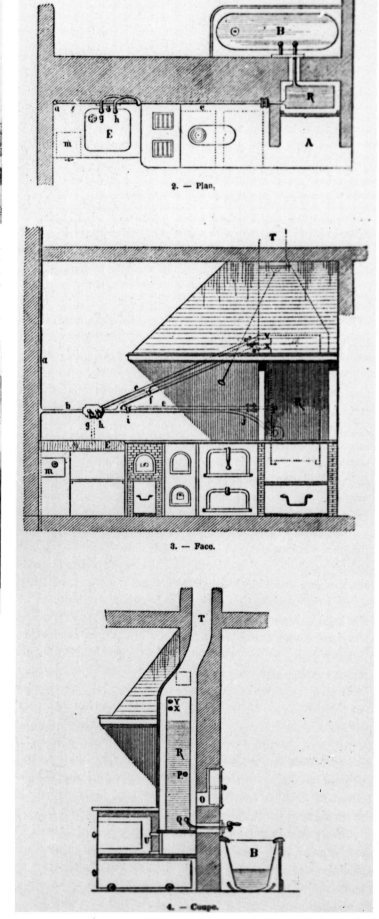

477 Amenities in the home: plan, elevation, section. 'M. Joly has had built some substantial apartment blocks in which each apartment has a bathroom.' After *Gazette des architectes et du bâtiment*, vol. VII, 1869–71, p. 5.

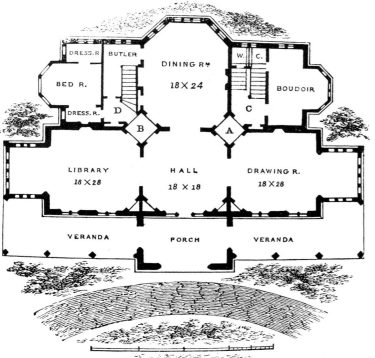

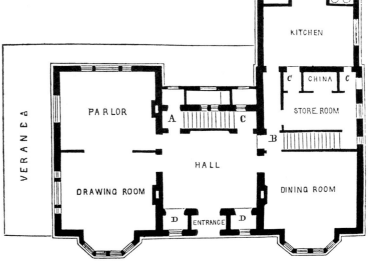

478, 479 Villa in the Pointed style: elevation and plan of the ground-floor; Alexander J. Davis. There is clearly a link with the collections of English models but the detail is undoubtedly more successful. After A. J. Downing, 1850, Pls. 160-1.

480, 481 Timber-framed cottage: elevation and plan of ground-floor; Gervase Wheeler. A variant on a house which the architect built at Brunswick, Maine. The necessity of building in wood gave rise, according to Wheeler, to 'a style which may almost be considered national'. After A. J. Downing, 1850, Pls. 130-1.

been international at the beginning of the century began to acquire a local accent: the neo-Norman style in France, 'Old English' in England, whereas the stick and shingle styles appeared to Americans to be indigenous growths. In the academic compass the Italian style, derived from the villas of the Renaissance, was accompanied by a range of national styles

– Elizabethan, Jacobean and Queen Anne in England, François I, Henri II and Louis XIII in France. In the United States certain architects, Robert Swain Peabody (1845–1917) and Arthur Little (1852–1925) prominent among them, became interested in colonial architecture and, from 1870 onwards, there was a colonial revival equivalent to the Queen Anne

481a House of William Watts-Sherman, Shephard Avenue, Newport; Stanford White, designed 1874, under the aegis of Henry Hobson Richardson.

482 Villa of Edward King, Newport, Rhode Island; Richard Upjohn, 1845–7. This villa, which is still extant, is according to Downing 'one of the most successful examples of the Italianate style in the United States' – a style which, to his mind, epitomizes the residence of a gentleman and a life of refined pleasure. After A. J. Downing, 1850, p. 317, Pl. 143.

483 Rest Cottage, Evanston, Ill., 1865. House of Frances E. Willard, organizer of the National Women's Christian Temperance Union and founder of the WCTU. A good example of 'carpenter Gothic', which was disseminated by sample books and virtually became a national style in the United States.

484 The Red House, Bexley Heath, Kent; Philip Webb, 1859–60, for William Morris. Hailed by Muthesius as 'the first house to be designed and built as a unified whole from the inside to the outside', the building is notable for the refinement of its red brick bonding and the freedom in the treatment of the tiled roof. Whereas we are struck today by the modern simplicity of the vocabulary, Morris saw his house in the thirteenth-century style and found a 'medieval' motif in the oculi lighting the upper floor.

movement in England. The Italians, however, remained faithful to their Florentine style, which had been international at the beginning of the century.

The choice of a style may have the value of a political or cultural manifesto, a sign of extravagance or the acquisition of a new social status or it may remain a question of taste, meriting the same somewhat superficial attention as the choice of a piece of furniture, a curtain or a suit. 'In what architectural style is a house to be constructed? Generally, the architect puts this question to his client at their first contact,' wrote Robert Kerr, whose book *The English Gentleman's House*, published in 1864, gives an exhaustive account of what the English expected of a country house in 1860. 'Following his intuition or his fancy, he must choose between half a dozen principal styles, all more or less antagonistic to each other . . . The perplexed client dares to suggest that he wants a simple and comfortable house without any style or again a comfortable style.' Problems of ventilation and heating and the installation of bathrooms and WCs preoccupied architects and interested their clients as much as questions of form.

In the typical middle-class house one finds on the ground floor, following the entrance hall which gives on to the staircase, the standard layout: drawing-room, dining-room, study, library or billiard room with the bedrooms upstairs. Whereas in France architects long remained faithful to the symmetrical designs of classical Italian villas, in Great Britain there was a preference for an irregular plan derived from rustic Italian pavilions or medieval houses. In 1800, in a preface to his *Sketches for Country Houses, Villas and Rural Dwellings*, John Plaw recalled (only to condemn) the view that 'some people think dwellings on a humble scale and cottages ought rather to be irregular in their forms and broken in their parts so that a new house has the patchwork and bungling appearance of an old one.' This is an idea that constantly

283

recurred and was put into effect throughout the century. George Devey (1820–86) at Betteshanger (1856–61) and Richard Norman Shaw at Grims Dyke (1872) sought to create the impression that 'the buildings composing it have not been constructed in one swoop and to a single unified design.' Viollet-le-Duc, who had made that comment on the Grims Dyke plan, went on: 'it is obvious that the owners of these dwellings were determined first and foremost to be comfortably and spaciously housed and did not set great store by attractive façades presented to the eyes of passers-by. Perhaps they were not mistaken!'

On the one hand the closer and deeper ties binding English civilization to the aesthetic of the picturesque, on the other the tradition of rationalist educational methods in France explain the contrast that existed throughout the century between English dwellings and continental villas. But about 1850 the two traditions began to converge: the neo-classical villa became less austere and the picturesque pavilion less artificial, and the outcome was the modern middle-class villa.

In America, Downing, whose architectural thinking was profoundly influenced by the picturesque tradition, shifted the emphasis for good to 'the villa', 'the most refined of America, the home of its most leisurely and educated class of citizens'. As to style, his preferences were for 'rural Gothic' with 'high gables, bay windows and other features full of domestic expression', and for the 'modern Italian with bold overhanging cornices and irregular outlines'. 'The former', he said, 'generally speaking is best suited to our Northern broken country, the latter to the hilly or flat Middle and Southern States, though sites may be found for each style in all portions of the Union.'

Downing's works were very widely disseminated: 'every young couple setting up home buys them'; but magazines were no less influential in forming a domestic architectural culture. Good examples are *Godey's Lady's Book and Lady's Magazine*, which, between 1846 and 1892, published more than 450 house designs; at first they were borrowed from English books illustrating the picturesque style (Papworth and Loudon in particular) but after 1859 they were original.

About 1850 the same interest began to be shown in the middle-class house in France. It is significant that in the first two volumes of his *Paris Moderne*, published in 1834 and 1843, Louis Marie Normand produced models exclusively of town mansions and apartment blocks, whereas in the third volume, which came out in 1849, he published several designs for suburban villas. In the years that followed numerous books of

this kind appeared: Victor Calliat, *Parallèle des Maisons de Paris*, 1850; Victor Petit, *Maisons les plus remarquables des environs de Paris*, about 1850; Théodore Vacquer, *Maisons les plus remarquables de Paris*, 1863; César Daly, *L'Architecture privée au XIXᵉ siècle*, vol. III, *Villas suburbaines*, 1864; Léon Marie Isabey and E. Leblan, *Villas, maisons de ville et de campagne*, 1864; and in 1875 the editor of *Nouvelles Annales de Construction* wrote: 'The ever increasing number of small country houses being built round the big cities has induced us once again to publish two small models of good practical design which may be of use to some of our readers who are architects or landowners.'

A number of designs were derived from the picturesque aesthetic, like the chalet on the shore of the Lac d'Enghien, published by Normand (vol. III, Pls. 82–3) which gives play to the contrast between bonded brickwork and a timber frame – stick style before its time; but most of them, with their grouped plans and their symmetrical layouts, are more in line with the typology of the classical country house and the neo-classical villa. In the years between 1845 and 1850 the architects Aimé Chenavard, P. C. Dusillon, J. S. Bridault and others remained faithful to the classical layout but reintroduced large dormer windows and mansard roofs, François I pilasters and brick piers decorated with stone rustication à la Louis XIII. This elegant and urban French style, striking a happy balance between classical tradition and the new picturesque taste, soon challenged the Italian style in the United States and Germany, and remained the predominant style in France.

However, the most interesting developments were taking place in Great Britain. By condemning picturesqueness for its own sake and pleading for variety based on a frank statement of materials and layouts, Pugin set a lasting direction for English secular architecture. 'Red House', the brick house which Philip Webb (1831–1915) built for William Morris at Bexleyheath in Kent in 1859–60, was hailed by the German architect Hermann Muthesius at the end of the nineteenth century as the first house of the new domestic culture. Remarkable though it was at the time for its furniture and décor, we today can see more clearly what its architecture owes to the vicarages which William Butterfield, George Edmund Street and William White built for the Ecclesiologists.

Roofs varying according to the part of the building they covered, staircase towers attached to the main structure, projecting chimney stacks, and the unconcealed use of local materials – these were all features

484a   House in Louis XIII style: view. After Isabey and Leblan, 1864, Pl. 51.

486   Residence, Händelstrasse 1, Berlin; E. Ihne. After *Architektonische Rundschau*, 1898, No. 2, Pl. 9.

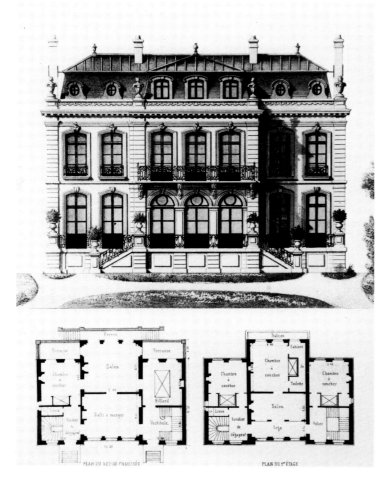

485   Manor-house in Louis XIV style: view and plans of ground-floor and the first storey. After Isabey and Leblan, 1864, Pl. 10.

487   Neuhabsburg Castle, Meggen, Lucerne, Switzerland; 1868–71. This building was erected by an unknown architect below the ruined castle of the same name.

488 Vicarage of All Saints Church, Boyne Hill, Maidenhead, Berkshire, England; George Edmund Street, 1854. With its asymmetric balance, its smooth surfaces and its bands of coloured brickwork, this vicarage is typical of the new line of neo-Gothic architecture in England.

489, 490 Villa Hahnenburg, Cologne: views of exterior and interior: 1870–2. The neo-classical building was erected by an unknown architect for Johann Herbert Hahn, owner of a brewery.

491 Residence, Stülerstrasse 1, Tiergarten, Berlin; Friedrich Hitzig, about 1855.

492 House of C. Kirsch, Maria-Theresienstrasse, Munich; A. Brüchle. A mixture of Early Renaissance features embodied in a picturesque composition (corner tower and porch, asymmetrical arrangement of gables). After *Architektonische Rundschau*, 1898, No. 2, Pl. 4.

493 Villa Dyes, Hildesheim, W. Germany, 1882. The Austrian consul-general and wholesale merchant had this castle-like building erected for himself when he retired. The architect's name is unknown.

of a picturesque style which arose from strict necessity and a well-marked external expression of the interior layout. Milton Ernest Hall, which Butterfield built in 1853–8 for his brother-in-law, is typical of this domestic architecture, whose severity is relieved only by a discreet use of colours.

In the 1860s certain architects like Alfred Waterhouse or William Burges kept their allegiance to this austere picturesque style, but a younger generation, Philip Webb, William Eden Nesfield (1835–88), Edward William Godwin and Richard Norman Shaw sought a less astringent elegance. To this end they turned on the one hand towards the architecture of the half-timbered house of the fifteenth century, the 'Old English' style, and on the other towards the domestic architecture of the early eighteenth century, the 'Queen Anne' style, which established a hold on them by their middle-class simplicity, rural freshness and freedom from architectural pomp.

The two styles are complementary: 'Old English' seemed to be particularly appropriate for country houses, 'Queen Anne' for suburban ones. Richard Norman Shaw adopted the first for Grims Dyke, which attracted the attention of Viollet-le-Duc, and the second for Bedford Park. This estate, in west London, where hundreds of houses were built between 1871 and 1881, attracted a whole colony of artists, writers and lawyers, who were appreciative of the aesthetic elegance of the designs provided first by Godwin and then by Shaw. 'Sweetness and light', to borrow the title of a study in 1877 by Mark Girouard recently devoted to this movement, typify these creations where the picturesque qualities of the materials and the silhouette and the historical references are perfectly mastered.

This quest for an architectural image of luminous purity sometimes ended up with almost abstract results, as in one of the plans submitted by Godwin for Tite Street, another of the major 'Queen Anne' construction sites. This design was set aside for another of a more conventional kind, but similar effects are to be found at the end of the century in the creations of Charles F. A. Voysey (1857–1941), who was the chief exponent of a new elegant simplicity. 'The fact', he wrote, 'is that we are overdecorated . . . Begin by casting out all the useless ornaments and remove the dust-catching flounces and furbelows . . . Eschew

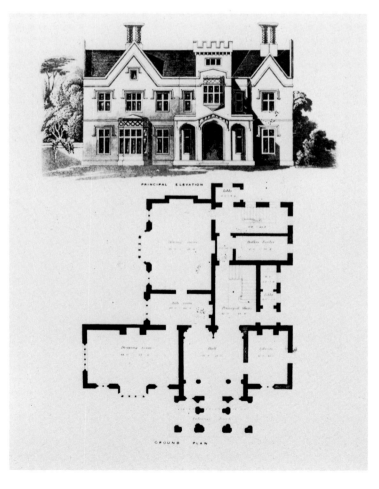

494 Villa Lenbach, Munich; Gabriel von Seidl, 1887–97.

495 Rectory: design; Francis Goodwin. Rectories, vicarages and rural schools are a favoured subject for Gothic secular architecture. After *Rural Architecture*, London, 1836, Pl. 14.

496 Milton Ernest Hall, Bedfordshire, England; William Butterfield, for his brother-in-law Benjamin B. H. Helps Starey, 1853–8. The picturesqueness of the front, which the large roof welds successfully into unity, corresponds to the internal layout; the polychromy (ochre stone and red brick) is less aggressive here than in some of Butterfield's other buildings.

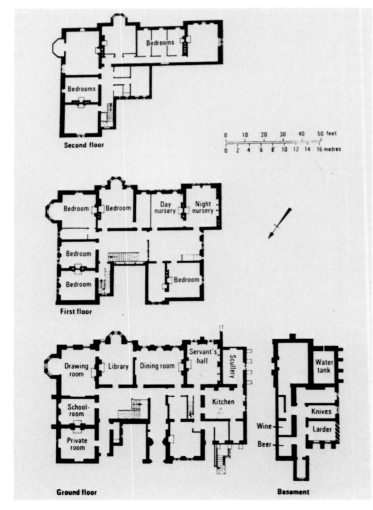

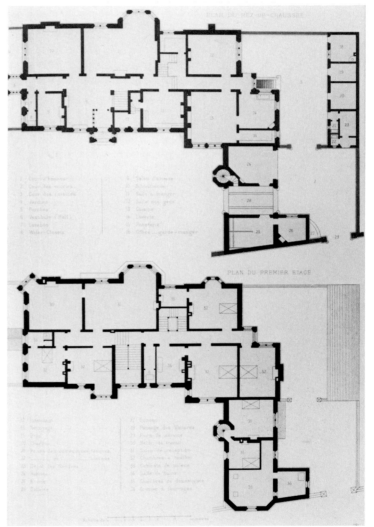

497 Milton Ernest Hall: plans of the basement, ground-floor, and first and second storeys; William Butterfield, 1853–8. After Girouard, 1979.

498, 499 Manor-house, Cambridge, England: view and plans of ground-floor and upper storey; Alfred Waterhouse. 'The faces are of brick and ashlar and, far from aiming at symmetry, favour great freedom in the overall composition and in the details.' A notable feature is the balance obtained between the solidity of the masses and the picturesqueness of the details (corner oriel and the window in the chimney). After Viollet-le-Duc, *Habitations modernes*, vol. II, Pls. 162–3.

FRONT ELEVATION.

500 House of Frank Miles, 44 Tile Street, Chelsea, London: preliminary design; Edward William Godwin, 1878. An abstract modern design with a hint of Japanese influence. The house was built to a very different design.

501   Grims Dyke House, Harrow Weald, Middlesex, England;
Richard Norman Shaw, 1872. One of the first examples of the
Old English style employed for a mansion; it should be borne in
mind, however, that it is an artist's house.

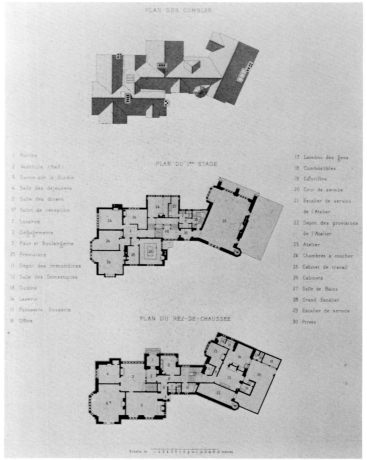

502   Grims Dyke House, Harrow Weald, Middlesex, England:
plans of the ground-floor, upper storey and roof; Richard Norman Shaw, 1872. After Viollet-le-Duc, *Habitations modernes*, vol.
I, 1875, Pl. 44.

503 Villa Weber, rue Erlanger, Auteuil, Paris: elevation; Paul Sédille. After Chabat, 1881, Pl. 67.

imitations. Strive to produce an effect of repose and simplicity.' ('The Art of Today', *British Architect*, November 1892.) Covering the bricks with white roughcast, Voysey rejects on aesthetic grounds the ideal of using local materials: on this point Voysey diverges from Prior, Lethaby and the Arts and Crafts movement, but what they all have in common is the quest not so much for an 'absence of style' as for a modern or personal style, emphatically simple. All look back to the example of Philip Webb, the hero of this younger generation.

In the 1870s there were somewhat similar phenomena in France even though they lacked the *éclat* of their British counterparts. They were distinguished by such features as the replacement of historicist and picturesque eclecticism by a modern aestheticism, 'free style', an interest in the abstract contrasts of vernacular materials, and a secularization of the Gothic vocabulary. Just as the aestheticizing medievalism of William Morris and John Ruskin opened the way to the free style of Shaw, Philip Webb and

Voysey, the Gothic rationalism of Viollet-le-Duc did the same for the free style of Paul Sédille and Hector Guimard (1867–1942).

French architects continued to view developments in domestic English architecture with reservations. In 1890, in his study *L'Architecture moderne en Angleterre*, Sédille criticized the 'unreflecting passion for the picturesque' displayed by the creators of the 'Queen Anne' style: 'the rhythm of the roof receives consideration before the needs of the interior have been satisfied; most of the accidental features of the exterior, by which I mean the projecting and re-entrant parts, are not justified.' However, he was alive to the special charms of English interiors, 'to which the numbers of bow-windows are not strangers' – interiors 'which are so well subdivided, machined, and equipped and so little cluttered up that one could imagine one was between decks on a ship'; he also appreciated 'the Japanese fragrance' that prevailed there.

If, after 1850, French architects introduced a certain asymmetry into their compositions, it always remained discreet, as for example in the house built by Émile Boeswilwald at Montigny in 1865. In his an-

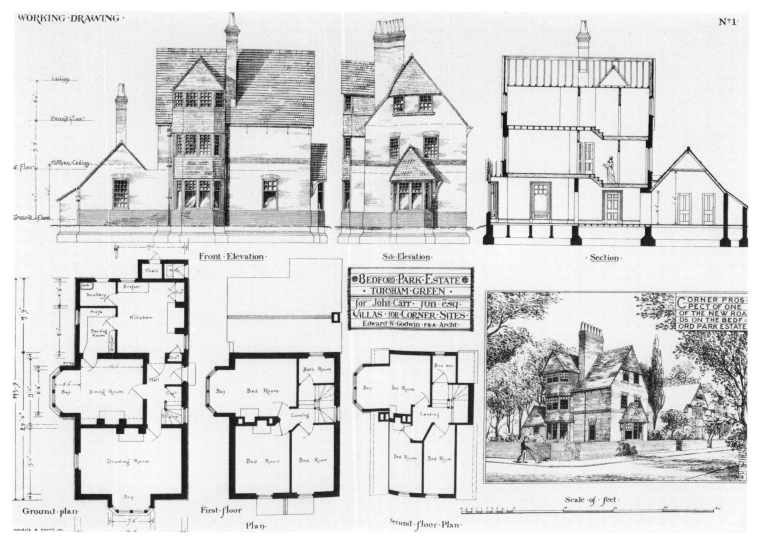

· Front · Elevation ·   · Side · Elevation ·   · Section ·

※ BEDFORD·PARK·ESTATE ※
· TURNHAM · GREEN ·
for · John·Carr · jun · esq ·
VILLAS·FOR·CORNER·SITES ·
Edward·W·Godwin · F·S·A· Archt ·

CORNER·PROS-
PECT·OF·ONE
OF·THE·NEW·ROA-
DS·ON·THE·BEDF-
ORD·PARK·ESTATE

· Ground · plan ·   · First · floor ·   · Second · floor · Plan ·   · Scale · of · feet ·

Plan·

504 Bedford Park Estate, London: design of villas for corner
sites; Edward William Godwin. In 1877 Godwin was replaced
by Richard Norman Shaw. After *The Building News*, 22 December 1876.

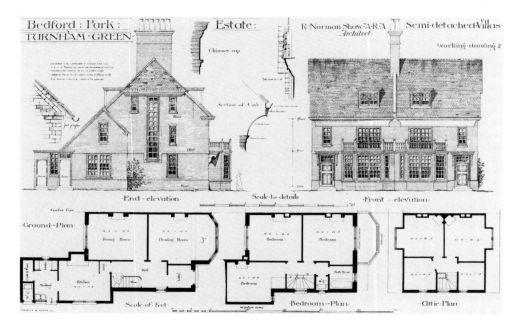

· Bedford : Park :   Estate :   R·Norman·Shaw·A·R·A·   · Semi·detached·Villas·
TURNHAM · GREEN ·   Architect   · Working · drawing · 2 ·

· End · elevation ·   · Scale · to · details ·   · Front · elevation ·

· Ground · Plan ·   · Bedroom · Plan ·   · Attic · Plan ·

505 Bedford Park Estate, London: design for semi-detached villas; Richard
Norman Shaw, 1877. By 1883, 490
houses had been built for this handsome
estate on designs supplied by Godwin
and Shaw. After *The Building News*,
16 November 1877.

294

506 Victor Horta house (today Musée Horta), Brussels: view of dining-room; Victor Horta, 1899.

thology, Viollet-le-Duc is, it would seem, captivated by the logic and the amenity of the English layout so clearly stated at Grims Dyke and at Milton Ernest Hall rather than by the visual charm of the compositions, which give play to the balancing of wilfully asymmetrical elements. Conversely, when French architects adopted a picturesque style, in seaside resorts particularly, they tended towards designs which

lacked the restraint and abstract elegance of their English counterparts.

In the United States the English domestic aesthetic naturally found a favourable cultural and social soil. The house of William Watts-Sherman on Shephard Avenue at Newport, designed in 1874 by Stanford White under the aegis of Richardson, bears witness to the immediate interest aroused in America by the creative designs of Shaw published in *Building News* and *The Builder*. Most of the American architects who passed through London in the 1870s and 1880s –

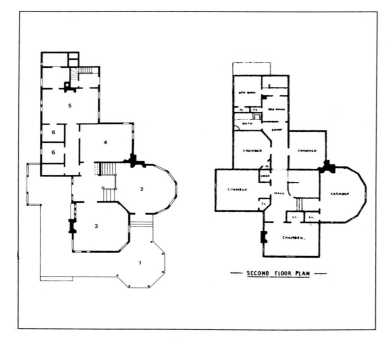

508 Morrill House, Bar Harbor, Mount Desert, Maine: front overlooking the sea; William Ralph Emerson. After *The American Architect and Building News*, 22 March 1879.

509 Morrill House, Bar Harbor, Mount Desert, Maine: plans of ground and first floors; William Ralph Emerson, about 1879. 1 veranda; 2 hall; 3 parlour; 4 dining-room; 5 kitchen; 6 utilities.

510 Morrill House, Bar Harbor, Mount Desert, Maine: interior view; William Ralph Emerson, about 1879. The handling of split levels and views from side angles and above are a harbinger of similar ventures by British Art Nouveau architects.

511 Stoughton House, Brattle Street, Cambridge, Mass.; Henry Hobson Richardson, 1882–3. The use of shingles, which reflect the interest in the domestic revival of traditional materials, enables smooth and continuous surfaces to be created which are in sharp contrast with the picturesque forms that preceded them.

512 F. L. Ames Gate Lodge, North Easton, Mass.; Henry Hobson Richardson, 1880–1. A modern variation on the traditional theme of a rustic building with bossed stonework. Richardson's taste for contrasting textures here attains its acme.

507 Morrill House, Bar Harbor, Mount Desert, Maine: seen from the drive; William Ralph Emerson, about 1879. One of the first adaptations of the Queen Anne style to the materials (shingles) and customs (large verandas) of North America.

513 Residence, 9 Priory Avenue, Bedford Park Estate, London; Richard Norman Shaw, 1880.

514 Bath Road, Bedford Park Estate, London: elevation of houses, shops and inn; Richard Norman Shaw, 1880. In this design, which was executed, Shaw succeeded in reconciling homogeneity and diversity. The oriels became one of the commonplaces of the Queen Anne style.

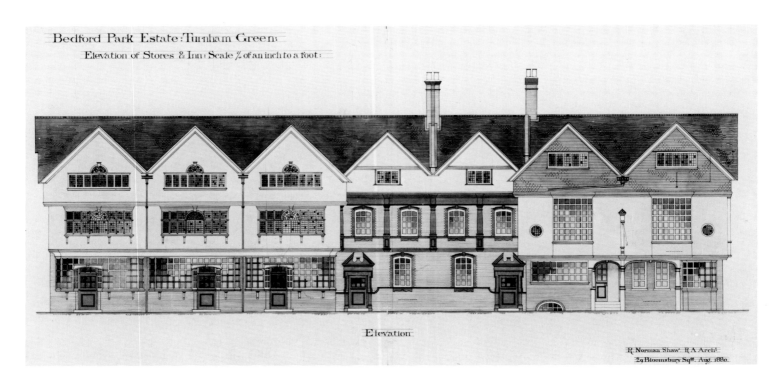

Bedford Park Estate: Turnham Green:

Elevation of Stores & Inn: Scale ½ of an inch to a foot:

Elevation

R. Norman Shaw, R A Archt
29 Bloomsbury Sqr. Aug. 1880.

515 Broadleys, Windermere, Cartmel, Lancashire, England: design; Charles F. A. Voysey, 1898. The genre of bluish-green pen-and-ink drawing, adopted by Voysey here, became fashionable in the following decade. This house which is still standing, with its white surface, marked horizontal lines and low roofs, is typical of Voysey's poetry.

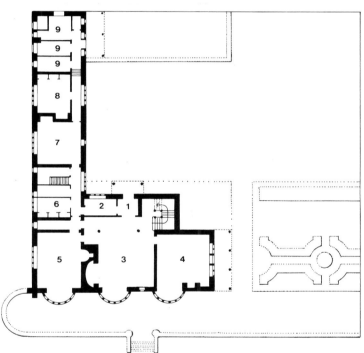

516 Broadleys, Windermere, Cartmel, Lancashire, England: plan (after the original design); Charles F. A. Voysey, 1898. 1 entrance; 2 toilet; 3 hall; 4 drawing-room; 5 dining-room; 6 pantry; 7 kitchen; 8 service room; 9 utilities.

Robert Swain Peabody in 1871 and 1876, Stanford White in 1879 and 1884, William Ralph Emerson in 1884 – certainly visited Bedford Park, where a whole colony of American artists was in residence. The articles by H. H. Holly on 'Modern Dwellings' in *Harper's Magazine* and those by Clarence M. Cook in *Scribner's Monthly*, 1875–7, published in 1878 under the significant title *The House Beautiful*, illustrate the fascination felt for these English creations.

English developments, however, served not so much as models in the narrow sense but rather as a stimulus to invention. The use of local materials (shingles) and more open plans, the interest taken in the Japanese house (a model shown at the Universal Exhibition in Philadelphia in 1876 made a great impression), and the return to the Colonial house all gave a specific character to the work of William Ralph Emerson (1833–1918), Robert Swain Peabody, Stanford White, Henry Hobson Richardson, Wilson Eyre (1858–1944) and many others.

These developments in American domestic architecture almost immediately caught the attention of

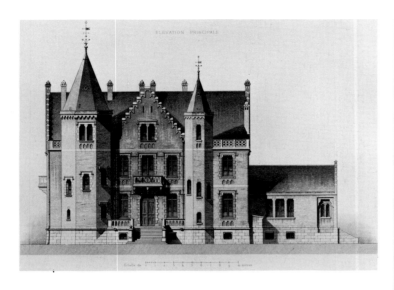

ELEVATION PRINCIPALE

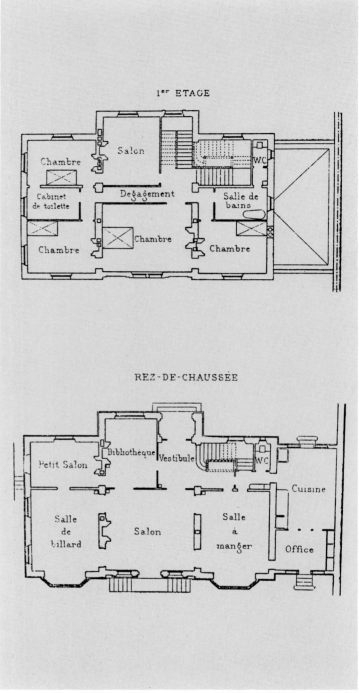

1er ÉTAGE

REZ-DE-CHAUSSÉE

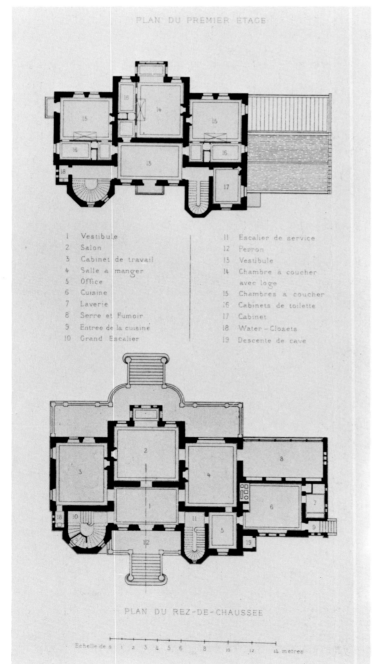

PLAN DU PREMIER ETAGE

1 Vestibule	11 Escalier de service
2 Salon	12 Perron
3 Cabinet de travail	13 Vestibule
4 Salle à manger	14 Chambre à coucher
5 Office	avec loge
6 Cuisine	15 Chambres à coucher
7 Laverie	16 Cabinets de toilette
8 Serre et Fumoir	17 Cabinet
9 Entrée de la cuisine	18 Water-Closets
10 Grand Escalier	19 Descente de cave

PLAN DU REZ-DE-CHAUSSÉE

Echelle de 0   1 2 3 4 5   6   8   10   12   14 metres

517 Villa Weber, rue Erlanger, Auteuil, Paris: plans of ground-floor and first storey; Paul Sédille. After Planat, n.d., Pl. 47.

◁518, 519 Country house, Montigny, Nord: elevation and plans of ground-floor and first storey; Émile Boeswilwald, about 1865. 'The architect of this country house, while seeking a balance between the masses in both plan and elevation, has nevertheless avoided absolute symmetry and has sensibly adapted his composition to the various functions to be performed.' In spite of the implicit allusion made by Viollet-le-Duc to the picturesque English layout, the symmetrical arrangement of French tradition is still readily discernible, particularly in the plan. After Viollet-le-Duc, vol. I, Pls. 102-3.

520 Casino, Newport, Rhode Island: front; McKim, Mead & White, 1879–81. In the centre of Newport the Casino forms a complex of shops, restaurants and cafés.

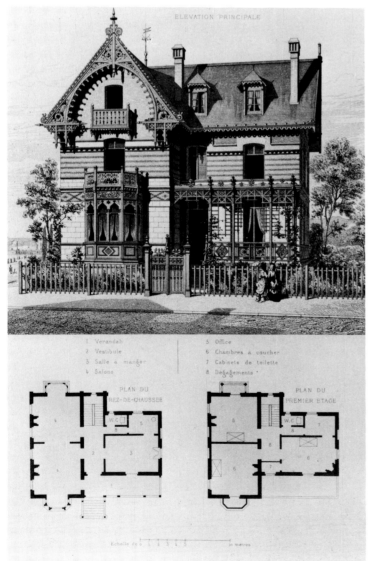

522, 523 Villas on the Beach, Walmer, Kent, England: elevation and plans; James Neale. Gables of brickwork with curved breaks, timber framing and projecting roofs, verandas and oriels: one example among thousands of this Queen Anne style which, in the 1880s, became the accepted style for English seaside resorts. After *The Builder*, 15 October 1887.

521 Villa, Deauville, Calvados, France: elevation and plans of the ground-floor and first storey; F. Hoffbauer. A typical example of the French seaside style; the layout is simple; the picturesque quality derives from the use of variously coloured materials and painted wood (openwork). After Viollet-le-Duc, vol. I, 1875, Pl. 41.

European architects, a first sign of a reversal in the direction of the cultural flow. In France, in spite of Sédille and Daly (*Villas américaines*, 1888), this interest did not rise above curiosity. German architects, who were to prove the most clear-sighted and the most attentive observers of English domestic architecture (Muthesius, *Das Englische Haus*), followed events in America more keenly. After spending a long time in the United States F. Rudolf Vogel (1846–1926) settled in Hamburg, where he built several villas in American style, whose designs he published in a number of articles. In Great Britain English and American culture was too intimately bound up for the tracing of influences to make any sense, but American designs appeared on the British cultural horizon and gave added impetus to the search for a free style. This was to find its most sophisticated expression at the end of the century in the designs of Charles F. A. Voysey.

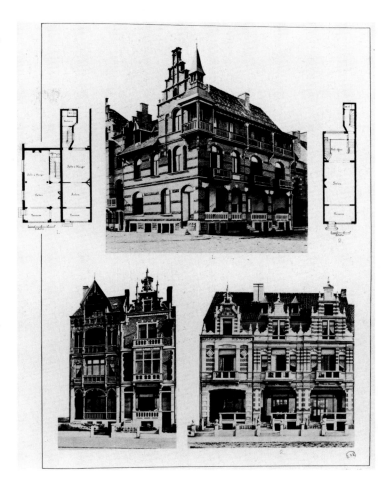

524   Villas, Middelkerke, Belgium; A. Dumont-Hebbelinck, 1887–91. After *L'Emulation*, 1892, Pl. 49.

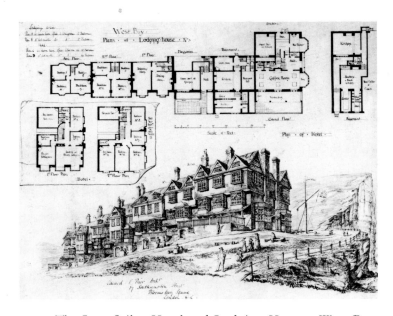

523a   'The Orchard', Shire Land, Chorleywood, Hertfordshire; C.A. Voysey for himself, 1899. With its walls of roughcast brickwork, its drip moulds unifying the façade from one window to another, its plain cross gables and its roofs of green slate, the house is typical of the gentle and rustic simplicity Voysey seeks.

525   The Lost Sailor Hotel and Lodging Houses, West Bay, near Bridport, Dorset, England: design (never executed); Edward S. Prior, 1885. Triangular gables and oriels, slates and white pebbledash walls – a typical example of Richard Norman Shaw's work.

Conclusion

'About 1900, a splendid gesture: Art Nouveau. The old fripperies of an ancient culture are being shaken,' wrote Le Corbusier in 1929. The founders of the modern movement clearly grasped the importance of the cultural breaks marking the end of the century. After half a century of marginal experimentation on concrete, the research of François Hennébique (1841–1921) ended in 1898 with the taking out of several patents that paved the way to a decisive new chapter in the art of building. New art reviews appeared everywhere (*L'Art moderne* in Belgium after 1884, *The Studio* in England after 1893, *Jugend* in Germany in 1896, *Art et décoration* in France in 1897) and testified to a new start. A new generation, Victor Horta (1861–1947) in Brussels, Antonio Gaudí (1852–1926) in Barcelona, Charles Rennie Mackintosh (1868–1928) in Glasgow, Otto Wagner (1841–1918), Josef Hoffmann (1870–1956) and Joseph Maria Olbrich (1869–1908) in Vienna, together with Henry van de Velde, Hector Guimard, Charles F. A. Voysey and many others who followed, gave definition to a new art ('modern style', *Jugendstil*, *style floréal*) which, in very varied forms, expressed the aspiration of breaking away from all harking back to the past. This European movement, which had all the vitality of a fashion and all its transience (1892–1914 and particularly 1896–1904), impinged most of all on the decorative arts and the forms of architecture most hospitable to the picturesque aesthetic – private houses and commercial buildings – and may thus be given a place in the eclectic hierarchy of styles. But, stressing the abstract vocabulary of the line, whether floral (Horta, Guimard) or geometrical (Mackintosh, Hoffmann), of surfaces, whether undulating and coloured (Gaudí) or smooth and white (Voysey), and of volumes (Otto Wagner, Adolf Loos), and by avoiding all cultural allusions these innovators broke with

the historical aesthetic of the nineteenth century, for which these values were always realized through the medium of a style adapted with more or less liberty; they rediscovered the universal elements and principles of architecture, and thus discreetly prepared the way for the modernist revolution of the 1920s.

Laying aside polemics and prejudices, one must acknowledge the extraordinary vitality of nineteenth-century architecture. Face to face with the advent of the new industrial and middle-class civilization, architects took up the challenge of meeting modern needs without forfeiting any of the traditional values; or rather, they satisfied the varied needs of a society in the midst of change while making use of a cultural horizon which they never ceased to push forward. The modernity of the nineteenth century rests in fact on a dual movement which is at once prospective and retrospective: while utilizing to the full and without prejudice the resources of new materials and tackling the problems raised by the new types of building needed by industrial society, these architects rediscovered the architectural values of different centuries, from Hellenic purity and Italian elegance at the start of the century to Baroque rhetoric in its middle years. Far from being an obstacle to creation, pondering over this heritage seemed to be a natural stimulant to the imagination, and cultural allusions a privileged instrument for expressing contrasts and significance in architecture. To satisfy the diverse needs of a society in the full flux of change, architects knew how to take advantage, with a remarkable sense of architectural character, of all the suggestions of this enormously broadened cultural horizon and, with the freedom bestowed by a living culture, to adapt designs, layouts, balanced masses and interlinked spaces to contemporary needs. If we pay as much attention to the differences as to the resemblances, we find that nineteenth-century architecture is no less inventive than that of previous centuries, and that its various styles are a language which expresses successfully the style of the era.

We are indebted to nineteenth-century architects for exploring the technical and aesthetic possibilities of new materials – cast iron, wrought iron and steel – and also for revitalizing the aesthetics of brick; they invented the covered, light-filled interior space and also breathed new and spectacular life into prestigious entrance halls and staircases, as conspicuous approaches to the intimacy of the interior; they showed a remarkable sense of decoration but also gave to the townscape a new scale, first that of the boulevards, which threw bourgeois towns into upheaval, and then that of the skyscrapers; they invented new types of architecture – shopping arcades and winter gardens, railway stations and department stores, skyscrapers and private middle-class houses – and they also cast traditional layouts and types in a new mould.

Select Bibliography

DURAND, JEAN NICOLAS LOUIS, *Précis des leçons d'architecture don-nées à l'École Polytechnique*, Paris, 1802-15, 1817, 1819-21; re-printed Nördlingen, 1981

DURM, JOSEPH (ed.), *Handbuch der Architektur*, 13 vols., Darm-stadt, 1880, in particular vol. 4 on various types of building

GUADET, JULES, *Éléments et théories de l'architecture*, Paris, 1902-4

KRAFFT, JEAN CHARLES, and DUBOIS, P. L. F., *Productions de plu-sieurs architectes français et étrangers relatives aux jardins pittores-ques et aux fabriques de divers genres qui peuvent entrer dans leur composition*, Paris, 1809

NODIER, CHARLES; TAYLOR, ISIDORE, and DE CAILLEUX, ALPHONSE, *Voyages pittoresques et romantiques dans l'ancienne France*, Paris, 1820

PAPWORTH, WYATT (ed.), *Encyclopédie de l'architecture et de la cons-truction*, 6 vols., Paris, 1888-1902

PEYRE, JOSEPH, *Œuvres d'architecture*, Paris, 1765, 2nd ed. 1795

SPRINGER, ANTON, *Handbuch der Kunstgeschichte*, vol. 5: *Das 19. Jahrhundert*, revised and enlarged by Max Osborn, 5th ed., Leipzig, 1905

STUART, JAMES, and REVETT, NICHOLAS, *The Antiquities of Athens*, London, 1762-1816

Surveys

BENEVOLO, LEONARDO, *Storia dell'architettura moderna*, Bari, 1960

COLLINS, PETER, *Changing Ideals in Modern Architecture, 1750-1950*, London, 1965

GERMANN, GEORG, *Neugotik, Geschichte ihrer Architekturtheorie*, Stuttgart, 1974

GROTE, LUDWIG (ed.), *Historismus und bildende Kunst*, Munich, 1965

HITCHCOCK, HENRY RUSSELL, *Architecture: Nineteenth and Twen-tieth Centuries*, Harmondsworth, 3rd ed., 1969 (The Pelican History of Art; paperback ed., 1971)

MIDDLETON, ROBIN, and WATKIN, DAVID, *Neoclassical and Nineteenth-Century Architecture*, 1st ed., Milan, 1977, New York, 1980

MORACHIELLO, PAOLO, and TEYSSOT, GEORGES (eds.), *Le macchi-ne imperfette, architettura, programma, istituzioni nel XIX secolo*, Rome, 1980

PATETTA, LUCIANO, *L'architettura dell'Eclettismo, fonti, teorie, modelli 1750-1900*, Milan, 1975

PEVSNER, NIKOLAUS, *Studies in Art, Architecture and Design*, vol. I, London, 1968

—, *Some Architectural Writers of the Nineteenth Century*, Oxford, 1972

ROISECCO, GIULIO, *L'Architettura del Ferro*, vol. I: *L'Inghilterra 1688-1914*; vol. II: *La Francia 1715-1914*; vol. III: *Gli Stati Uniti*, Rome, 1973-80

SUMMERSON, SIR JOHN (ed.), *Concerning Architecture: Essays on Architectural Writers and Writings Presented to Nikolaus Pevsner*, London, 1968

WAGNER-RIEGER, RENATE (ed.), *Historismus und Schlossbau*, Munich, 1975

ZANTEN, DAVID VAN, *The Architectural Polychromy of the 1830s*, New York and London, 1977

[Exhibition catalogue] *Le 'Gothique' retrouvé avant Viollet-le-Duc*, Caisse Nationale des Monuments Historiques et des Sites, Paris, 1979

Types of Building

PEVSNER, NIKOLAUS, *A History of Building Types*, London, 1976, paperback ed., 1979

Bridges

DESWARTE, SYLVIE, and LEMOINE, BERTRAND, *L'Architecture et les ingénieurs, deux siècles de construction*, Paris, 1980

MEHRTENS, GEORGES, *Der deutsche Brückenbau im 19. Jahrhundert*, Berlin, 1900

RUDDOCK, TED, *Arch Bridges and their Builders, 1735-1835*, Cam-bridge, 1979

Conservatories

HIX, JOHN, *The Glass House*, Cambridge (Mass.), 1974, paper-back ed. 1981

KOHLMAIER, GEORG, *Das Glashaus: ein Bautypus des 19. Jahrhun-derts*, Munich, 1981

Hospitals

BURDETT, HENRY C., *Hospitals and Asylums of the World*, London, 1891-3

DEGESS, L., *Der Bau der Krankenhäuser*, Munich, 1862

FOUCAULD, MICHEL, FORTIER, BRUNO, et al., *Les Machines à gué-rir aux origines de l'hôpital moderne*, Brussels, 1979

MURKEN, AXEL, *Die bauliche Entwicklung des deutschen allgemeinen Krankenhauses im 19. Jahrhundert*, Göttingen, 1979

TOLLET, CASIMIR, *Les hôpitaux modernes au XIXᵉ siècle*, Paris, 1894

Prisons

BALTARD, LOUIS PIERRE, *Architectonographie des prisons ou parallèle des divers systèmes de distribution dont les prisons sont susceptibles*, Paris, 1829

DUBBINI, RENZO, 'Carcere e architettura in Italia nel XIX secolo', in *Le macchine imperfette*, by Morachiello, Paolo, and Teyssot, Georges (eds.), Rome, 1980, pp. 218-44

FOUCART, BRUNO, 'Architecture carcérale et architectes fonctionnalistes en France au XIXᵉ siècle', *Revue de l'Art*, 1976, No. 32, pp. 23-56

GRAUL, H. J., *Der Strafvollzugsbau einst und heute*, Düsseldorf, 1965

JOHNSTON, NORMAN, *The Human Cage. A Brief History of Prison Architecture*, New York, 1973

KROHNE, KARL, and UBER, R., *Die Strafanstalten und Gefängnisse in Preussen*, Berlin, 1901

—, *Instruction et programme pour la construction de maisons d'arrêt et de justice*, Plans of prisons by Abel Blouet, Harou-Romain and Hector Horeau, Paris, 1841

Railway Stations

BERGER, M., *Historische Bahnhofbauten in Sachsen, Preussen und Thüringen*, Berlin, 1980

BINNEY, MARCUS, and PEARCE, DAVID (eds.), *Railway Architecture*, London, 1979

CHABAT, PIERRE, *Bâtiments de chemins de fer*, Paris, 1860

KUBINSKY, M., *Bahnhöfe Europas*, Stuttgart, 1969

MEEKS, CARROLL, *The Railroad Station*, New Haven and London, 1956, rev. ed. 1978

PASTIELS, P., *Gares d'antan*, Brussels, 1978

PERDONNET, AUGUSTE, *Traité élémentaire des chemins de fer*, Paris, 1856

—, *Nouveau portefeuille de l'ingénieur des chemins de fer*, Paris, 1857-66

—, and POLONCEAU, CAMILLE, *Portefeuille de l'ingénieur des chemins de fer*, 3 vols. and atlas, Paris, 1843-6

SCHADENDORF, WULF, *Das Jahrhundert der Eisenbahn*, Munich, 1965

—, 'La arquitectura de las estaciones en España', *El Mundo de las Estaciones*, Madrid, 1981, pp. 137-230

—, *L'Espace du voyage: les gares*, Paris, 1978 (Monuments historiques de la France, 6)

Shopping Arcades and Department Stores

DEAN, D., *English Shop Fronts, 1792-1840*, London, 1970

FERRY, J. W., *A History of Department Stores*, New York, 1960

GEIST, JOHANN FRIEDRICH, *Passagen. Ein Bautyp des 19. Jahrhunderts*, Munich, 1969

MARREY, BERNARD, *Les Grands Magasins*, Paris, 1979

WIENER, ALFRED, *Das Warenhaus*, Berlin, 1911

Villas and Country Houses

DOWNING, ANDREW JACKSON, *The Architecture of the Country House*, New York, 1850; reprinted New York, 1969

ISABEY, LÉON, and LEBLAN, E., *Villas, maisons de ville et de campagne*, Paris, 1864

KERR, ROBERT, *The Gentleman's House or How to Plan English Residences*, London, 1864; reprinted New York, 1972

LOUDON, JOHN CLAUDIUS, *Encyclopaedia of Cottage, Farm and Villa Architecture and Furniture*, London, 1833

PLANAT, PAUL, *Habitations particulières*, Paris, n.d.

VIOLLET-LE-DUC, EUGÈNE-EMMANUEL, *Habitations modernes*, Paris, 1875; reprinted Brussels, 1979

World Exhibitions

BEUTLER, CHRISTIAN [Exhibition catalogue] *Weltausstellungen im 19. Jahrhundert*, with a contribution by Günter Metken, Munich, Die Neue Sammlung, Staatl. Museum für angewandte Kunst, 1973

CORNELL, E., *De Stora Utställningarnas Arkitekturhistoria*, Stockholm, 1952

DOWNES, CHARLES, *The Building Erected in Hyde Park for the Great Exhibition of ... 1851*, London, 1852; reprinted London, 1952

—, *Exposition universelle de 1878, monographie des palais et constructions diverses de l'Exposition universelle de 1878*, Paris, 1882

COUNTRIES

Austria

KORTZ, PAUL, *Wien am Anfang des 20. Jahrhunderts*, 2 vols., Vienna, 1905-6

LUTZOW, C. VON, and TISCHLER, L. (eds.), *Wiener Neubauten*, Vienna, 1876-80

NOVOTNY, FRITZ, and WAGNER-RIEGER, RENATE (eds.), *Die Wiener Ringstrasse*, 11 vols., Vienna, 1969-81

WAGNER-RIEGER, RENATE, *Wiens Architektur im 19. Jahrhundert*, Vienna, 1971

Belgium

[Exhibition catalogue] *Polaert et son Temps*, Institut supérieur d'Architecture Victor Horta, Brussels, 1980

Denmark

ELLING, C., and FISCHER, K., *Danish Architectural Drawings, 1600-1900*, Copenhagen, 1961

LUND, HAKON (ed.), *Danmarks arkitektur*, 6 vols., Copenhagen, 1979

France

CHABAT, PIERRE, *La Brique et la terre cuite*, 2 vols., Paris, 1881

DECLOUX and NOURY, *Paris dans sa splendeur*, Paris, 1862

DEROUET CHRISTIAN, *Grandes demeures angevines au XIXᵉ siècle, l'œuvre de René Hodé, 1840-70*, Paris, Caisse Nationale des Monuments Historiques, n.d.

DREXLER, ARTHUR (ed.), *The Architecture of the École des Beaux-Arts*, London, 1977

GOURLIER, CHARLES; BIET, GRILLON, and TARDIEU, *Choix d'édifices publics projetés et construits en France depuis le commencement du XIXᵉ siècle*, 3 vols., Paris, 1825-36

HAUTECŒUR, LOUIS, *Histoire de l'architecture classique en France*, vol. 5: *Révolution et Empire*; vol. 6: *La Restauration et le Gouvernement de Juillet, 1815-1848*; vol. 7: *La Fin de l'architecture classique en France, 1848-1900*, Paris, 1953-7

LACROUX, J., *Constructions en brique, la brique ordinaire du point de vue décoratif*, 2 vols., Paris, 1878

MIDDLETON, ROBIN (ed.), *The Beaux-Arts and Nineteenth-Century French Architecture*, Cambridge (Mass.), 1982

NARJOUX, FÉLIX, *Paris, monuments élevés par la ville, 1850-1880*, 4 vols., Paris, 1880-3

NORMAND, LOUIS MARIE, *Paris moderne*, 4 vols., Paris 1834-57

PINEAUX, DENISE, *Architecture civile et urbanisme à Auxerre, 1800-1914*, Auxerre, 1978

VEILLARD, JEAN-YVES, *Rennes au XIXe siècle, architectes, urbanisme et architecture*, Rennes, 1978

Les Monuments Historiques de la France, 1974, No. 1

— 'Architecture et décors à Lyon au XIXe siècle', *Travaux de l'Institut d'Histoire de l'Art de Lyon*, 1980, No. 6

[Exhibition catalogue] *Touraine Néo-gothique*, Musée des Beaux-Arts, Tours, 1978

[Exhibition catalogue] *Le Siècle de l'Eclectisme, Lille 1830-1930*, Brussels and Paris, 1979

[Exhibition catalogue] *Pompéi, travaux et envois des architectes français au XIXe siècle*, E.N.S.B.A., Paris, 1981

[Exhibition catalogue] *Paris-Rome-Athènes. Le voyage en Grèce des architectes français aux XIXe et XXe siècles*, E.N.S.B.A., Paris, 1982

Germany

BOISSERÉE, SULPIZ, *Ansichten, Risse und einzelne Theile des Doms zu Köln*, Stuttgart, 1821

—, *Domwerk: Geschichte und Beschreibung des Doms zu Köln, 1823-32*, 2nd ed. 1842

BÖRSCH-SUPAN, EVA, *Berliner Baukunst nach Schinkel, 1840-1870*, Munich, 1977

BRINGMANN, MICHAEL, *Studien zur neuromanischen Architektur in Deutschland*, Hanover, 1969

BRIX, MICHAEL, *Nürnberg und Lübeck im 19. Jahrhundert*, Munich, 1981

GROTE, LUDWIG, *Die deutsche Stadt im 19. Jahrhundert*. Epilogue by N. Pevsner, Munich, 1974

HERRMANN, WOLFGANG, *Deutsche Baukunst des 19. und 20. Jahrhunderts*, pt. 1, Stuttgart, 1932; reprinted Stuttgart, 1977

LICHT, H., *Architektur Deutschlands*, Berlin, 1882

MANN, ALBRECHT, *Die Neuromanik. Eine rheinische Komponente im Historismus des 19. Jahrhunderts*, Cologne, 1966

MILDE, KURT, *Die Neorenaissance in der deutschen Architektur des 19. Jahrhunderts*, Dresden, 1981

MUTHESIUS, STEFAN, *Das englische Vorbild. Eine Studie zu den deutschen Reformbewegungen in Architektur, Wohnbau und Kunstgewerbe im späteren 19. Jahrhundert*, Munich 1974

RATHKE, URSULA, *Preussische Burgenromantik am Rhein*, Munich, 1979

REIMANN, G. J., *Deutsche Baukunst des Klassizismus*, Leipzig, 1967

STÜLER, FRIEDRICH AUGUST, *Entwürfe zu Kirchen, Pfarr- und Schul-Häusern*, Potsdam, 1846

TRIER, EDUARD, and WEYRES, WILLY (eds.), *Kunst des 19. Jahrhunderts im Rheinland*, vol. 1: *Architektur I (ecclesiastical buildings)*; vol. 2: *Architektur II*, Düsseldorf, 1980

WEYRES, WILLY, *Zur Geschichte der kirchlichen Baukunst im Rheinland von 1800 bis 1870*, Düsseldorf, 1960

Great Britain

CROOK, JOHN MORDAUNT, *The Greek Revival*, The RIBA Drawing Series, London, 1968

— (ed.), *Victorian Architecture, a Visual Anthology*, New York and London, 1971

—, *The Greek Revival, Neoclassical Attitudes in British Architecture, 1760-1870*, London, 1972

DARLEY, GILLIAN, *Villages of Vision*, London, 1975

DIXON, ROGER, and MUTHESIUS, STEFAN, *Victorian Architecture*, London, 1978

EASTLAKE, CHARLES, *A History of Gothic Revival*, London, 1872; reprinted New York, 1978

FERRIDAY, PAUL (ed.), *Victorian Architecture*, London 1963

GIROUARD, MARK, *The Victorian Country House*, 2nd ed. London, 1979

—, *Sweetness and Light, The 'Queen Anne' Movement, 1860-1900*, Oxford, 1977

GOMME, ANDOR, and WALKER, DAVID, *Architecture of Glasgow*, London, 1968

HERBERT, GILBERT, *Pioneers of Prefabrication. The British Contribution in the Nineteenth Century*, Baltimore and London, 1978

HITCHCOCK, HENRY RUSSELL, *Early Victorian Architecture in Britain*, 2nd ed. New Haven, 1972

LINSTRUM, DEREK, *West Yorkshire Architects and Architecture*, London, 1978

MACAULAY, JAMES, *The Gothic Revival, 1745-1845*, Glasgow, 1975

MUTHESIUS, STEFAN, *The High Victorian Movement in Architecture, 1850-1870*, London and Boston, 1972

PEVSNER, NIKOLAUS, *The Buildings of England*, 46 vols., Harmondsworth, 1951-74

PORT, M. H., *Six Hundred Churches. A Study of the Church Building Commissions, 1818-1856*, London, 1961

STAMP, GAVIN, and AMERY, COLIN, *Victorian Buildings of London, 1837-1887, an Illustrated Guide*, London, 1980

SUMMERSON, SIR JOHN, *Victorian Architecture. Four Studies in Evaluation*, New York, 1970

YOUNGSON, A. J., *The Making of Classical Edinburgh, 1750-1840*, Edinburgh, 1966

[Exhibition catalogue] *Marble Halls, Drawings and Models for Victorian Secular Buildings*, Victoria and Albert Museum, London, 1973

[Exhibition catalogue] *Plans and Prospects, Architecture in Wales 1780-1914*, The Welsh Arts Council, Cardiff, 1975

[Exhibition catalogue] *The Triumph of the Classical: Cambridge Architecture, 1804-1834*, Cambridge 1977

Greece

TRAVLOS, J., *Neoclassical Architecture in Greece*, Athens, 1967

Italy

FUSCO, RENATO DE, *L'Architettura dell'Ottocento*, Turin, 1980

MEEKS, CARROLL, *Italian Architecture, 1750-1914*, New Haven and London, 1966

Poland

ZACHWATOWICZ, JAN, *Architektura Polska do Polowy XIX Wieku*, Warsaw, 1956

Spain

NAVASCUES PALACIO, PEDRO, 'Del neoclasicismo al modernismo. Arquitectura', *Historia del Arte Hispánico*, vol. 5, Madrid, 1979, pp. 1-147

—, *Arquitectura y arquitectos madrileños del siglo XIX*, Madrid, 1973

Switzerland

BIRKNER, OTHMAR, *Bauen und Wohnen in der Schweiz, 1850-1920*, Zurich, 1975

CARL, BRUNO, *Klassizismus, 1770-1860*, Zurich, 1963 (Die Architektur der Schweiz, I)

MEYER, ANDRÉ, *Neugotik und Neuromanik in der Schweiz. Die Kirchenarchitektur des 19. Jahrhunderts*, thesis, Zurich, 1973

United States

ANDREW, WAYNE, *American Gothic*, New York, 1975
CARROT, RICHARD G., *The Egyptian Revival, its Sources, Monuments and Meaning, 1808-1858*, Los Angeles, 1978
CONDIT, CARL W., *American Building Art: The Nineteenth Century*, New York, 1960
—, *The Chicago School of Architecture. A History of Commercial and Public Building in the Chicago Area, 1875-1925*, Chicago, 1964
HAMLIN, TALBOT, *Greek Revival Architecture in America*, New York, 1944; paperback ed. 1964
HITCHCOCK, HENRY RUSSELL, and SEALE, W., *Temples of Democracy. The State Capitols of the U.S.A.*, New York, 1976
KAUFMANN, EDGAR (ed.), *The Rise of American Architecture*, New York, 1970
SCULLY, VINCENT, *The Shingle and Stick Style*, New Haven, 1971
STANTON, PHOEBE, *The Gothic Revival and American Church Architecture, an Episode in Taste, 1840-1856*, Baltimore, 1968

Architects

Baudot, Anatole de
BOUDON, FRANÇOISE, 'Recherches sur la pensée et l'œuvre d'Anatole de Baudot', *Architecture, Mouvement, Continuité*, 1973, No. 28, pp. 1-67

Bindesbøll, Gottlieb
BRAMSEN, H., *Gottlieb Bindesbøll, liv og arbejder*, Copenhagen, 1959

Brunel, Isambard Kingdom
ROLT, L. T. C., *Isambard Kingdom Brunel*, London, 1967

Brunt, Henry van
Architecture and Society, Collected Essays of Henry van Brunt, Cambridge (Mass.), 1969
HENNESEY, W. J., *The Architectural Work of Henry van Brunt*, New York, 1978

Burges, William
CROOK, JOHN MORDAUNT, *William Burges and the High Victorian Dream*, London, 1981
[Exhibition catalogue] *The Strange Genius of William Burges*, National Museum of Wales, 1981

Butterfield, William
THOMPSON, PAUL, *William Butterfield*, London, 1971

Chateauneuf, Alexis de
LANGE, G., *Alexis de Chateauneuf*, Hamburg, 1965

Cockerell, Charles Robert
WATKIN, DAVID, *The Life and Work of Charles Robert Cockerell*, London, 1974

Davioud, Gabriel
[Exhibition catalogue] *Gabriel Davioud, architecte de Paris*, Délégation de l'Action Artistique de la Ville de Paris, Paris, 1981-2

Emerson, William Ralph
ZAITZEVSKY, CYNTHIA, and MILLER, MYRON, *The Architecture of William Ralph Emerson*, Cambridge (Mass.), 1969

Engel, Johann Carl Ludwig
[Exhibition catalogue] *Carl Ludwig Engel*, Berlin, 1970

Fellner, Ferdinand
HOFFMANN, HANS CHRISTOF, *Die Theaterbauten von Fellner und Helmer*, Munich, 1966

Ferstel, Heinrich von
WIBIRAL, N., and MIKULA, R., *Heinrich von Ferstel*, Wiesbaden, 1974

Fontaine, Pierre François Léonard
BIVER, M. L., *Pierre Fontaine, premier architecte de l'Empereur*, Paris, 1964

Furness, Frank
O'GORMAN, JAMES, *The Architecture of Frank Furness*, Philadelphia, 1973

Garnier, Charles
STEINHAUSER, MONIKA, *Die Architektur der Pariser Oper*, Munich, 1969

Gärtner, Friedrich von
HEDERER, OSWALD, *Friedrich von Gärtner, 1792-1847, Leben, Werk, Schüler*, Munich, 1976

Godefroy, Maximilien
ALEXANDER, ROBERT L., *The Architecture of Maximilien Godefroy*, Baltimore, 1974

Hansen, Theophil von
WAGNER-RIEGER, RENATE, 'Der Architekt Theophil Hansen', *Anzeiger der österreichischen Akademie der Wissenschaften*, 114 (1977), pp. 260-76

Helmer, Hermann
HOFFMANN, HANS CHRISTOF, *Die Theaterbauten von Fellner und Helmer*, Munich, 1966

Hittorff, Jacques Ignace
HAMMER, KARL, *Jakob Ignaz Hittorff. Ein Pariser Baumeister, 1792-1867*, Stuttgart, 1967
SCHNEIDER, DONALD DAVID, *The Works and Doctrine of Jacques Ignace Hittorff, Structural Innovation and Formal Expression in French Architecture, 1810-1867*, New York, 1977

Horeau, Hector
DUFOURNET, PAUL, *Horeau précurseur*, Paris, 1980
[Exhibition catalogue] *Hector Horeau, 1801-1872* (Cahiers de la Recherche Architecturale, No. 3, suppl.)

Hunt, Richard Morris
BAKER, PAUL R., *Richard Morris Hunt*, Cambridge (Mass.), 1980

Jappelli, Giuseppe
GALIMBERTI, N., *Giuseppe Jappelli*, Padua, 1963
[Exhibition catalogue] *Giuseppe Jappelli e il suo tempo*, Padua, 1977

Klenze, Leo von
LIEB, NORBERT, *Leo von Klenze, Gemälde und Zeichnungen*, Munich, 1979

Labrouste, Henri
SADDY, PIERRE, *Henri Labrouste architecte, 1801-1875*, Caisse Nationale des Monuments et des Sites, Paris, 1976

Lassus, Jean-Baptiste
LENIAUD, JEAN-MICHEL, *Jean-Baptiste Lassus ou le temps retrouvé des cathédrales*, Geneva, 1980

Loudon, John Claudius
GLOAG, JOHN, *The Life and Work of John Claudius Loudon and his Influence on Architectural and Furniture Design*, Newcastle, 1970

Moller, Georg
FRÖHLICH, MARTIN, and SPERLICH, HANS GÜNTHER, *Georg Moller, Baumeister der Romantik*, Darmstadt, 1959

Morris, William
BRADLEY, JAN, *William Morris and his World*, London, 1978

Nash, John
DAVIES, TERENCE, *The Architecture of John Nash*, London, 1960
TEMPLE, NIGEL, *John Nash and the Village Picturesque*, Gloucester, 1979
SUMMERSON, SIR JOHN, *The Life and Work of John Nash, Architect*, London, 1980

Paxton, John
CHADWICK, G. F., *The Works of Sir John Paxton*, London, 1961

Peabody, Robert Swain
HOLDEN, WHEATON, A., 'The Peabody Touch, Peabody and Stearns of Boston, 1870-1917', *Journal of the Society of Architectural Historians*, 1973, pp. 114-31

Pearson, John Loughborough
QUINEY, ANTHONY, *John L. Pearson*, New Haven and London, 1979

Poccianti, Pasquale
— *Pasquale Poccianti, architetto 1774-1858. Studi e ricerche nel secondo centenario della nascita*, Florence, 1977
[Exhibition catalogue] *Firenze e Livorno e l'opera di Pasquale Poccianti nell'età granducale*, Rome, 1974

Post, George Brown
WEISMAN, WINSTON, 'The Commercial Architecture of George B. Post', *Journal of the Society of Architectural Historians*, 1972, pp. 176-203

Potter, Edward T. and William A.
LANDAU, SARAH B., *Edward T. Potter and William A. Potter, American High Victorian Architects*, New York, 1979
WODEHOUSE, LAWRENCE, 'William A. Potter, 1842-1900, Principal Pasticheur of Henry Hobson Richardson', *Journal of the Society of Architectural Historians*, 1973, pp. 175-92

Pugin, Augustus Welby
STANTON, PHOEBE, *Pugin*, London, 1971

Richardson, Henry Hobson
HITCHCOCK, HENRY RUSSELL, *The Architecture of Henry Hobson Richardson and his Times*, Cambridge, 1935; reprinted 1966
RENSSELAER, MARIANA GRISWOLD VAN, *Henry Hobson Richardson and his Work*, 1888; reprinted New York, 1969

Root, John Wellburn
HOFFMANN, DONALD, *The Architecture of John Wellburn Root*, Baltimore, 1973

Ruskin, John
OTTESEN GARRIGAN, KRISTINE, *Ruskin on Architecture*, Madison, 1973
UNRAU, JOHN, *Looking at Architecture with Ruskin*, London, 1978

Schinkel, Karl Friedrich
PUNDT, HERMANN G., *Schinkel's Berlin, a Study in Environmental Planning*, Cambridge (Mass.), 1972

RAVE, PAUL ORTWIN, and KÜHN, MARGARETHE (eds.), *Karl Friedrich Schinkel, Lebenswerk*, Berlin, 1939
—, *Karl Friedrich Schinkel, Sein Wirken als Architekt*, Stuttgart, 1981
[Exhibition catalogue] *Karl Friedrich Schinkel, Werke und Wirkungen, Martin-Gropius-Bau*, Berlin, 1980

Schmidt, Friedrich von
PLANNER-STEINER, ULRIKE, *Friedrich von Schmidt*, Wiesbaden, 1978

Scott, George Gilbert
COLE, DAVID, *The Work of Sir George Gilbert Scott*, London, 1980

Semper, Gottfried
FRÖHLICH, MARTIN, *Gottfried Semper*, Basle, 1974
[Exhibition catalogue] *Gottfried Semper, 1803-1879, Baumeister zwischen Revolution und Historismus*, Staatl. Kunstsammlungen Dresden, 1979, Munich and Fribourg, 1980

Shaw, Richard Norman
SAINT, ANDREW, *Richard Norman Shaw*, New Haven and London, 1976

Soane, John
STROUD, DOROTHY, *The Architecture of Sir John Soane*, London, 1961

Strickland, William
GILCHRIST, A. A., *William Strickland, Architect and Engineer, 1781-1854*, Philadelphia, 1950

Sullivan, Louis Henry
MORRISON, HUGH, *Louis Sullivan, Prophet of Modern Architecture*, 1935; reprinted Westport, 1971
SULLIVAN, LOUIS, *The Autobiography of an Idea*, 1924; reprinted New York, 1976

Telford, Thomas
ROLT, L. T. C., *Thomas Telford*, London, 1958

Thomson, Alexander
McFADZEAN, ROLAND, *The Life and Works of Alexander Thomson*, London and Boston, 1979

Viollet-le-Duc, Eugène-Emmanuel
BEKAERT, GEERT (ed.), *A la recherche de Viollet-le-Duc*, Brussels, 1980
[Exhibition catalogue] *Centenaire de la Mort*, Lausanne, 1979
[Exhibition catalogue] *Viollet-le-Duc*, Réunion des Musées Nationaux, Paris, 1980

Vitry, Urbain
[Exhibition catalogue] *Urbain Vitry, architecte, 1802-1863*, Palais des Beaux-Arts, Toulouse, 1981

Voysey, Charles F. A.
GEBHARD, D., *Charles F. A. Voysey*, Los Angeles, 1975

Waterhouse, Alfred
GIROUARD, MARK, *Alfred Waterhouse and the Natural History Museum*, New Haven and London, 1981

White, Stanford
BALDWIN, C., *Stanford White*, New York, 1931; reprinted New York, 1971

Wilkins, William
Liscombe, R. W., *William Wilkins, 1778-1839*, Cambridge, 1980

Wimmel, Carl Ludwig
Hannmann, Eckhart, *Carl Ludwig Wimmel, 1786-1846*, Munich, 1975

Wyatt, Matthew Digby
Pevsner, Nikolaus, *Matthew Digby Wyatt*, Cambridge, 1950

PERIODICALS

France

Encyclopédie d'architecture, 1851-1862, 1872-1892
Gazette des architectes et du bâtiment, 1863-1886
Moniteur des architectes, 1847-1900
Revue générale de l'architecture et des travaux publics, 1840-1889

Germany

Allgemeine Bauzeitung, 1836-1918
Deutsche Bauzeitung, 1868-1942
Deutsches Baugewerksblatt, 1881-1899 (previously: *Zeitschrift für praktische Baukunst*)
Zeitschrift für Bauwesen, 1851-1931
Zeitschrift für praktische Baukunst, 1841-1881

Great Britain

The Architect, founded 1869
The Builder, an Illustrated Weekly Magazine, 1842-1966
The Building News, 1855-1926 (from 1926 absorbed in *The Architect*)
The British Architect, 1874-1917

United States

The American Architect and Building News, founded 1876
The American Builder, founded 1869
The Inland Architect, founded 1877

Index

List of monuments reproduced in this volume

Photo Credits

The publishers wish to express their gratitude to the photographers listed below as well as to the following libraries, museums and other institutions which made other photographic material available. The figures refer to the numbers of the plates.

The illustrations were kindly obtained by Ingrid de Kalbermatten.

Alexandria, Scottish Colorfoto Laboratory: 384
Amsterdam, Ned. Doc. centrum v.d. Bouwkunst: 200
Ashville, North Carolina, The Biltmore Company: 160
Athens, Commercial Bank of Greece: 255
Augsburg, Stadtbildstelle: 276
Berlin, Bildarchiv Preussischer Kulturbesitz: 448
Berlin, Landesarchiv: (Karl H. Paulmann) 379, 462
Berlin, Landesbildstelle: 376, 488
Berlin, Helmut Maier: 68
Berlin, Technische Universität, Hauptbibliothek: 66
Berlin, Technische Universität, Universitätsbibliothek, Plansammlung: 67, 197; (H. E. Kiessling, Berlin) 138, 274
Berlin (GDR), Institut für Denkmalpflege, Messbildarchiv: 172, 190
Berlin (GDR), Staatliche Museen zu Berlin, Kupferstichkabinett und Sammlung der Zeichnungen: 65, 71, 72
Bottmingen, G. Germann: 111, 112, 162-5
Brookline, Mass., Myron Miller: 512, 513, 515
Brussels, Archives d'Architecture Moderne: 316, 317, 324, 460; (H. Wieser) 170, 180-2
Budapest, Hungarian Studio of Commercial Photography: 238-240, 456
Caen, Conservation régionale des Monuments Historiques de Basse-Normandie: (M.-H. Since) 372, 373
Cambridge, Mass., The Houghton Library, Harvard University: 242, 245, 247, 248
Cambridge, Mass., Harvard Law School, Harvard University: 243
Charlottesville, Virginia, University of Virginia Library, Manuscript Department: 44
Chicago, Harold Allen: 367
Chicago, Carson Pirie Scott & Co., Publicity Department: 424-6
Cologne, Rheinische Bildarchiv: 83, 84
Cologne, Wallraf-Richartz-Museum, Ludwig Coll.: (Kunst- und Museumsbibliothek, Cologne) 129
Copenhagen, Ny Carlsberg Glyptotek: (Ole Woldbye, Copenhagen) 282
Copenhagen, Royal Danish Academy of Fine Arts: (Jørgen Watz, Lyngby) 128, 463
Daventry, Northamptonshire, Christopher Dalton: 443

Dresden, Deutsche Fotothek: 63, 64, 76, 109, 110
Düsseldorf, Landesbildstelle Rheinland: 330
Edinburgh, Edinburgh University Press: 39
Edinburgh, The Royal Commission on the Ancient and Historical Monuments of Scotland: 38, 40, 73, 74, 186, 188, 201, 331
Evanston, Illinois, National WCTU: 483
Florence, Alinari: 30, 34, 175, 257, 405, 409, 410
Florence, Gabinetto Disegno e Stampe degli Uffizi: (Guido Sansoni, Florence) 31-33
Frauenfeld, Thurg. Denkmalpflege und Kunstdenkmälerinventarisation, C. Walder Coll.: 169
Fribourg, Leo Hilber: 297
Gauting, Bavaria Verlag: (M. Storck) 149
Glasgow, School of Art, Library: 185
Hamburg, Staatliche Landesbildstelle: 60, 62, 97, 145, 237
Hanover, Niedersächsisches Landesverwaltungsamt, Landesbildstelle: 113
Helsinki, The Museum of Finnish Architecture: (Karhumäki) 27; (A. Salokorpi) 28; (Iffland) 29
Hildesheim, Stadtarchiv: 490
Karlsruhe, Landesdenkmalamt Baden-Württemberg: 436
Koblenz, Landesbildstelle Rheinland-Pfalz: 98 (aerial photograph No. 2599-2, Bezirksregierung für Rheinhessen)
London, The British Library: 86, 207, 249, 301, 318, 403, 437, 465, 502, 503
London, The British Museum (Natural History): 224
London, Country Life: (Alex Starkey) 106
London, Gillian Darley: 474
London, A. F. Kersting: 36, 85, 101, 118, 206, 427a, 442, 484, 523a
London, National Monuments Record: 2, 35, 37, 75, 89-92, 99, 102, 103, 123, 125, 142, 143, 159, 183, 189, 202, 204, 205, 208, 209-15, 222, 223, 225, 226, 283, 286, 292, 315, 344, 370, 414, 444, 445, 468, 469, 493, 496, 505
London, The National Trust: 296, 471, 472
London, Public Record Office: 119
London, Royal Institute of British Architects, British Architectural Library: (Geremy Butler, London) 104, 219, 220, 302, 348, 349, 500, 525
London, The Science Museum: 294, 328, 427, 428
London, Sir John Soane's Museum: 79
London, Victoria and Albert Museum: 87, 221, 303, 468a, 506; (Eileen Tweedy, London) 304, 504, 522
Lucerne, Kantonale Denkmalpflege: 487
Mainz, Landesamt für Denkmalpflege Rheinland-Pfalz: 116, 117
Marburg, Bildarchiv: 16, 17, 23, 139, 148, 277, 423
Milan, Archivio Fotografico dei Civici Musei, Castello Sforzesco, Raccolta delle Stampe Achille Bertarelli: 407

Munich, Bayerisches Landesamt für Denkmalpflege: (Maria Linseisen) 96
Munich, Bayerische Verwaltung der Staatl. Schlösser, Gärten u. Seen: 57
Munich, Deutsches Museum: 295
Munich, Martin Herpich & Sohn: 161
Munich, Sigrid Neubert: 291
Munich, Werner Neumeister: 491
Munich, Staatliche Graphische Sammlung: 14, 15, 137
Munich, Stadtmuseum: 323
Munich, Technische Universität, Architektursammlung: 146, 147, 307, 431
Munich, Zentralinstitut für Kunstgeschichte: 24; (Römmler and Jonas, Dresden) 25; (Margrit Behrens) 196
Nantes, Photo Studio Madec: 95
Newport, R. I., Salve Regina College: 481a
New York, N. Y., Museum of the City of New York, Photo Library Department: 346, 347, 418
Orléans, Inventaire Général des Monuments et des Richesses Artistiques de la France: (J.-C. Jacques & R. Malnoury) 114
Oxford, Oxfordshire County Council, Central Library: (John Peacock, Abingdon) 216, 217
Paris, Académie d'Architecture: 308, 404
Paris, Archives Photographiques/S.P.A.D.E.M.: 115, 435, 438; (J. Feuillie) 56, 166, 168, 251, 309, 311
Paris, Pierre-Yves Ballu: 19, 20, 176
Paris, Bibliothèque nationale: 1, 3, 288, 298, 473
Paris, J. E. Bulloz: 51, 260, 261, 459
Paris, Studio Chevojon: 326, 335, 338, 339, 417, 419, 420, 461
Paris, Connaissance des Arts: (P. Hinous) 43, 511; (R. Guillemot) 400
Paris, B. Doucet: 54, 356, 477
Paris, École Nationale Supérieure des Beaux-Arts: 127, 158, 271, 281, 289, 293, 312, 322, 382, 383, 385-7, 397, 520, 521, 524
Paris, Gilles de Fayet: 4, 7-13, 42, 47, 49, 53, 55, 80-2, 100, 107, 120, 121, 126, 131, 155, 192, 193, 203, 227, 230, 233-5, 241, 265, 266, 313, 341, 342, 350, 351, 353, 354, 356-9, 362, 378, 380, 388-93, 396, 401, 406, 416, 432-4, 447, 451, 452, 454, 458, 475, 478-82, 484a, 485-6, 489, 492, 497-9, 501, 507-10, 519

Paris, Claude Mignot: 18, 21, 52, 132, 167, 244, 250, 262, 263, 299, 352, 394, 395, 516, 517
Paris, Réunion des Musées Nationaux: 364
Paris, Étienne Revault: 41, 45, 267, 325
Paris, Christiane Riboulleau: 133-5, 194, 259, 314, 398, 399
Paris, H. Roger Viollet: 5, 6, 58, 69, 70, 94, 122, 136, 140, 141, 150, 151, 171, 173, 174, 178, 179, 184, 199, 229, 236, 264, 268, 269, 272, 273, 275, 279, 287, 306, 319, 320, 329, 332, 333a, 336, 337, 340, 343, 355, 381, 402, 408, 412, 448, 449, 453, 455, 466
Potsdam-Sans Souci, Staatliche Schlösser und Gärten: 22
Salzburg, Oskar Anrather: 108
Stuttgart, Landesbildstelle Württemberg: 59, 61
Toledo, Ohio, The Toledo Museum of Art: 152
Vienna, Landesbildstelle: 153
Vienna, Museen der Stadt Wien: 464
Vienna, Österreichische Nationalbibliothek, Bildarchiv: 154, 156, 157, 195, 198, 284, 334
Washington, D. C., Library of Congress: 46, 48, 93, 270, 305, 518
Wuppertal, Dieter Leistner: 256, 494, 495
Würzburg, Amt für Öffentlichkeitsarbeit: 360
York, National Railway Museum: 439, 441
Zurich, ETH Zurich, Institut GTA, Archiv für Moderne Schweizer Architektur: 144 (Semper 20-82-1-1); 252 (Semper 20-58); 253 (Semper 20-196); 254 (Semper 20-89); 476 (Semper 20-171-1-6)
Zurich, Jelmoli: (J. Meiner & Sohn, Zurich) 422

After: Hermann Ziller, *Schinkel*, Bielefeld and Leipzig, 1897: 77, 78
After: Anton Springer, *Handbuch der Kunstgeschichte*, Leipzig, vol. V, 5th ed., 1909: 191, 278, 280
With kind permission of the Baugeschichtliches Archiv, Zurich: 411

All other illustrations are from the author's collection.

The plans were redrawn by Christian Huvet.